DAI GREATCOAT

T0333419

DAVID JONES IN 1964   *photo: Mark Gerson*

DAVID JONES

Dai Greatcoat

A Self-Portrait of David Jones
in His Letters

Edited by
RENÉ HAGUE

i am of my otes it is this wurk I know it will
bring me to deaths door i know it will . . .

WILLIAM PENROSE TAPLOW

FABER & FABER

First published in 1980
by Faber & Faber Ltd
The Bindery, 51 Hatton Garden
London EC1N 8HN
This paperback edition first published in 2017

Printed in England by TJ Books Limited, Padstow, Cornwall

A CIP record for this book is available from the British Library

ISBN 978-0-571-33952-5

4 6 8 10 9 7 5

Contents

————————————*————————————

Illustrations

———————————— * ————————————

Plates 1–8 are reproduced here by kind permission of the Trustees of the Estate of David Jones and Mr. Anthony d'Offay as administrator of the copyrights. They form a sequence, illustrating various places in which David Jones worked during the years 1921–74.

Preface

———————————*———————————

Where does 'Dai Greatcoat' come from? He is a Welsh soldier who appears on three occasions in David Jones's long, poetically contrived, at times lyrical, narrative of the Great War, *In Parenthesis.* When the Queen of the Woods cuts 'bright boughs of various flowering' for those who died in Mametz Wood, during the Somme offensive, on 10 and 11 July 1916: 'Dai Greatcoat, she can't find him anywhere—she calls both high and low, she had a very special one for him.' Earlier, he is Malory's Dai 'de la Cote Mal Taile',[1] whose 'over-garment sat over-thwartly' and again, and more grandly, he is the Dai of the great Boast, given the life of the spoken as well as the written word by the skill of Dylan Thomas and Douglas Cleverdon in the radio production of the poem. At the same time he is David Jones himself, for though it is not David in person who 'adjusts his slipping shoulder-straps, wraps close his misfit outsize greatcoat' and starts, 'My fathers were with the Black Prinse of Wales at the passion of the blind Bohemian king', it is David who uses the old sweat as his mouthpiece. And there is a further reason: in 1930–3 David Jones spent a good deal of time at Pigotts in Buckinghamshire, the home of Eric and Mary Gill, living in a small cottage there with a young couple, me and my wife Joan. He liked, or at least was greatly amused by, a little drawing which represented him lashed-up in his greatcoat against the Chilterns cold; it was entitled 'Greatcoat Lurker', and it was thus (for David was then working hard both at *In Parenthesis* and at his watercolours) that the Greatcoat became attached to the Dai of the Boast. And anyone who reads the letters that make up the larger part of this book will see how apt the greatcoated figure

[1] The name of Malory's knight (*Morte Darthur,* Book IX) was in fact Breunor le Noire.

is as a symbol for one who both endured and sought protection for so many years.

The plan of this book changed as it was being put together. It was to have been more of a biography illustrated by letters; but, as happens so often when one makes anything that one thinks will depend upon the maker's judgement, the material itself took control and determined the form. It very soon became clear that, left to himself, David would both record the progress of his life (for one small but important detail we have to be specially thankful: he always put at the head of his letter the full address from which he was writing, and the date) and at the same time portray his character and personality. What David writes about are all the things that those who love and admire him most wish to know: where he is, of what he is thinking, what he is reading, what work he is doing or cannot succeed in doing, what he likes and dislikes, what moves him to joy or rage, what will interest the friend to whom he is writing—often with great profundity, but often, too, particularly in the earlier years, with lightness and humour.

The letters chosen for this collection have been taken almost entirely from four series, addressed to four friends: David's contemporary Jim Ede (H.S.E. in the text), and three others born in the next decade who, with the passage of time, became more or less contemporary, Tom Burns (T.F.B.), Harman Grisewood (H.J.G.) and me (R.H.), with my wife (J.H.). This means that what is printed concentrates on a single aspect of the man. He may well (indeed, I know that he does) speak in a different tone, and so present a different person, to others with whom he had a different relationship. I felt, however, that I could not bring myself to copy and print anything which I could not fully understand, could not fully get the feel of, because it went into intellectual, emotional, literary, historical or religious fields, and attitudes to those fields, that were in any degree foreign to me. I wished to print only what was said in a tone of voice that was completely familiar to me. I could feel sure of my ground only if I knew David's correspondent well enough to understand how what David wrote would be received and understood.

Had I felt otherwise, a vast range of correspondence would no doubt have been open to me; sooner or later someone, I hope, will undertake the great task of hauling in the wider net.

I have, on one or two occasions, gone further afield and have printed letters, for example, to T. S. Eliot and W. H. Auden. These I happened to have by me at home, and although I was anxious not to burden the book with material of professional or literary interest, it seemed mean not to include them. There are some passages too, from letters to a younger man, Colin Hughes, and the reader will see that these contain some of David's most valuable memories of the war, just as part of a letter to Saunders Lewis illuminates David's own way of thinking at a particular time. The opening letter, to Philip Hagreen, another contemporary of David's, could not be spared, because it is the earliest in date (1925) and in it can be seen the first indications of David's later 'direction' and, slight though it is, of what was to be his more fully elaborated epistolary style. A very different sort of book could have been compiled, and a very different aspect of the writer could have emerged, from his letters to the classical scholar Jackson Knight, for example, to his patron Helen Sutherland, to other women friends, and to his many friends and acquaintances in the academic world.

I am every day more amazed at the enormous mass of David's correspondence. The four series from which this comparatively brief selection has been made must amount to something between a quarter of a million and half a million words. The 37-page *List of Letters by David Jones* compiled by Tony Stoneburner (Granville, Ohio: Limekiln Press, 1977), though admittedly incomplete, must contain at least twice as much, I would guess, as the sources upon which I have drawn. When it is remembered, too, that David would often write several drafts of the same letter, and perhaps keep a copy, and that these drafts and copies could be very long,[2] we see how much time he must have spent, particularly in his later years, in this endless self-imposed task, and we must wonder how he was able to do any other work.

[2] See below, p. 145, for a fuller account of these re-draftings.

Anything, therefore, that David says about his physical or spiritual incapacity or exhaustion should be interpreted in the light of this achievement.

For all the many re-draftings, David's letters were written rapidly, and not read through or corrected. A common postscript runs 'Forgive all the lacunae and inconsistencies and meanderings . . .'. The syntax, therefore, is often irregular and the punctuation spasmodic. The sense, however, is nearly always perfectly obvious, and no change has been made except when there seemed to be a real danger that the writer might be misunderstood. The spelling *has* been corrected.

Since David wrote at such length, a book as long as the present one could have consisted of no more than a dozen or fifteen letters, each written round a central theme, with many digressions and annotations. Such a book, however, would not have provided so complete a biographical portrait. In mutilating such letters and at times other shorter ones, as I have been obliged to do, I have tried to bear in mind that the excellence of a letter depends to some degree on the mixture of the apparently trivial and the profound. To see the letter as a whole construction, the 'Thank auntie for the dripping and we hope her leg is better' is as important as a discussion of Marcion's distortion of Pauline theology. Marcion tends to win towards the end, but David is too entertaining a guide to exclude the lesser things that give pleasure.

R.H.

Shanagarry, Co. Cork
June 1979

Acknowledgements

————————————*————————————

I have many to thank for the help they gave me when I was compiling this book. I could have done nothing without the permission, sweetened by encouragement, of the Trustees of the Estate of David Jones (whom I prefer to think and speak of as Mollie Elkin, Stella Wright and Tony Hyne) and of the owners of the letters I have used, Jim Ede, Tom Burns, Harman Grisewood, Philip Hagreen, Colin Hughes, William Blissett—a double debt to that last, for the sharpness of his eye matches the generosity of his nature. I could write at length of the kindness shown to me by other friends, all of whom know what gratitude I bear to them and why: Diana Austin, Catharine Carver, Douglas Cleverdon, Nicolete Gray, Walter Shewring, Stanley Honeyman, Peter Orr, Vincent Sherry, my sister-in-law Petra Tegetmeier, Robert Buhler, Anthony d'Offay and Caroline Cuthbert, Valerie Wynne-Williams, Michael Richey; to move even closer to my heart, my nimble-fingered daughter Rosalind Erangey and, in the very penetralia, my wife Joan.—With well-managed coincidence, what a delightful house-party we would enjoy.

R.H.

I

INTRODUCTORY
1895—1925

---*---

Brockley, the Great War, Ditchling Common,
Capel-y-ffin, Caldey Island

I have said that in his letters David writes his own biography, though from time to time some annotation or intrusion is demanded of the compiler. But the letters gathered here start in 1925, and although David looks back in later years to his youth and childhood and gives much detail about, for example, his years in the army, some sort of biographical framework has to be provided for the years from his birth in 1895 to the time when he joined the circle of friends whom he is addressing later.

Fortunately we have, thanks to his friend Peter Orr, at least the short autobiographical piece 'In Illo Tempore',[1] which was written, or rather recorded, between 1966 and 1973. It covers the years up to 1917, and is the beginning of what would have been not a chronological account but a rambling contemplation of his life. In 1935 David had written for the Tate Gallery, at Jim Ede's request, the less decorative but more factual account of his earlier life from which I quote below.[2] This can be supplemented by information from David's nieces, Stella Wright and Mollie Elkin, and his nephew Tony Hyne, children of his sister, Alice Mary ('Cissie') Hyne, born in 1891. The following account was written, it should be noted, two years before the publication of *In Parenthesis*, and there is therefore no mention of the writings which were to become as important as, if not (because they necessarily reach a wider audience) even more important than, his painting.

Father: James Jones [1860–1943] printer's manager on the staff of Christian Herald Publishing Company Ltd., resident in London since 1883; worked previously on *The Flintshire Observer*; a native of Holywell; of the family of John Jones, master plasterer, of farming stock from Ysceifiog, below the Clwydian Hills, North Wales.

Mother: Alice Ann Bradshaw [1856–1937], daughter of Ebenezer Bradshaw, mast- and block-maker of Rotherhithe in Surrey, of an English family of Thames-side shipbuilders, of Italian extraction on her mother's side.

[1] Published in *The Dying Gaul*, pp. 19–29.
[2] Printed in the catalogue of the Memorial Exhibition of David's work held at Kettle's Yard, Cambridge, in February 1975, not long after his death.

1895: Born on 1 November 1895, at Brockley in Kent.

Childhood: Backward at any kind of lesson and physically feeble. No enthusiasms other than drawing. Received from parents every possible encouragement within their power to foster this inclination. One of my earliest recollections is of looking at three crayon drawings of my mother's, one of Tintern Abbey, another a Donkey's Head, and the third of a Gladiator with curly hair. She drew extremely well in the tradition of Victorian drawing masters. Among other childhood things are remembrances of my father singing a Welsh song—(and I have always cherished, through him, a sense of belonging to the Welsh people)—and of his reading the *Pilgrim's Progress* to us on Sunday evening, which impressed me a good bit.

1903: The first drawing I can positively remember making was of a dancing bear seen in the street at Brockley (drawing still extant). Exhibited with the Royal Drawing Society; work confined to animals—lions, tigers, wolves, bears, cats, deer, mostly in conflict. Only the *very earliest* of these show any sensitivity, or any interest whatsoever. . . .

1909–14: Became a student at Camberwell School of Art under Mr. A. S. Hartrick, Mr. Reginald Savage, and the late Mr. Herbert Cole. Owe debt of gratitude to A. S. Hartrick (he had known Van Gogh and Gauguin in Paris, and from him I first heard of the French movement—felt very proud to know a man who had studied in Paris) for counteracting the baleful, vulgarian influences of magazines, etc., and the current conventions of the schools—in short, for reviving and fanning to enthusiasm the latent sense of drawing for its own sake manifest earlier. Also to Mr. Reginald Savage for a certain civilizing influence, and for his introducing me to the great English illustrators of the nineteenth century: Pinwell, Sandys, Beardsley, etc.; and the work of the Pre-Raphaelites and the Frenchman, Boutet de Monvel. *Sad result*—ambition to illustrate historical subjects —preferably for Welsh history and legend—alternatively to become an animal painter. Remained completely muddle-headed as to the function of the arts in general.

1914–18: Enlisted in the Royal Welsh Fusiliers in London on

2 January 1915. Served as a private soldier with them on the West Front from December 1915 to February 1918. Demobilized in December 1918.[3]

During this period did small drawings in pocket-book in trenches and billets ... They are without *any sense of form and display no imagination.* But the *War landscape*—the '*Waste Land*' *motif—has remained with me*, I think as a potent influence, to assert itself later.

1919: Obtained Government grant to attend Westminster School of Art under Mr. Walter Bayes. ... Interested in the ideas and work of the various English artists associated with the movements theorized in Paris. ... Enthusiastic about Blake and the English watercolourists. Was profoundly moved by the first appearance of the El Greco *Agony [in the Garden]* on the walls of the National Gallery in 1919. ... Mr. Bernard Meninsky, whose life class I attended, was also of great help and encouragement.

1921–4: Received into the Roman Church on 7 September 1921. ... Attempted to learn the trade of carpentry under Mr. George Maxwell, carpenter and builder. At the same time I learned the use of the engraver's tools from Fr. Desmond Chute and Mr. Eric Gill. Discovered I was no use as a carpenter, and gradually became able to engrave tolerably enough to do small jobs for Mr. Hilary Pepler's private [St. Dominic's] Press. Did a small watercolour drawing from time to time. ...

1925: Went to live with Mr. Eric Gill and his family, now removed to Capel-y-ffin.

Looking back at the above we may make some additions and corrections:

The address with which one associates David and his family in Brockley is 115 Howson Road, S.E.4. David, in fact, was born in Arabin Road, near by, and the family moved a couple of times before they settled in 115. He would always emphasize his frailty as a child and lament the lack of formal education. In both these matters, I believe, he exaggerates. His sister used to say that, being the youngest child, he

[3] David's Certificate of Transfer to Reserve on Demobilization is dated 15 January 1919.

was spoilt and that if he missed school the reason, as often as not, was that his mother yielded to his complaint of one of those mysterious pains that often afflict indolent children as the hour for school approaches. If I say that to the end of his days he was to be similarly spoilt by his friends, I do not mean either that his friends ever grudged the special treatment he called for—far from it—or that he did not, for reasons that will be apparent later, suffer from a real spiritual distress for which there were good reasons, and which required affectionate protection. Physically, however, he was always robust; but he hoarded his store of well-being, rather as, in later years, he hoarded many pictures the sale of which would have relieved him from financial worry. (I should, in fairness, add that he had a further reason, and a good one, for refusing to sell anything. He believed that a man's work made one whole and that it should remain intact, both the good and the relatively bad. What was not so good must be seen with and in the light of the better, but must on no account be isolated.)

In the matter of formal education, what David says is an example of how much greener is the grass on the other side of the hedge. He probably exaggerates when he says that he learnt practically nothing at school, for he did win at least one prize: a book called *Birds I have Known*. Inside we read, 'Brockley Road School. Awarded to Walter Jones for Grammar, July 1907. Alfred Garside'. To which David has added, 'Always known as David by his family and, subsequently, David Jones the only signature'—which is not quite true, since his earliest published drawing is signed 'W. David Jones' (as were his cheques, to avoid confusion), and there were occasions after he was received into the Roman Catholic Church when he signed himself 'David Michael' or 'David Michael Jones'.

It is remarkable and admirable that David was able to go, and that his parents were willing that he should go, to the Camberwell School of Art at such an early age as fourteen, 'in knickerbockers and Eton collar'; and what he learnt from the teachers of whom he speaks with such gratitude must surely have been of more value to him in later years than learning Greek irregular verbs: not as 'art school' training but as an introduction to all sorts of literary and historical studies that he was to pursue until the end of his life and which were to provide the material for his poetry.

David had an older brother, the eldest of the three children. He died young, and David seldom spoke of him. It was of his sister that he would speak, and although in his middle years he moved in a world that was separated from the world of his family, he and his sister remained close and came even closer in their old age—Alice died in February of the year in which David himself died, 1974.

His father and his mother both had an enduring influence on his way of thinking and working, drawing him in different directions. The former was Welsh, the latter very English: and it was James, the father, who won when it came to choosing a Welsh or an English name for David. The elder brother was given the Saxon name of Harold, and so he remained, for his second name, Peart, was a family name and not a Christian name. Though David started with the Teutonic name of Walter, the Welsh pressure was constant and Walter, as we have seen, was abandoned for David. On the other hand it was the mother who won in determining the character of David's writing—and of his painting, if we consider its essential quality and not the introduction at times of Welsh themes and subject matter. In spite of all David's attempts to Cambrianize his work, in spite of all he says with such pathos and eloquence, and in spite of his devotion to a great Welsh myth, it was the English tradition that was most completely assimilated, and everything in his work that is most convincing, sincere, and based on real knowledge and understanding is English. And the core of that English tradition, lying in the riverside and city of London, came to him from his mother and her memories of her youth in Rotherhithe. Even his father, in spite of his love of Wales, helped by first turning David towards the main current of English literature.

The conflict could be seen when James Jones's Welsh relatives came to visit Brockley. Alice would behave like Mrs. Joe Gargery in reverse. Mrs. Joe, you will remember, would, when deeply moved, turn Joe and Pip out of the room and busy herself vigorously with bucket and mop, broom and duster. Alice Jones would leave the others in the 'front room' and make a great clatter in the kitchen, banging saucepans and slamming doors.

It was a great sorrow to David that he was cut off from Wales, but he was cut off from a Wales for which he had no more than a sentimental love. He was widely read in Welsh history, but the Wales he loved ended with the death of Llywelyn ap Gruffyd on 11 December 1282 (one date in Welsh history that none of David's friends could fail to memorize) and reached back into a Wales of myth and not of fact. This statement would, I fear, have brought from David the ultimate and most damning reproach of Nominalism. He held fast to the reality of universals, and among his universals was 'Welshness'. Of modern

Wales he had little or no knowledge. He was seldom in the country except at Caldey Island and Capel-y-ffin, which are almost completely anglicized, and he could never have lived there; and he had few Welsh friends (fond though he was of those he had). Worst of all, in spite of years of application, he could never learn the language; and this was the cause of the most serious blemishes in his poetry. His ingenuous use of Welsh words as though they had some magical quality reminds one of the Saxon invader in *The Anathemata* (p. 112) who will 'latin-runes tellan', and very often such words or corresponding Welsh references are introduced with a crudity that he would not tolerate when using English. (The same applies to Latin and German.)

When James Jones married Alice Ann Bradshaw of 11 Princes Street, Rotherhithe, on 20 September 1888, in Christ Church, Rotherhithe (this is taken from a copy of the marriage certificate), he was twenty-eight and she was thirty-two. He describes himself as a compositor and she describes herself as a governess. Quite apart from schooling, David grew up in an environment of persons who were well read and well educated in an old-fashioned way—Bunyan on Sunday evenings, and Milton's 'Hymn on the Morning of Christ's Nativity' at Christmas-time. His father would bring home many papers and magazines from the printing office at the end of the week. His mother, later, reproved David for his letters from the Western Front: 'The spelling is a disgrace to the family.' His father was promoted to overseer or foreman, and later became production manager of the *Christian Herald*.

Most readers will be familiar with, or will easily be able to picture to themselves, the domestic circumstances of the suburban class in which David grew up: frugal, careful, but by no means poor in the sense that attached to poverty in those days. This is admirably illus-trated in such pictures as David's *The Sitting Room*, in the group o Brockley back gardens, interiors and exteriors, *The Suburban Order*, or in *The Maid at No. 37*, even though the date of that watercolour (1926) is considerably later. At Mrs. Jones's, across the road from No. 37, there was a servant who came in every day, all day, another who 'did the rough', a woman who came on Thursdays to do the washing, and —a phrase that captures the whole climate and atmosphere—'the Saturday step-girl'. In those years not long after the Great War, David was already looking at such scenes as an outsider. The comment con-tained in his work is such as would never have come into his mind in the years before the war when he himself was native to the scene.

In thinking of that society I am always reminded of the Grossmiths'

Diary of a Nobody: not that there was anything ridiculous about Mr. and Mrs. Jones, but the type of house, the period, the way of living, the relationships with friends, the word with the parson—here Jim Jones as a lay reader was well ahead of Charles Pooter—the emphasis on the gentlemanly, the attitude to tradesmen, the biscuit barrel, the nightly rice pudding, all these bring the house in Holloway and the house in Brockley very close to one another. David had a special affection for that book, and must have understood perfectly the target at which its kindly humour is directed.

Two virtues in David's parents should, in view of what has just been said, be emphasized: their great dignity, and their humour, tolerant in his father, caustic in his mother—and the absence of anything that could be called 'cockney'. The cockney accent, habit, humour, tradition, became well known to David but only as to one who stands apart from it. He learnt that from some of the Londoners with whom he served in the London Welsh, but his two close friends in the army, Reggie Allen and Leslie Poulter, were, as he tells us himself, middle class, from the society in which he himself had originally been at home. Both his mother and his father would have been horrified by anything incorrect or 'common' in his speech or behaviour.

From Camberwell to the army. In his autobiographical fragments David speaks very briefly of the war years. *In Parenthesis* gives a close and, subject to the qualifications imposed by the nature of the writing, accurate account of his experiences from his departure for France until he was wounded in the small hours of the night of 11–12 July 1916. This can be checked and very much amplified by his later letters, and, from the point of view of the military historian, by A. C. Hughes's *Mametz, Lloyd George's 'Welsh Army' at the Battle of the Somme, 1916.*[4] If David's letters can be regarded as providing a life of the poet (I always include the painter in the word), the life they provide is, it will be found, written almost in reverse. As the memory grows older it concentrates more and more on the past, and overlooks today and yesterday. Most of the memories of the war and of childhood appear

[4] This work is as yet, unhappily, unpublished, but a copy of the typescript can be consulted in the Ministry of Defence Library, Whitehall, and at the Imperial War Museum. It includes good maps and photographs; and it has the great advantage that it was inspired by an admiration for *In Parenthesis* and was written partly to illuminate, and always with an eye on, David's book. See also Hughes's shorter essay, 'David Jones: The Man who was on the Field', published by the David Jones Society (German Dept., The University, Manchester) in 1979.

in David's later years and letters; the picture, which starts a little tentatively, is then filled in and rounded off as it returns almost to its beginning.

It may be useful to summarize the chronology of the war years. First, enlistment. David must have decided to join up very soon after the outbreak of the war, for in September 1914 his father wrote to Lloyd George's Private Secretary asking about the formation of a London Welsh battalion of the Royal Welsh Fusiliers.[5] David writes of the 'illusions' that he shared with others of his generation, and spoke of being influenced by the posters that read 'Remember Louvain!'. The following is taken from an undated draft or copy of a letter:

It was now getting towards 1914 and I was seriously concerned with what I should do, for I was determined if possible to avoid becoming a 'commercial artist', and as I refused to do the exams necessary to qualify as an art master, that occupation was closed, but I obviously could not go on indefinitely living on my parents and allowing them to pay the fees required by the art school. But my difficulties were solved by the outbreak of World War I. I tried to enlist in the Artists' Rifles, but was rejected as deficient in expansion of chest—they kept up the Regular Army standard very strictly and to the letter in the early months of the war.[6]

Actually I had wanted to join a Welsh regiment of some sort. And there was being raised a unit called 'The Welsh Horse', and I think it might amuse you to hear of my attempt to join them. It had always been my ambition to ride a horse—preferably a cavalry horse—and I thought here was my chance, so I went to some place in the Inns of Court, I think, where I was taken before a perfectly round man wearing an eye-glass, and this

[5] See below, p. 195. For the change, in 1919, to the spelling 'Welch' Fusiliers, see Robert Graves, *Goodbye to All That* (1929), p. 121.

[6] In conversation David would describe how he used to trot through the streets of Brockley and Lewisham, in running shorts, in order to build up his slight but resilient physique. Though no athlete—I doubt whether he played any game at all until 1947, when his doctors introduced him to medicine ball and badminton—he was in later years a great, and a swift, walker, and after the 1914–18 war made what was then still called a 'walking tour', leaving Brockley to join the pilgrims' road from Winchester to Canterbury.

followed: 'Can you ride?' 'No, sir.' 'Do you know anything about horses?' 'Well, not really, sir.' 'But y'r a Welshman, I take it?' 'My father is a North Welshman, my mother English.' 'I see, that's all right, Welsh enough, and we'd like to have you, but between ourselves, if you'll take my advice, you'll enlist in some infantry mob—Welsh, by all means, but if you know nothing about horses this set-up is no place for you. We see to the care of mounts first and men second. You can please yourself, but I think you'll find it pretty tough—there'll be plenty of time and opportunity to join up, I assure you, and my advice to you is the infantry.'

On 2 January 1915 David enlisted in the 15th (London Welsh) Battalion of the Royal Welsh Fusiliers.[7] Nearly the whole of 1915 was spent in training, first in billets at Llandudno and later at Winnol Down near Winchester. The battalion crossed over to France on 1 December 1915. From 5 to 19 December they trained at Warne, some eight miles south-east of St. Omer, and had their first spell in the trenches, in the La Bassée sector, from 19 to 30 December.

With so much detail available elsewhere and in later letters, it is sufficient here to say that after six months in the trenches the Division marched south through the hills of Artois towards the Somme. This was from 11 to 25 June 1916. Then followed the attack on Mametz Wood in which David was wounded. This is the end of *In Parenthesis* as a source. He was taken to hospital in Birmingham, and then to a nursing home to convalesce, near Shipston-on-Stour. (See below, p. 258, for his misadventure there.) He was back in France just before his twenty-first birthday, i.e. at the end of October, but found himself posted from his own company, B, to D Company. The battalion was then in the Boesinghe sector, north of Ypres, and David would have been involved in the attack on Pilckem Ridge which opened the Passchendaele offensive, had he not been kept back in 'battalion nucleus'—a posting he tried, unsuccessfully, to get out of. The eleven months spent in that area and the next five months in the more southerly Bois Grenier area are referred to in letters. In February 1918 David had a severe attack of trench fever. He was sent back to England,

---

[7] Llewelyn Wyn Griffith was for a time a company officer in the same battalion, and his *Up to Mametz* (1931) covers exactly the same period, in the same areas, as *In Parenthesis*.

and I have not been able to learn where he was in hospital or for how long. He speaks of 'some months', after which he was posted to Limerick, and of a 'couple of months' in Limerick. Since he was in Limerick until the beginning of January 1919, the 'couple' of months must have been more like six. He says little in his letters about this period, and nothing, for example, about his relationship with or view of the Irish—and it was on the eve of the very troubled years. From his conversation I have myself only a vague recollection of David's speaking of going to tea at a Church of Ireland Rectory (I think) and a still vaguer one of the unpleasantness of being jeered at by women when on guard duty at the barrack gates. One of his memories is among the most beautifully contrived of his marginal annotations ('red girl', p. 255).

From Limerick David went to Dublin, to be demobilized in mid-January 1919. I may anticipate now what I shall emphasize later, that his four years in the army, the months in the trenches and the bloody battle of the Wood left him spiritually and psychologically unscarred and even invigorated: and for a short time at least ready for more soldiering. After demobilization he wished at first—until dissuaded by his father—to join the British forces in Russia.

The years 1919–21, at the Westminster School of Art, were to lead to an important change in David's life and thought. In the trenches, he says, he had been a Catholic at heart, and he had from early childhood been drawn, without knowing it, towards the sacramental teaching of the Church. He speaks highly of the R.C. chaplain to his battalion, Fr. Daniel Hughes, S.J., M.C. (the Fr. Martin Larkin of *In Parenthesis*), and hints that Fr. Hughes may have influenced him in this direction; and he describes at some length (see pp. 248–9) the deep impression that was made on him when by chance he saw Mass being celebrated by candlelight in an old building close to the front line. At the Westminster he had some Catholic friends, and although they failed to understand what David meant when he said that post-Impressionist theory in the arts fitted in with what he saw in the Church's teaching about the Mass as a making of a real thing, of the liturgy as an artefact, of the sacraments as effectual signs, I cannot help suspecting that it was one of those friends who introduced him to Fr. John O'Connor of Bradford. We know that it was Fr. O'Connor who suggested that David should go to Eric Gill at Ditchling Common, and that he first went there in January 1921. He spent some time with Fr. O'Connor in Bradford, and, as the Certificate of Baptism shows, was received by him into the Catholic Church on 7 September 1921. It was then that he took the further Christian name of Michael, his use of which depended upon his varying attitudes to pious practices.

Eric Gill writes rather ominously to Fr. O'Connor on 13 September 1921: 'We are delighted about David and hope he'll come back afore long (then we'll have to keep him up to the mark and knock some corners off him D.V.).'[8] This, I believe, shows that David visited Ditchling Common more than once during 1921 and finally went to live there soon after his reception into the Catholic Church. I have not found it possible to determine the exact date. Keeping David 'up to the mark' meant cutting him off from all art-school tradition and habits and trying to make him a 'workman'. He was put to work at first with George Maxwell, the carpenter and builder, and it is hardly surprising that this was a complete failure. On the other hand, he learnt from Eric Gill and from Desmond Chute how to engrave on wood, and he gradually and at first almost surreptitiously went back to water-colours.

Philip Hagreen, who was very close to David at Ditchling, writes:

'My main memory of David at Ditchling is of his utter goodness. He had an awful lot to put up with and he never blamed anyone or complained; the discomfort amounted almost to torment. He was lodged in a stable that was one brick thick and had a sloping brick floor. Around and under it clay—the dregs of Noe's flood not yet drained off. David's mattress grew mildew and I don't know why he did not get rheumatic fever. Our workshop was a hut without lining or ceiling. The wind blew between the weatherboards and the floorboards. David pulled his belt tight to make his clothes hug him and kept on working. At that time he produced an astonishing quantity of engravings, drawings and carvings. He followed Eric in working old blocks into reliefs. He made a *Mater Castissima*, a tiny thing of monumental majesty. But when he wanted to make a base he was flummoxed. To fasten two pieces of wood together was almost carpentry. I had to do that.

'Eric used to come into our shop and remonstrate with David about his methods—or want of method. Eric told him that his table was the altar on which he offered his work to God. As the priest he should have nothing on the table but the tools for the job in hand and they should be in a regular order. Also David should keep accounts. He should know how many hours he spent on each job and what the materials cost. David did not rebel. He would have obeyed if he could, but his

[8] *Letters of Eric Gill*, ed. Walter Shewring (1947), p. 148.

table continued to bear a mound of books, tools, brushes, papers and paint box with cigarette-ends in it.'

The stable—though 'barn' might be a better word—in which David lived, was in the grounds of a house called Woodbarton which had been built for Desmond Chute. David shared this with Reggie Lawson (now a Dominican lay brother in Rome), who taught the three Gill girls to sing; and at times with others. They provided and cooked their own rations. A rough billet. Joan Gill, golden-haired milkmaid, would deliver their milk every afternoon. 'The term "Sorrowful Mysteries" was used', writes Philip Hagreen, though he is not speaking of David and Reggie, 'for the misfits and rolling stones that drifted to Ditchling. Mostly they had been sent by Fr. Vincent McNabb. Some were broken men and some were cracked. Eric was invariably kind, but there was little he could do. Some were given shelter in the stable, which thus got its name.' It was on the wall of that building that David painted his *Entry into Jerusalem*.[9] Later the building was made into a dwelling house, with an upper floor, and the wall painting was obliterated.

There were two separate but allied organizations at Ditchling Common, the Guild of craftsmen (printer, stone-carvers, carpenter and builder, engravers) and the association of members of the Third Order of St. Dominic. David was a Dominican tertiary and attended the Little Office that was sung or recited at regular hours in the chapel. It was this that introduced him to many of the psalms in the Vulgate version that were important to his work. He was never at the heart of the endless Guild discussions and internal politics, and never, so far as I can ascertain, a full member of the Guild. A minute of 2 March 1924 in the then current Guild minute-book says, 'It is agreed that David Michael Jones, T.O.S.D., is eligible as a postulant if he should desire membership', and then on 6 April 1924, 'David Michael Jones is elected as a postulant of the Guild, to be received at the next convenient occasion'—such an occasion being the holding of a ceremony of reception in the chapel. Qualifications for Guild membership included earning one's living by creative manual work, owning one's tools and one's work. As regards work David's status was that of a learner; and at the meeting on 2 March they would have been discussing whether by that time he possessed the above qualifications. There is no record of his having advanced beyond postulancy, and he

[9] Reproduced in Robin Ironside's *David Jones* (1949), in the Penguin Modern Painters series.

is not mentioned again in the minute-book after his presence was recorded at a Guild meeting on 1 May 1924.[10]

Ditchling provided David with a period of rest and reorientation. It will be noticed that he often speaks of 'direction'. If his work is going well it is 'in the right direction', if it is going badly he has lost his 'sense of direction'. Direction implies a starting-point, and he found a starting-point at Ditchling in Eric Gill's views on industrialism, in the Scholastic philosophy of art as presented by Jacques Maritain— in particular in Maritain's treatment of the artefact as sign or symbol, the other half of Gill's view of the artefact as a thing made 'according to right reason'—and above all in what David took most to heart, the notion of the gratuitousness of the Creation and the analogical gratuitousness of the work of man-the-artist: the theme of much of his later writing.

In June 1924 David became engaged to Eric Gill's second daughter, Petra, the first and undoubtedly the most beautiful of his cult figures. Two months later, after a split in the Ditchling Guild, Gill and his family moved to the monastery at Capel-y-ffin in the Black Mountains on the Monmouthshire–Breconshire border. With them went the Hagreens (who did not stay long); the Attwaters were already living in one part of the monastery. At the time the Gills arrived, most of the monastery was empty and partly derelict. It belonged to the Benedictine community of Caldey, from whom Gill rented his part of the buildings and the land that went with them.[11] He repaired the place with the particular skill he had for such work.

I was living then in a house about three or four hundred yards away, built by Fr. Ignatius for his mother, which we called Plas Geneviève or, more often, the Grange. My companions were two Caldey monks, Fr. Joseph Woodford, who lived there for the sake of his health, and Brother (later Dom) Raphael Davies, pattern of all masculine and monastic virtues, who cared for Fr. Joseph and was supposed to profit in some way from such little knowledge as I possessed. I had been

[10] I am indebted to Valentine Kilbride, the present secretary of the Guild, for this information. A fairly, but not completely, accurate account of Ditchling, the ideals and the manner of life, and David's position in that group, may be found in Robert Speaight's *Life of Eric Gill* (1966) and in Donald Attwater's *A Cell of Good Living* (1969).

[11] Donald Attwater gives an excellent description of the building and the valley at the head of which it lay, in his *A Cell of Good Living*; anyone interested in the founder of the community that once lived there should read his *Father Ignatius of Llanthony* (1931).

eagerly awaiting the arrival of the Gills, because I knew that there were three girls; the heart of the eldest, Betty, had already been given to David Pepler, son of Hilary; Petra was engaged to David Jones; but the youngest? . . . my memory therefore of Capel-y-ffin is a golden glow of Arcady. It did not take me long to infiltrate the Gill household, although all I could bring to it was a readiness to learn from Eric. And if Eric had an enduring influence on David's thought—if little or none on his work—he determined my life.

David himself did not come to Capel until just before Christmas 1924. It was then that I first met him, and I found, as others of his friends have found, that friendship was immediate. This was because, if he was going to be bothered with a person at all (and he knew at once whether there would be anything of value to share with any particular person), he immediately established a direct relationship. This, I believe, explains how it was that, even more than most of us, he would keep different friends or different circles of friends, in different compartments. I do not mean that he in any deliberate way kept his friends separated from one another—indeed, one of his greatest joys lay in the sharing of friendships—but to each individual he communicated, as though for that person alone, one particular segment of his own self.

It was at Capel on Christmas Eve 1924 that, as he was to remember for so many years, the two of us 'released the waters', as David describes in *The Anathemata* (p. 238). I have a clear memory of him sitting, trench-coated, at a high, deep window sill, engraving; of long conversations in the evenings; of discussing Malory (the Waste Land theme had been with him for years); of taking tea up to his cell or cubicle in the early morning ('Ah, gunfire! Thank you, china!')—for I was then working for a local sheep farmer, and Laurie Cribb, the stone mason, Eric's assistant, and I would be the first to rise in the mornings; and I could take tea up to the youngest Gill daughter, Joan, only by the excuse of taking it to all the others.

That first winter at Capel was a hard one. David did a great deal of work, muffled against the cold in scarf and tightly lashed trench-coat. He was engraving and making small boxwood carvings; he painted the large crucifix and long inscription in what was at first the chapel and was later Eric's workshop, and the metal tabernacle still in the present chapel. He returned seriously to watercolours. One, I was astonished to see as I looked at our collection of photographs of his pictures, was painted out of doors in February: a tribute to his hardiness. At Capel, where this first emancipated flowering began, he moved out of doors in two senses: literally, in that he was working in the open air, and metaphorically, in that, after taking many fundamental principles from Eric Gill, he was beginning to develop and express them in his own way and, more particularly, in his own vocabulary.

At Capel David might have realized his ambition to ride a horse or —what, indeed, he might have thought even more romantic—a Welsh hill pony of the type he was later to associate with the mobile striking force of Romano-Britons under the leadership of an Arthur. Such ponies, ridden or drawing a float, were the only means of transport, apart from Dom Raphael's 1913 Austro-Daimler, which was frowned on by the purity of our elders. The nearest that David came to horse-management was to drive the float the eleven miles to Llanvihangel to meet Petra. He found it difficult to force the obstinate pony, Jessie, into a smart trot, even though he stood up like an ancient charioteer and urged her on with loud cries and sharp blows from the slack of the reins.

David had no contact with the inhabitants of the valley. It is true that in that very much anglicized border-land no Welsh is spoken—or was then—but the people of the valley were very Welsh in their intonation and very different in their ways, in much of their vocabulary, in their domestic economy and social habits, from the corresponding English country people. The Englishman, Donald Attwater, came to know them well. So to some degree did I, the Irishman, in the year or more I worked for the sheep farmer. David can hardly have even spoken to any of them. He found them strange and frightening—just as he says later (p. 106) that he found the English working class frightening.

David was at Capel until March 1925, when he paid his first visit to Caldey Island, as the letter printed below records. He went there at the suggestion of Philip Hagreen who, having enlisted on the very first day of the war and been discharged in 1916 on medical grounds, had gone to Caldey to recover his health. David stayed in the monastery, where he knew a number of the monks, including the Prior, Dom Wilfrid Upson (later Abbot), and, more particularly, Dom Theodore Bailey. He had seen a good deal of the latter at Capel, knew his work (even if he had no great admiration for it) and loved his gentle and sensitive nature. Some of Dom Theodore's painted lettering can still be seen in the chapel at Capel.

David had begun the engravings for the Golden Cockerel Press edition of *Gulliver's Travels* when he went to Caldey.

To Philip Hagreen, 26 March 1925   *The Abbey, Caldey*

... I have done a good deal of drawing since my arrival. The weather has been so good that I simply felt that Gulliver or no Gulliver I must take the opportunity and do some outdoor work, as it would be absurd to leave here without having done some work. ... I wish I could bring the results of my labours to show you—not that they are at all good—but merely rather interesting. I like the stone walls and the murderously sharp rocks that

do this only much more so. Only I find the *form* most infernally difficult to correlate—if you follow. I have never before drawn the sea—it is difficult not to be led up various impressionistic and realistic and otherwise dangerous paths when faced with sea—or —even worse, to fall back upon some dead convention.

There is also a superb plantation of new trees here, which is thrilling, very thrilling—like the Garden of Gethsemane and the Garden of the Tomb and the Garden of—well—the other sort of garden, where Venus disports herself. In fact it is, as 'B' [Belloc] would say, 'a garden universal, a garden Catholic'—not that it is a flower garden, but a garden of small trees and winding paths—but oh! so difficult to seize hold of when one tries to draw it. I have nearly been demented trying to capture its beauty even but vaguely—I have made four or five furtive attempts—one in oils I have sent to the 'Unknown and Unowned' Artists' show—one something like this [*see facing page*] only, I think, better. It is pink and green and brown and blue.

I am glad you have sent your Madonna to the Goupil.[12] Dom

[12] The Goupil Gallery in Regent Street, owned by William Marchant, who was Eric Gill's agent.

1. THE GARDEN ENCLOSED (Ditchling) 1924. Oil on panel, 14 × 11¾ in.
Tate Gallery

2. DOG ON THE SOFA (Brockley) 1926. Pencil and watercolour, 21 × 15 in.
National Museum of Wales

Theodore, I am pleased to say, has sent three crucifixes and two paintings—one painting of a Madonna which I think is in the right direction and a small still-life he did in Paris which is rather nice.

I am grieved to hear that the situation at Capel is not any easier—what a world—it is incredibly difficult—I pray for you— I wish I could do something. I agree about fasting—anything that causes a definite and prolonged breach of charity should be avoided—if people can't fast and remain charitable and normally polite it seems to me sheer rot to go on fasting—seeing that the role and only point in any mortification of the flesh is to *increase* charity and kill selfishness—which it does do in saints completely. Forgive all this quite unnecessary amateur theology—I am sorry —and in any case 'I may be wrong' [Belloc again, the 'r' to be rolled]! At all events I can't see it in any other way at present.

Now Desmond [Chute] has written to say he likes the block and has sent a cheque for £4, and seems very pleased and wants 100 printed.[13] What do you think? Shall I have the block sent

[13] Probably the book plate listed as no. 31 in *Word and Image IV*, ed. Douglas Cleverdon, the catalogue of the 1972 National Book League exhibition of David's work.

to Hilary [Pepler], or could you print them on your press on that paper of Eric's and send me a bill?—less fag to send them to Hilary—do whichever you feel inclined—I will explain to Desmond.

Eric Gill writes to Desmond Chute on 23 May 1925, 'David J. is at Caldey—he's been there since beginning of Lent—painting and engraving. I don't know what will happen to him. He's so determined to earn his living off his own bat—but he's so incapacitated by his temperament and unworkmanlike training.' Now that David was engaged to Petra, at the back of his mind must have lain the dread of having to earn a living for more than one; but Eric's remark, characteristic of his attitude to all forms of art not directed to an immediate practical end (a principle which, when applied to his own work, he interpreted at times by a somewhat devious casuistry), shows little understanding; for, in the exercise of his talents, David was most workmanlike. His trouble, of which we shall hear more in later letters, was entirely different. He was to spend years trying, not to deny any role to the artist in modern society, as Eric denied it, but to explain and justify the importance of such a role: and this because of his own awareness of his gifts and his determination to use them, in spite of great difficulties, to carry out what he regarded as an inevitable duty.

II

EMERGENCE, ACHIEVEMENT, ADVERSITY 1925—1946

---*---

Caldey, Pigotts, Sidmouth, London, Bowden House

The place in which David lived—his immediate surroundings—in later years, especially, what he could see from his window—was always of great importance to him and to his work. What he wrote about Capel-y-ffin has often been quoted: 'It was at this propitious time'—1924-6—'that circumstances occasioned my living in Nant Honddhu, there to feel the impact of the strong hill-rhythms and the bright counter-rhythms of the *afonydd dyfroedd* which make so much of Wales such a "plurabelle".'[1] Similarly he writes of Caldey, 'On Caldey Island I began to have some idea of what I personally would ask a painting to be, and I think that from 1926 onwards there has been a fairly recognizable direction in my work.' Of Pigotts, too, and of Rock Hall, Alnwick: 'The rambling, familiar, south, walled, small, flower-beddedness of Pigotts and the space, park, north, serene, clear silverness of Rock in Northumberland both did something.' As he needed this sense of stability in nature, of a starting-point from which he could determine a *direction*, so he needed the support and reassurance of his nearest companions. Of several friends he writes that he *leaned* on him or her. And this, I believe, partly explains why at certain times and in certain places he was desolate. At Sidmouth, for example, he was comfortable enough in the Fort Hotel, but he cared little for the immediate countryside and was often alone. He was at times cheered by the company of those who joined him, but they came for comparatively short visits and he was greatly cast down when they left. David needed his friends to be constantly at hand. It was the same in 1942, when he settled in Sheffield Terrace, off Church Street, Kensington, with little to look at from his small room, and friends who were attentive but could not be living with him. On the other hand, among the happiest days were the two Chelsea periods—in the late 1920s when, while living in Brockley, he was often at the Burns house in St. Leonard's Terrace; and in the early part of the war (between Sidmouth and Sheffield Terrace) when he was in Tom Burns's house in Glebe Place, when Harman Grisewood was round the corner, and others were close at hand and often seen. He was never, I believe, happy in any particular place without some particular person. And it should be added that in any household or gathering David gave, in return, even

---

[1] See *Epoch and Artist*, p. 30.

more than he received, for he acted as a leaven to activate the intelligence of his friends and repaid their love many times over.

It may be well to say a word or two about David's finances. Anyone who is really interested in what porridge had John Keats might well, with patience and industry, find out exactly what David earned himself and what he received from his friends, and when. I am satisfied with a much more general picture. Until David joined the army he was dependent on his parents. Then for four years, from the beginning of 1915 to the beginning of 1919 he lived as a soldier. From 1919 until he went to Ditchling Common in 1921 he was partly dependent on his parents and partly on his government grant. At Ditchling he certainly earned his living, meagre though it may have been, by engraving. And the same is true of his time at Capel-y-ffin, Caldey and Brockley in 1924 to 1930, and at Pigotts and Brockley—with Helen Sutherland, too, at times, at Rock Hall—until 1933. During all this time there was always a base at which he could be housed and fed. He sold a certain amount privately and this supplied him with anything else he needed. Things became more difficult when he gradually ceased to use his parents' home and moved briefly to Hartland Quay, then to Sidmouth, and then, after the outbreak of war, to London. It was about this time that both Helen Sutherland and Jim Ede (others, too) began to give him regular help.

1925—1935

David was back at Capel during the summer of 1925, and spent a good deal of 1926 there, as we know from dated pictures, for example *Mr. Gill's Hay Harvest*. His base was still his parents' home in Brockley, where he did a good deal of signed and dated work in these years. In 1926 he stayed at Waltham St. Lawrence in Berkshire, with Robert and Moira Gibbings of the Golden Cockerel Press. He was at Caldey again in 1927, in Bristol, and in that year too he first stayed in and painted from his parents' bungalow on the very edge of the sea, at Hove. In 1928 he was in France, visiting the Gills at Salies-de-Béarn and the Hagreens at Lourdes and Arcachon.

At the same time he formed a number of new and important friendships that were to last all his life: with Jim Ede, who was then at the Tate Gallery; with Tom Burns, whom he had met first in 1922 when Tom as a schoolboy—he was always half a generation ahead of his contemporaries—visited Ditchling Common, and who was now invigorating the world of serious publishing; with Harman Grisewood, then starting his career at the BBC; with Helen Sutherland, so long to be David's patron, where the difference in age, background and means produced a different type of relationship. There was Bernard Wall, too, who was a great extender of horizons, and Louis Bussell, who kept his savagely destructive intelligence in the background (I can still hear nothing praised without thinking of Louis and the line from one of David's favourite poems, Browning's *Bishop Blougram's Apology*, 'Where sits Rossini patient in his stall'). Letters written from, and pictures of, Bristol remind us of the entry (through Eric Gill) of Douglas Cleverdon, whose enthusiasm and patience, in years to come, were to bring David's work to the wider audience of the Third Programme.

I had left Capel fairly early in 1926, and met David again when I was working in London (in very odd, arduous, amusing circumstances) at the end of that year. David would come in from Brockley two or three times a week—maybe oftener—to see his friend Frank Medworth, Jim and Helen Ede, Harman Grisewood, Tom Burns, or me, or to meet any number of different friends at the Burns house, 40 St. Leonard's Terrace, Chelsea.

My memory of those days is one of great gaiety and energy.[2] What a roaring time we had, Tom writes many years later—and what girls! 'Everybody was desperately falling in and out of love as far as I can see —except the only steadies, you and Joan.' One could, perhaps, count David as an 'unemployed steady', for his engagement to Petra Gill had been broken off at the beginning of 1927. Vastly though he was attracted by the many lovely girls he was to meet, and much as he delighted in their company and enjoyed their intelligence (which seemed oddly to coincide with good looks), he was not to 'fall in love' again for some time—if that phrase can describe what happened to him on two later occasions.

David was in close touch with Philip Hagreen when he heard from Petra, who solved the problem David would never face, that she was to marry Denis Tegetmeier. Philip believes that it was a shattering and permanent blow. 'Langland said', he writes in a recent letter, '—"Let bring a man in a bote amiddes a broade water"—David's boat was

[2] The feel of the time, and of the intellectual, religious, philosophic climate of the mid-1920s, is admirably conveyed in Harman Grisewood's *One Thing at a Time* (1968), which may be supplemented by the early part of Bernard Wall's *Headlong into Change* (1969).

sailing with a fair wind towards a clear horizon. Then in January 1927 the mast snapped. Thereafter he could only row. He rowed bravely but, pulling at the oars, he could not see ahead. Denied the vision of hope he could only see what lay behind—the smouldering ruins of man's history and a litter of broken things. Throughout all that happened David was angelically good.'

Joan and I have always been inclined to minimize the distress caused by Petra's decision. It was so obvious that marriage was out of the question, and that not only for financial reasons but also because David had known even from his teens that his vocation would never allow him to marry. He had lived in a convenient and agreeable day-dream, and after the shock of awakening he must have felt that a great burden of responsibility had been removed. Confirmation may be found in the quality and quantity of his work at that time, which included what was literally, no doubt, a look into the past but artistically a venture into the future, the beginning of *In Parenthesis*.

A few fragments of letters survive from the late 1920s, including one to Jim Ede:

To H.S.E., Sunday 2 October 1927　　　　　*Coburg Hotel, Tenby*

Here am I a prisoner not being able to say to the sea be still—I cannot reach Caldey until the weather changes! It's very depressing—anyway being alone in a hotel always really drives me mad! Tenby is rather charming of course—but it is fiendishly windy and a beastly drizzle.

... I have not got your letter with me as I write but I was a little amused about 'the kind of letter your philosophy would tear up'—I wonder if you think the C[atholic] C[hurch] tends to suppression—it really does not—it only (ideally) shapes and modifies and rightly orders the emotions as an artist rightly orders and makes significant the forms of his picture—you understand I speak ideally—but even in practice I believe it occasionally shows itself in some people! Of course anyone might say—Yes! but I don't like the 'shapes' the C.C. makes of people's lives—well, that's another story—I mean like saying of a man playing tennis that one prefers rugby football.

... [Arthur] Howell [of the St. George's Gallery] liked only the good pictures I took him—he's getting quite a good critic!!

I wish he was easier to get on with as a human being. I mean I admit I find him a little trying to converse with. . . . There are very few people in this hotel and no one of my kind. I mean, you know, no one to talk to. Well, there is a parson of some sort who told me all about red sandstone before breakfast! *Love to you both.*

The first exhibition of David's work was in 1927, at the St. George's Gallery off Hanover Square. David had been introduced to Arthur Howell, owner of the gallery, in 1925 by Eric Gill and Jim Ede, but at first Howell was puzzled by the style of David's watercolours. 'I waited', he says, 'for the colours to take form in my mind. This they gradually did. Three quarters of an hour passed before I felt capable of passing an opinion. It was favourable.' To David's evident disappointment, however, Howell refused at the time to do more than include two of his pictures in an exhibition of the Modern English Watercolour Society. These attracted little notice. Months later, David returned to the gallery with more watercolours. 'After he left I opened the portfolio and took out what was in it. The work seemed to me exquisite. Quite apart from the colour, and the design into which it was woven, there was here a charm, an imponderable delicacy and gentleness of vision, maturely handled, that was entirely personal.'

The result, two years after David's first visit to Howell, was a most successful exhibition: 'Many spectators were drawn. Most of the pictures were sold.'[3] One can only guess at the approximate amount of money David received. The prices, which included the cost of the frames and the dealer's commission, probably ranged from £6 or £7 to, most exceptionally, £15: a total, perhaps, of £250, which would certainly have kept him alive as a bachelor, and even in reasonable comfort, for a year. What was sold, however, was the work of several years, and all he had earned besides this were the paltry fees he received for his engravings.

To Helen Ede, 2 November 1927   5 Western Esplanade, Hove
. . . I left Caldey last Thursday—went to Bristol—came to London for one night and then on here where the parents are enjoying the sea—and I attempting to draw the same. A more

[3] Howell's account is from his *Frances Hodgkins: Four Vital Years* (1952), pp. 5-10.

difficult thing! God knows how I am going to answer all my letters—it's quite hopeless. I wrote *none* at Caldey—it's hideous.

As to Gin—I reverted to that habit solemnly today—it was excellent! A month at Caldey, nearly—drink—one whisky and soda, one Grand Marnier, two glasses of port—and a great deal of water and tea. So you see temperance could hardly go further.

. . . The sea roars outside this house which is builded upon the tide line—which is rather fun. *How are you?* I hope happy—I look forward to coming to Hampstead simply tremendously, it *will* be nice—so glad you liked the St. George's Gallery show. *Au revoir* for now. God bless you.

To H.S.E., 4 November 1927   *5 Western Esplanade, Hove*
. . . I wonder what you will think of my work when you return. I do hope you will like some of it—I did an immense amount of tearing up at Caldey but one or two of the remaining ones I myself like—and indeed think them in a curious way the best things I have done so far. (This is probably rubbish—some of them are awful.)

. . . I agree I think with what you say in your letter to a large extent—It may be I personally am too concerned with 'inhibitions'—the whole question of sublimation—suppression—'canalization' and the rest is a very vexed one—and hideously complicated for me—Complicated largely by there being no general standard of practice, or accepted ethics in the world at the moment—everyone means different things by the same words and everyone interprets ideas and actions so diversely that one is more scrupulous I suppose than one might normally be if there were a real civilization builded upon some understood philosophy—were it Catholic, Buddhist, Protestant, pagan or what you will—but we of the modern world all are a mixture of these 'isms' and consequently are shy and alarmed at each other's notions. *This is probably all nonsense*—at any rate it is ill put. I *told* you it is no use my writing letters—but I will post it.

. . . As to what you say about my thinking all these energies can be turned into spiritual channels—I *know* this is *only the vocation of the few*—I know, we *all* admit that God alone can satisfy our affection but clearly it is only the 'mystic' who is able to 'suit the action to the word', so to say, in the full degree.

I loathe the word mystic—it might mean anything—anyway, I mean by it here that human being who is more *directly* in union with God than are most of us—for most, of course, rightly and properly, have to be content with loving God *through* created things.

I think you're off the track about the kind of person I am!—I can't imagine anyone more bound up in terrestrial comforts etc. than I am—it revolts me to think of it.—About 'angels'—the C[atholic] C[hurch] when she speaks of angels means beings of pure intelligence—whose *wills* are *fixed*—heavens above! here am I on the verge of discussing all the business about Lucifer—the Fall—anyway, all I mentioned angels for was that the Church means by the word angel—just that—a being without any body and existing purely as a separate intelligence—whereas she says man is *incomplete* without body—hence, the 'Resurrection of the body'—by which she means that the soul must have some counterpart—which we call 'body'—whatever is 'essential' to body, of course, I do not know—but she says that whatever *is* of the 'essence' of our bodies (and not merely accidental) we shall have for all eternity—as separate individuals.

Angels on the other hand never (she postulates) had 'bodies' although sometimes appearing in bodily form—as at the Annunciation etc.—Enough of this amateur theology!

To H.S.E. and Helen Ede, 21 May 1928
c/o Philip Hagreen Esq., Chalet St. Vincent,
Monastère des Dominicaines, Lourdes

... I came on here [from the Gills at Salies-de-Béarn] when Eric came back to England. . . . This little house is just outside the enclosure of a convent of Dominican nuns—who sing the office with a more marvellous beauty than I have before heard—and their French-Latin—no, I spoke of that before—but it is *so* wonderful. I did a kind of picture of a nun picking roses with mountains behind and a white wall, which I don't mind in some ways—but I've achieved nothing new or thrilling—I wonder if you will hate them. I notice the trees are so much more upright here and taller than in England, even up in the mountains.

To H.S.E., 24 October 1929   *115 Howson Road, Brockley*
... I'm reading a very interesting book, called *From Ritual to Romance*, a learned book about the Grail legend—very *Golden Bough*ish but I think, in the main, sound, by a woman called Jessie Weston—a bit trying in places. It's very interesting to me at the moment, with this Arthur business in my head.

... Sickert has rather a nice painting in the London Group— the only thing there that seemed to have an 'idea'—isn't it awful —these yards of 'able' paintings of various kinds that seem only seen with the eye of the flesh.

The 'Arthur business in my head' in the above letter could refer, in a general way, to the drawing upon Malory for some of the imagery of *In Parenthesis*, and, in a more particular way, to Douglas Cleverdon's plan for a *Morte Darthur*, to be illustrated by David. This did not get beyond a single dry-point, preliminary to an ambitious series of engravings on copper—*Lady with wounded knight by seashore*. The 'but' attached to Frazer (the content of whose work fascinated David) is interesting.

In the spring or summer of 1929 I rejoined the Gills at Pigotts, the Buckinghamshire farmhouse to which they had moved in 1928, and started printing with Eric. David was at Pigotts for some time in 1929 and thereafter was there a great deal until the autumn of 1933.

The house, built round a central yard, lay at the top of a steep hill some five miles from High Wycombe, above the village of North Dean. It was primitive by modern vulgar standards—David had no cause to complain of the 'utile' electric light or heat or the ugly wasteful tap. But Eric, repairing and building, had made it into an admirable working haven. The 'Big House' (the adjective is relative), where Eric and Mary Gill lived (and during 1930, or most of it, David and I and Joan and her brother Gordian and various other persons from time to time), occupied one side of the quadrangle and part of another. David and I shared a bedroom over the long room in which Eric engraved— our 'billet', from the window of which David drew *Pigotts in Storm*.[4]

[4] Reproduced in Robin Ironside's *David Jones*.

There was a chapel and two large stone workshops; a house along another side in which Petra and Denis Tegetmeier lived after their marriage in January 1930, and where Denis had his workshop. Another side was mostly taken up by my printing office and a wash-house. And there was a very small cottage, a sort of addendum, into which Joan and I moved after we were married in November 1930, and where David then joined us.

Christmas of 1930, however, David spent with his parents in Brockley, writing to Harman Grisewood from there:

To H.J.G., Christmas Day, 1930   115 Howson Road, Brockley
Thank you so much for the Eliot poem ['The Journey of the Magi'], which I like *immensely*—and for your letter, which I was delighted to get. . . . Midnight Mass *was* good—an *incredibly* packed church and a general mêlée of atrocious music, vestments, candles and heat—but jolly fine: it always astonishes me how the liturgy 'comes through' these wads and layers of stuff—but it seems to.

My father gave me Gerard Manley Hopkins's poems for Christmas—for which I am delighted.

Thank heaven it's been a day free from any attempts at 'Festivities' on a large scale, which is what I really dread about this season. It's been quite deliciously quiet for me—I do hope you have not been too hopelessly subjected to the slings and arrows of anything particularly outrageous.

I came 'out of the trenches' for the first time fifteen years ago today—it makes me feel incredibly ancient. I remember seeing field-artillerymen sitting astride the muzzle of a field-gun, singing carols (very badly!) on the La Bassée road.

That Christmas scene was to be stored and to reappear many years later on p. 216 of *The Anathemata*. Had David cast his mind back another five years, to 1910, he would have recalled a 'festivity' typical of his youth. A programme survives of the fourth annual entertainment given by the 'Dalrymple Concert Party' in the Dalrymple Hall, Brockley: David and his sister, with their cousins the Bradshaws, grandchildren of Ebenezer Bradshaw, mast- and block-maker of Rotherhithe. 'Master W. Jones' recited 'Griffith's answer to Harold' and passages from *Henry V*; and the 'Grand Torchlight Procession' included Britannia (his sister) and 'Cadwal, a Briton' (Master W. Jones). The cover of the programme (minstrel, harp, dog, much holly etc.) was designed by David. This is the only glimpse I have had of his brother Harold, soon to die of tuberculosis, bravely and touchingly lying on the sofa and shouting 'Encore!'. The Dalrymple Hall was, in fact, the family's 'front room'.

In the very small cottage Joan and I shared with David at Pigotts, we had to pass through his cabin-like bedroom to get into ours, and after our first son, Michael, was born David would come into our room at bed time and sit on the bed talking—and the most revealing conversations are about nothing or everything and so impossible to recall —or reading us lumps of *In Parenthesis*. What I remember most of such readings is his constant dread of excessive rhetoric.

Even later, in 1933 when David was at his most strained, a conversation with him was never miserable or depressing. A good example of this dual attitude may be read in *In Parenthesis* (p. 153), where one of the men comes close to a breakdown as the moment for the dawn attack approaches: 'He found him all gone to pieces and not pulling himself together nor making the best of things. When they found him his friends came on him in the secluded fire-bay who miserably wept for the pity of it all and for the things shortly to come to pass and no hills to cover us.' It could be a description of David himself as he faces the blank sheet of Whatman or unlined foolscap; yet I would wager that it is the first 'He' and not the next pronoun, 'him', that refers to the poet himself. Immediately, however, he turns to a jest that is light-hearted and full of memories of his childhood: '... you see Cousin Dicky doesn't cry nor any of this nonsense—why, he ate his jam-puff when they came to take Tiger away—and getting an awfully good job in the Indian Civil.' I can never forget the laughter in our little cottage at Pigotts when David first read those lines to us: his delight in the jam-puff—the perfect juxtaposition with the terror of anticipation—David's description of that particular sort of children's tea party in the 'front room' of the house in the London suburb—the added force and amusement of the cat Tiger—a Capel-y-ffin cat who would leap through the window as one of the girls called 'Tiger, Tiger, Tiger!'—and David would say, 'You'd be uncommon surprised if Blake's Tyger, burning bright, answered your call'—and then, on one occasion, drew a charming illustration of the scene.

He was what is called 'good about the house', making his bed in 'reg'mental style', fetching sticks for the fire, drying up and 'putting away'. He had, from Joan's point of view, only two serious faults: being a swift and neat dryer-up, he would not allow our pewter plates to shed the excess of water naturally, but would bang their edges on the draining-board; and, in spite of being often reproved, he broke the rims of many of them. The other fault was his standing to work by a window where he completely blocked a short narrow passage that led from the living room into the kitchen.

The letter that follows was written while Joan and I were staying with Donald Attwater in Machynlleth—hence the reference to Dafydd ap Gruffyd, brother of Llywelyn, and the red-haired banditti. David remained in our cottage and was in charge of the dog Jock. On our return we found that David had made Joan a most beautiful board on which to hang her saucepans, painted and numbered and lettered JOAN'S SAVSEPAN BORD—which still shows how uncertain are the foundations of his distinction between 'use' and 'sign'.

To J. and R.H., 28 July 1931   *Pigotts*

Thanks so much for your letter. Awfully glad you are finding painting exciting. I hope I got the range of palette you like.[5] As for me, the document has not advanced much further—been trying to paint but with no result save intolerable annoyance and rage.

Stayed in London from Saturday last until Wednesday. Now it's Saturday again!

So far from shouting at the dog Jock, he has attached himself to my person with an unique devotion. He was very unhappy for the first two days after your departure, but seems better now and will without doubt give you a terrific welcome when you return.

I am very anxious to see your painting. I'd forgotten about that bloody traitor Dafydd Gom.

No news, I think. If only one could get some work done! No. Harman merely brought news and I wrote of the financial mess in Germany and Hungary, that was all.

[5] The colours David gave me were cerulean blue, aureolin, vermilion, alizarin ('madder' was to appear quite often in his later writing, too), viridian, chinese white, ivory black.

Charles [Burns] came today. Tom [Burns] has gone to Cumberland. Petra has a cold.

I tried to do a painting from the scullery in your cottage—ghastly mess—can't see anything, you know—gone.

Now going to try and paint usual flower business in sitting-room at H.Q. [the 'Big House']. I want a new vision—so tired.

Joan's p.c. just arrived. Thank you *so* much, Joan. What a place—I remember it—amazing.

Find out what you can about the red-haired banditti of Mawddwy. Must stop. Forgive dull, dull letter. . . . Everybody sends love.

Look forward to seeing you both very much. I return to London for Rock [Helen Sutherland's house in Northumberland] very soon. Now for another try at the most desperately difficult of all the arts.

Lots of love.

DAVID

P.S. Much love to Donald from me. I write this from your printing shop—the dog Jock sitting scratching his hindmost parts outside window.

The next letter is preceded by an inscription, the words of which are taken from the blessing of the candle on Holy Saturday: 'Nihil enim nobis nasci profuit, nisi redimi profuisset' (for to be born had been no boon to us, had there not been the boon of redemption) (*see facing page*).

To J. and R.H., Holy Saturday (26 March) 1932   *Brockley*
To thank you both ever so much for both your letters. I was so very pleased to get them this morn. I'm sorry to repeat the same text as I sent to Petra but it seems to me jolly good and I hadn't noticed it before. Also I was pleased to notice that St. Augustine in a bit of his sermon used for the sixth lesson of the Matins for Good Friday, has a good word for Pilate—or do you suppose that is just anti-'Perfidious Jew' stuff because of his being Roman in sympathy—no—I think it's all right. I managed to get out to part of the vegetation rites of the Redeemed this morning,

NIHIL ENI
IMM NOBIS
NASCI P
RO FVIT
NISI RED
IMI PRO
FVISSET

otherwise I've been to nothing. Was sorry that some bastard in the choir did Caruso (don't know how to spell his name but you know, the macaroni-merchant) stuff just a bit too precious and swallowed up the Celebrant's commencing of the Magnificat at the end of Mass, which is one of the plums of the year, I think—however. Yes, wasn't it beastly not being able to get off with the lads on Tuesday it was *horrible*—and everything packed ready and all things ready—these crashing colds on top of each other are becoming a nightmare. Nothing really to tell you. Am going to Rock sometime soon. Glad to hear from Petra that David P[epler] is a little better.

How goes the gun-pit fatigue [the making of a tennis court at Pigotts]? Suppose by the time I come down you'll have 'em all in position. . . . Where do you do your pre-Fall lumber-camp stuff? Do you wear boots? . . . By what act of the will supported by what direction of the intelligence were you enabled to take the first plunge—does it excite, above his nature, the dog Jock. Don't let him nip 'em.

It rains here now—I was wondering if you were getting to be without water in the cisterns—but I think Eric told me there was plenty and I hear a great black bath is being installed at H.Q. Suppose they'll allow the Company to go across and use it, when they come out of the line. Eric said Michael Mary Emmanuel [our son] was flourishing like the rose. I'm awfully glad.

I was so hoping to get some watercolours done at Caldey—I don't really quite know now what I shall do—I don't know exactly when the boys come back—Tom [Burns], I think, on Tuesday. If I get all right quickly I might go next week although I don't much fancy going alone. It's really an awful curse this everlasting getting ill and it's worse every year.

I must do a terrific lot of painting this year because I'm going to have a show at the Leicester Galleries in the spring, or if I'm ready in the late autumn.

The book [*In Parenthesis*] proceeds at a very slow pace—but does just proceed. I don't think I have read much new. Been looking at Butcher and Lang's translation of the *Odyssey* but can't get on with it much—translations never are 'things'—no, that's absurd, of course they *can* be—well anyway this isn't—I mean the B and L isn't—to me. Give my love to Eric and Mary and everybody and thank Petra for her letter—I was terrifically pleased to get it. Thank you, Joan, *mostly awfully* for asking me to come and stay—I will as soon as ever I can, but I shall have to go to Rock I expect first—but I do look forward to coming when I can. *Au revoir*. God bless you.

In the following, and in some later letters to Joan and me, a certain amount of language picked up from William Penrose Taplow (of Hamish Maclaren's *The Private Opinions of a British Bluejacket, 1929*), from children and from domestic sources, begins to appear. It should present no difficulty to the intelligent and well-disposed reader.

To R.H., May Day 1933   Rock Hall, Alnwick, Northumberland
I may say what a maye dai an all—wind E.N.E. straight from the Skager Rak and raining into the effin bargain—what of it? Went out to lunch into Scotland to Coldstream where the Guards come from—it's a lovely place on the north bank of the Tweed. Nise family nise ma and three nise nise daughters and a little boy.

Drove there in car—Balls nearly frozen off but warm burgundy helped to restore them. Two of the above pritishcar daughters (one only *really* P.C. (Second Grade) but all terribly nice) coming to lunch tomorrow here (D.V.)—What of it?

Yes I meant I was on the *wrong* side of his wire with whole herd of great bulls and bullions—'big cow' by buggered—[*drawing on following page*] lots like this only much more fierce and evil eyed.

I am writing this alone in library. Just finished dinner—Helen [Sutherland] being out. Bertie Read's new book [probably *The Innocent Eye*] before me and huge ivory paper knife.

I don't feel any more well—in spite of open air and all that and no immediate pressure of anything unpleasant, so it *must* be some evil in my blood I think, don't you? So kind of you to send paper. I'm terribly sorry but I fear I shan't use it after all—and I know the *awful* curse of packing it up—but I *can't* do a painting yet, just can't be done. Alacks and alas. I wish I wasn't putty-coloured and felt it.

I want to talk about the other proof of Book—I shall have to wait till we meet—terribly kind of you to make it up to pages —it looked more noble on the big sheet of course—perhaps a bigger page or something (this does not mean I didn't like the pages—merely that the other in column looked so superlatively impressive and lovely)—or more margin?[6] Thanks for sending *Unemployment* [a 32-page booklet by Eric Gill]. I hurriedly went through it this morn, seems to me jolly good—I can't really understand the engraving—I mean except in a general way because of the Greek—'Making' and what—It's lovelyly printed— but I don't like the red colour of the cover somehow or other— much. Please give my lots of, nay all of my love to Petra and say I'm writing—explain that I have to write to you because of business matters, which is true. Seen [Richard] de la Mare lately? Burns is on the briny, I understand—I return to London on Thursday. Lots of love to Joan and the Big House.

[6] I was then setting specimen pages for *In Parenthesis*. What David really wanted was a two-column crown folio, which indeed looked very noble. Richard de la Mare of Fabers persuaded us that a demy octavo would be more reasonable.

David had been working with increasing intensity and, in spite of what he says himself, success, up to a peak in the summer and early autumn of 1933. He was then at Pigotts, still living with us in our cottage; and it was there that he had his first 'nervous breakdown', to use for convenience the term that was then commonly applied to such attacks. One spoke also of 'neurosis' and 'neurasthenia'. (With Tom Burns it was personified as 'Rosy', with us it was 'the old misrubbs'.) The form it took was an increasing quietness, a brooding, outward signs (in language and behaviour) of an exasperated bafflement: 'I can't work: it's a fair sod: the whole thing's a monumental bollux, a first-class buggeration'. From this time dates his last engraving, *He frees the waters* (1932), that one of which he thought the most highly; and as, later, the first version of his *Tristan and Iseult* watercolour was to be savagely mauled, so that engraving shows the marks of angry jabs with a tool that refused to express his intention. Gaiety fled, but a wry and rueful humour remained. Joan and I were young at the time—not that David, at the age of thirty-seven, was even beginning to be middle-aged—and took his distress more lightly, perhaps, than we should have done. 'Goodnight, Dai,' one of us might say, passing through his bedroom, 'for God's sake don't gnaw your blanket—there's enough mending as it is.' He did not, I am sure, think that we were heartless, and understood that had the three of us succumbed to united wailing and lamentation his life would have been even more difficult to endure.

The misery of enforced and frustrating idleness increased until Tom Burns was called in. Tom took decisions. 'You know, David, and you have often said, that the chief act of art is to *judge*. Remember now that the chief act of prudence is to *command*!' Tom took him to London, where his brother Dr. Charles Burns sent him to Dr. Woods, a neurologist who had specialized in the treatment of what was then called 'shell-shock'.

Meanwhile Tom had been in touch with Ralph and Manya Harari in Cairo and arranged that David should go and stay with them for some weeks. The journey would be made by sea, and Tom would accompany him. Tom saw to all the business of providing money, packing, arranging dates, times, tickets, cabins, transport to Tilbury. Dr. Woods believed that such a voyage and holiday would be of much more benefit to David than any treatment in London. And so it proved. At the very last moment there was nearly a tragic peripeteia: David refused to move, because he had no 'little coat' to wear in place of his tweed jacket when the weather should become warmer: 'No, Tom, it's no good—no little coat . . . I can't face it without a little coat; it's too late, too difficult . . . drop the whole thing.' Tom swept this aside, and carried David off, with a promise of a little coat at Gibraltar: a promise which he kept, and I used the little unlined light jacket for many years afterwards.

Dr. Woods was right. Tom says that no sooner was the ship in calm and sunny waters—for the Bay was kindly—than David was leaping about the deck playing deck tennis, all his misery gone. Always careful to keep in store a safe margin of ill-health as a protection against outside interference, he would be loath to admit this himself. 'The sea trip', he wrote many years later to Saunders Lewis, 'had done me a great deal of good, but I was still not up to much.' 'Not up to much' would, in fact, rank fairly high in a less cautious person's scale of well-being.

In the same letter, of April 1971, to Saunders Lewis (quoted here from a copy David retained), David described his visit to Jerusalem, where he went after Cairo to stay with Eric Gill and Thomas Hodgkin in the Austrian Hospice; they were joined later by Eric's wife Mary and by Joan. The weather was extremely hot and that in itself was enough to confine David to his quarters. The indefatigable Eric, who would have marched uncomplainingly with Lucan's Cato through the North African desert, was greatly annoyed that David should stay indoors reading *Barchester Towers*.

. . . In 1934 I went, or was taken, to Cairo to stay a few weeks with Ralph and Manya Harari, because the sea trip was considered good for my blasted breakdown, and from Egypt I went by air to Lydda and by car to Jerusalem, where it so happened I had two friends staying. Eric Gill was making some sculptures for I think the Hebrew Library or museum [assisted by Laurie Cribb]—can't remember, and Tommy Hodgkin was on the staff of the Governor of Palestine, then British mandated territory—so there were two familiar faces to meet me. . . . I hardly moved out of the Holy City, but used to watch from my window which faced south, with the Mount of Olives on my left and east, and the 'Mosque of Omar' in the middle distance and the tangle of meandering streets from immediately below and stretching away to the west; and I used also to meander about in the densely crowded and incredibly noisy streets and the Suq—chaps on donkeys or mules—Palestinian Arabs in ceaseless argument over the price of anything and everything from a melon to a tin kettle—(the colour of brass but seemingly most skilfully contrived out of discarded petrol tins)—then suddenly I caught sight of a figure who carried me back a couple of decades or thereabouts, the very familiar stance of the figure, rather bored, indifferent glance towards a closely grouped fiercely gesticulating half-dozen Palestinians.

Or, may be, one chanced to come close upon a couple off duty: 'Gotta gasper, mate? . . . Christ, what a sod of a place.' It might have been a rain-soaked Givenchy duck-board trackway instead of a sweltering Hierosolyma by-street.

But occasionally I saw either from my window or in mooching around, a squad of these figures that seen singly evoked comparisons of twenty years back, in the Nord or the Pas de Calais or the Somme. But now in their full parade rig, the light khaki drill shirts, the bronzed arms bare from above the elbow to the wrist and pale khaki shorts leaving the equally bronzed legs bare from above the knee to the brief ankle socks, the feet in heavy field-service hob-nailed boots, but above all the riot shields aligned to cover the left side and in each right fist the haft-grip of a stout baton, evoked not the familiar things of less than two decades back, but rather of two millennia close on, and the ring of the hob-nailed service boots on the stone sets and the sharp commands—so they were a section from the Antonia, up for duties in Hierosolyma after all!

And as the days and weeks passed this analogy I would say increased, but became established—there was a good deal else to think on. I did go to Bethlehem, which is, or *then was*, very beautiful.

David's letter to Saunders Lewis then goes on to say that 'not only *The Anathemata*, but best part of' all his various later separate pieces, such as 'The Wall', 'The Tribune's Visitation', 'The Fatigue', and even in roundabout ways 'The Dream of Private Clitus' and 'The Tutelar of the Place', derived from this 'forced' visit to Jerusalem in 1934: ' "Forced" because of illness, for it is certain I should never have gone to Palestine off my own bat,' he wrote; 'for I hate what our American friends call "going places".'

It has often been said that David's breakdown in 1933 was caused by his war experiences. For my own part, I believe this to be completely untrue. David enjoyed the war. He loved soldiering and comradeship. (What he says about being 'a knocker-over of piles, a parade's despair' is all nonsense: he was somewhat offended when a young friend of his took this too seriously—which of us, indeed, has known, or could tolerate, a serviceman who claimed efficiency? Good form dictates a certain ineptitude.)

His happiness in the ranks was largely due, I believe, to the absence of responsibility and of any need to make decisions. What the private soldier has to do is always the easiest thing: even if he has to overcome fear, he can only stay where he is and do what he is told to do. Discomfort, however great, is relative and has the consolation that the smallest alleviation, negligible in normal conditions, is exaggerated into a luxury. I find confirmation for this view in *In Parenthesis*. This is not an exposition or condemnation of the horrors of war, even if it is concerned with them. A careful reading of the Preface shows a pride and delight in the type of war that, by David's reckoning, ended in 1916; and the core of the book is the goodness of 'the intimate, continuing, domestic life of small contingents of men, within whose structure Roland could find, and for a reasonable while, enjoy his Oliver'.

Stronger confirmation comes from David's conversation and letters. In neither was there ever any attempt to avoid any aspect of his war experiences. There were no nightmares, no horrors that could not be mentioned, no noises, smells, scenes that made wounds bleed afresh. There was only pleasure in the searchlight of memory, the recapture of half-forgotten detail, the link with tradition, the re-creation of personality, the analogy with the problems of ordinary social and domestic life—and above all humour.

On the other hand, the difficulties he met in his work, and the accompanying at times paralysing mental and spiritual stress, will be patent to every reader of his letters and published work. Of those difficulties there were three aspects or stages. First, there was the initial problem encountered by every person who seriously tries to make any thing in the way most fitted to its end: a problem that becomes more grave as the definition of the end becomes more elusive, so that it is much more serious for the painter than it is for the carpenter.

In philosophic mood, David would speak of the imposition of form upon matter, or the wedding of form and content; more colloquially, this would simply be a matter of 'getting the bloody thing right'. This in itself can 'give you', as he might say, 'a right twisting'.

The second stage was the enlargement of the content. This entailed the introduction of every sort of allusion, belief, tradition, hope, love, on top of, or incorporated in, the subject-matter of his work. At first this could be done in a simple way by a suggestion conveyed in the title. Thus four very similar pictures dating from these years (1927, 1929 and 1931), all drawn from the sea-lapped bungalow at Hove, and all in content pure seascapes, are entitled *Terrace Overlooking the Sea*, *Portslade, Eisteddfa Calupso* and *Manawyddan's Glass Door*. The evangelist—and I use the word in no derogatory sense—is already at work. The next step was to incorporate in the picture itself all that David felt to be contained in a 'live' as opposed to a 'dead' title. (He notes, incidentally, of a title such as *Violin with Flowers*, 'a dead title'.) The greater complexity brought infinitely more work, as will be seen in the long letter of 1949 to Mrs. Ede (pp. 149–52) about that great historical essay and statement of belief, *Vexilla Regis* (1947). As he struggled to include more and more and yet retain the fluidity of his earlier work—'fluid', as the opposite of 'tight', is his own word of praise—the tension increased. He took *Aphrodite in Aulis* (1941) more or less in his stride, relatively speaking, but was driven nearly to distraction by the preliminary attempts at, and final version of, *Tristan and Iseult* and, even more, by *A latere dextro*. The reader will know for himself how this development is paralleled in David's writing.

The final stage was the attempt to find an historical and philosophical justification for his view of the function of the artist in every society; to explain it to countless correspondents; and, what caused him endless worry and disappointment, to present it to a wider audience in his published essays. In spite of, or perhaps partly because of, his piratical raids on antiquity, which he looted for key words that he adapted to his own purpose (*poiesis, anamnesis, signum, gens, res*) and used as unreliable props for what was basically a sound structure, he ended his days with a bitter feeling that few had understood what he meant in 'Art and Sacrament', 'Use and Sign' and other such papers. To my mind, there can be little doubt but that this accumulation of problems was an almost intolerable burden and a sufficient explanation of his neurosis.

In the autumn of 1934 David was back in England, and staying with Helen Sutherland at Rock:

To R.H., 4 October 1934   *Rock*

Can you beat it—General Wauchope has just arrived for bed and breakfast. They're rumbling about in the vaults for the '78 burgundy and the '72 port and so on—he's got a hule blaze-make in his apartment and a picture of Caldey Island over the mantel-shelf, it being considered one he might not find too poll. mod. or non fig., also a nigh boulk of florgies—He looks a nice kind of bloke he's in a check Harris suity and very salmon-weirish—the domestics quake in their double garments. Mary beams at such great lords to make narrow beds for.

The heating by the mercy of God was got going yesterday—outside it is pretty parki but very beautiful.

Tommy Hodgkin's father (an authority on Anglo-Saxon England) hurried from Wessex by the night train to be here. I write this in my bedroom—it's 7.15 and I'm pretty well inclined to go and bawl through the baize door 'please sup—supjibs!' Can't imagine what we shall talk about—this queer party of four—if I get enough of the bubbly stuff I might sing 'Who'll have a lump'—he's in the bloody Jocks of course.

Monday 8th. Sorry I did not send this last whenever it was—yes last Thursday—he came and went, I mean the Gen'ral—he rather put the fear of God into me—he was awfully like a mixture of Colonel Bell R.W.F. and Dr. Woods—very queer. He adores Eric, from what he saw.[7] Couldn't get any war talk out of him, he was badly wounded at Magersfontein. I'm here alone—Helen has gone to London till Thursday or Friday—Lord of the bloody manor in a manner o' speaking. How I wish you and Joan were here, it would be fun. Don't think I shall go abroad till after Christmas as it's difficult to arrange a long enough trip.

CAN you beat it, young Barbara [Hepworth] has given birth to *three* (3) great big bouncing boilers—or boilerines maybe. I don't half feel jolly sorry for them—it really does seem *too* awful a thing to be possible—*poor* Ben [Nicholson]—well you

---

[7] General Wauchope was British High Commissioner in Palestine when Eric was working there in 1934; see Robert Speaight, *Eric Gill*, p. 252.

want to be very careful—woof, it's a most surprising phenomenon.

I visit the Vicar every day, who lies ill with asthma—he's
terribly nice and has a night nurse to look after him. He tells me
all about Dean Inge and other back-chat. It's cold here and very
Northumbrian—I've just read all about the Glencoe business—
it's terrific. I *wish* my book was finished—I had a letter from de
la Mare asking me if it was ready the other day. I gave the
printed bit [i.e. early proofs] to Helen S. to read the other day
—she *likes* it, it seems—I thought she would *not*. Kit Dawson
wants me to stay with them on the way back south. I hope I
can. Dear René, how are you I wonder—please write to me.
I do hope Joan is all right and Michael—give Joan *lots of love*
from me—how is all the upheaval of the Clans[8]—and my
dearest Petra and everybody.

I've drunk red wine and can't really be very much good at
writing tonight. I think of you a lot and did love being with you.
I so hope you can take some holiday.

I want this to catch the morning post—I'm having my breakfast in bed for a bit and hear the postman puff up on his little
motorcycle.

Good night now. God bless you. Much love to you and Joan.

DAVID

I'm about the same—not much cop some days—it's a lousy
business.

Manya [Harari] wants to see you sometime and talk about
social credit. I told her you knew about it.   D.

Later that year he wrote from Berkshire, where he was staying with
the Laurence Binyons, friends of Helen Sutherland. David retained as
a metaphor the infantryman's envy of the supposedly more comfortable quarters of the R.A.

To R.H., 22 November 1934   Westridge Farm, Streatley, Berks.
. . . these artillery blokes here are nice and snug with central

---

[8] The move of Betty Pepler, recently widowed, with her children to the
monastery at Capel-y-ffin. The buildings and land had been bought by Mary
Gill from the Caldey community.

heating—it's a nice farmhouse and the country near lovely—
real chalk down neolithic scrub country just above—'spect the
population is 90 per cent Celtic too if one went into the matter.

It's much the most remote-feeling place I've been in for a
long time, and so near London. I went out for a walk this afternoon with L[aurence] B[inyon]—he is most awfully nice—I
would like to talk to him a lot about the graphics but you know
how difficult it is to talk to great men of the decade just past—
you get curiously shy and feel an awful little impostor, I never
quite know why. I wish you were here. I've found two illustrations by old Solly [Reginald Savage] in a book here—one for the
Ancient Mariner and another called in real Solly language
'Sidonia and Otto von Bork on the Waterway to Stettin—a few
drawings by Reginald Savage'. They are in a thing called *The
Pageant* 1896 (I was a year old then, raising hell in Brockley, I
suppose. It appals me to think that my dear mother has lived at
B. ever since then—the Boer War—the G. War and all the rest
of it—cooking mending nursing every day without rest almost
—it's terrific) Sturge Moore, Ricketts, Shannon, Rossetti,
Whistler, Burne-Jones—poem by Paul Verlaine and a story by
John Gray called 'Niggard Truth' which opens authentically
'Harriet came of farmers. The stout race hesitated and hoped in
the strong girl; at last, for she never had any children, finished
with her. . . . At the time when Harriet first had a real existence,
symbolism might have called the grand-dad Silenus, the father
Gambrinus, the brother Dionysos . . .' and so on. It's already
getting towards *Park* and the writing we know—isn't it—the
careful punctuation and slight specialness—I can almost hear his
Nobis quoque peccatoribus and the throat-clearing—I suppose
there would never be any interest in his collected works?—no I
think not—it would now be nice to have them.[9] This house has
been lousy with Anglican priests—uncles of Nicky [Nicolete

[9] For John Gray, poet of the 1890s and friend of Wilde and Beardsley, later
Canon Gray of Edinburgh, see the volume of essays, *Two Friends, John Gray
and André Raffalovich*, ed. Fr. Brocard Sewell, O.Carm. (Aylesford, Kent: St.
Albert's Press, 1963). We printed at Pigotts a small edition of Gray's *Park, a
fantastic story* (1932) and of his *Poems 1931* (1931).

David was always moved by any trick, eccentricity or beauty of voice. The

Gray, *née* Binyon]—nice blokes—one of them had been on the canal bank at Wipers when I was there, because he came to see the Colonel of my battalion—a pal of his—may have stepped off the bloody duck-board to let him pass for all I know. He reminded me that we used to call Festubert 'Festering Hubert'—which I had forgotten—pretty nice, I think. (N.B. for incorporation or inversion.)

... I went to Mass with Nicky in a nice snug church with a stove.—Yes, I told you over the phone about old [Herbert] Cole preaching about the leaven etc. Nicky had a nice little fur coat and looked sweet. Nice dear girl. ... Penelope [Betjeman] is coming for me on Saturday morning. I hope I like being there —it's right against the White Horse where Alfred bollocked up the black heathen men—that old G.K. carried on about. I always wanted to see the White Horse Vale.

... I met Donald [Attwater] in the Commercio[10] the other day. ... I also went to see David Mathew [Fr., later Archbishop] to fling some Welsh stuff—he asked about you and wanted to know what you thought of the Laxton do.[11] I told him—he roared with laughter, his fat sides shaking. Poor Joan, I do hope she is getting better now ... did she say damn and blast this great big knashing bounder of a tooth. I suppose Eric is still with the North Welshmen [he was lecturing at University College, Bangor]—if it's at all clear he will see Snowdon and the fastnesses

---

throat-clearing noted here in Canon Gray is attributed to Fr. John O'Connor in parts of the 'mass-sequences' associated with *The Kensington Mass*:

> Loudly he clears his throat:
> Brother Ass must belch for all his
> May Day rosette — the belly murmurs
> though it serve Melchisedec.

[10] The Commercio was a restaurant we frequented in Frith Street, waited on by the lovely Francesca. Fastidious David would rarely order anything but 'a plain omelette with spinach *en branche*', that there might be no possibility of his dinner's being 'messed about'.

[11] Robert Speaight (*Eric Gill*, p. 253) writes of the gathering in the Dominican house at Laxton, briefly and inaccurately. Donald Attwater makes it a little more interesting in his *A Cell of Good Living*, pp. 177-8.

of Gwynedd. . . . I like your 'rude colleges', because Bangor in Welsh means college—in Irish, too, I believe. Sup is shortly coming up so I must just wash and straighten my tie. I like about Joan's tum. 'Well now you might take your pencil and make a careful loving study—you will do well to notice the delicate contours—you can't steal a march on nature—some of you students think you can invent and invent without going to the fountain-head—mother nature. I strongly advise you to spend some hours each evening of careful observation—the great Ruskin, as you may know, made the most careful drawings and Mr. Savage went even further: the point of his pencil conveyed the utmost veracity'—(woofing without).[12]

Sup. finished. Wouldn't old B[inyon] think this awful balls if he read it—I expect it is, but it amuses us in a hard world. They're most awfully kind to me and it's nice and peaceful. It was lovely seeing Prudence [Pelham].

. . . Well dear dear René I must go to bed—I feel not so bad but not to say primb—feel I'm not making much headway—all right as long as I do nothing and think of nothing and nothing happens. Hope I emerge some day, God I *do wish* I could get something done—Well anyway God bless you and Joan and lots of love to you both—Bon swores all, my love to my dear Petra.

1935—1940

Lady Prudence Pelham, mentioned above, was a close friend of David's during these years. Her father, the sixth Earl of Chichester, and her elder brother, the seventh Earl, both died in 1926, and their memorial stone (in Stanmer Park, Sussex) was made and incised by Eric Gill and Laurie Cribb at Pigotts in 1929. It was then that Prudence came to Pigotts and met David. She stayed for some time during 1929–30, learning stone-carving from Eric.

After David began in early 1935 to stay for long periods at the Fort Hotel in Sidmouth, Prudence was frequently with him there. To my

[12] Herbert Cole, one of David's teachers at the Camberwell School of Art, is being mimicked in this passage, the 'woofing' being supplied by another teacher, Reginald Savage.

mind, this friendship was the most important personal relationship in David's life.

To H.S.E., 7 March 1935   *Fort Hotel, Sidmouth*

... I did love Hartland[13] and it's been lovely being with Prudence —she's gone now. Sidmouth I like too, but of course it's not grand nor a desert place like Hartland—but Victorian on the tiny esplanade—and a *very* comfortable hotel.

I think I'm better—have ups and downs. It would be nice to talk with you. It still takes very little to unsettle me. I still can't work.

Prudence and I found a marvellous stone knight in a church near here [Ottery St. Mary] and we are having it photographed by a local chemist. I do hope he does it well—it's absolutely grand—one of the most moving Gothic carvings I've ever seen —it's like all the Round Table dead. ... It's [i.e. Malory] a supreme book. I still think Chap. 1 Book XX is about the limit ... the packed small room, the impotence of Gawain, Gareth and Co., the venom of Agravaine and the sense of imminent ruin in the space of the Hampstead tube lift. In fact from then on to the end of the book it's all simply matchless.

I've just read *David Copperfield*. I think a good bit about that —If *only* Dickens (it always seems awful to me when he, Dickens, speaks through his characters. He does come some crashers!) had had a religion and a philosophy instead of a filthy tenth-rate emotional 'morality' I should have been obliged. But it is grand in places. Miss Betsy Trotwood's grand. ...

P.S. I don't much like the red cliffs about here. On some days it's like living under a vast baulk of chocolate—they turn the bitter sea also into a kind of cocoa lake, however.

To R.H., 14 March 1935   *Fort Hotel, Sidmouth*

I sit in the window corner at the Marine ... it was particularly nice of you to write because you knew I should be sad with sweet high bright Prudence going again. I've just written to her

[13] Hartland Quay, in North Devon, where David had stayed for some weeks at the Quay Hotel.

—I shall be glad when I hear from her that she is well and happy. I have not done any book—I wish I had—I can't settle to it—but I'm all right.

Tom [Burns] phoned last night—he's gone in an airplane to Paris: wonder what he's doing now—bugger twelve times—ink failing, will write with Gingies, bugger you can't. Yes, I do hope Lady C[hichester] is nice to dear Prudence and doesn't make her misrub. I miss her. Must go home to dinner and a primb feed. I could fair gnaw some type of animal.

Back at the old Fort—asparagus and butter: wish you were here. . . . I had a nice letter from Helen Sutherland—terribly nice—she sang a veritable Benedicite omnia opera dominum. . . . I go in the afternoon and hear the nuns say compline which I like and see the little Dawson girls [daughters of Christopher and Valery] from behind. So old man O'Connor has been about has he—you want to be careful with the hassocks. And wasn't he the bold priest and wasn't I the poor victim. One of the swans from the Sid (you remember that miserable stream) came sailing white and proudly on the sunny waves the other day—a marvel to see before sitting down to meat. Thanks for the nice label in your letter. Write to me when you have strells. Poor René how awful is that period of half-well half-ill—the buggers will give you light duty quick as a stoat if you don't watch them. It's been cool and grey today and the sea losing its shape in mist—I rather like it—the sun made me quite sick and a headache two days ago—it's odd how the sun gives me that pain on the top of me head, even with hat on.

Friday morning. Damnation brought foolscap purposely to continue this letter in pub and have left it behind. Nice morning, but no letter from Prudence. I shall make dole if I don't hear before Sunday—I do hope I do. I like the thing about the red and green busmen talking of their jennies and the cold frosts blast her bit and how he'd reckoned wrongly. Wish I'd got me paper, this meagre piece cramps me style. . . .

I'm sending you, from Prue, a little [Alfred] Wallis picture—she asked me to send you one, she gave me some—you won't get it till Monday now—I do hope you get this tomorrow—I

3. MR. GILL'S HAY HARVEST (Capel-y-ffin) 1926. Pencil and watercolour, 22½ × 15 in. *Private collection*

4. VESSELS SHELTERING (Caldey Island)1927. Pencil and watercolour, $13\frac{3}{4} \times 10\frac{1}{4}$ in. *Arts Council of Wales*

wonder. Look after yourself and be careful of light duty. It's a bugger. . . .

I write this as I eat hake and egg sauce, a very meagre tipe of food. Bloody boring letter after all, I'm sorry.

Started re-reading the Sailor [Taplow] in bed this morning. Have neglected him for some time. Been trying old Blake and you would laugh at his comments on Sir J. Reynolds's discourses, such as 'O yes', 'Damned Fool'—'Liar'—'Impostor'—wish he would rise to 'Bollocks', but no. This bar, where we used to come, is absolutely choked with chaps talking awful balls —God it is depressing—what a world—heavenly lovely nice wodged in with bloody desolate old lachrymarum valle.

Fr. John O'Connor, mentioned above in connection with hassocks, was irascible, for all his kindly nature. David would relate how, when serving Fr. O'Connor's Mass, he neglected to move to one side the cushion at the foot of the altar steps when the priest was about to move up to the altar. 'He looked at it for a moment', said David, 'and then booted the bloody thing across the sanctuary.'

To R.H., 28 March 1935   *Fort Hotel, Sidmouth*

This is from Mr. Joyce's report on the first Court of the season in today's *Times*.

For Mrs. E. A. Strachan a classical gown of pearl-tinted satin with diamanté embroidery and a train of chiffon and satin. For Miss Patricia Rose a Victorian gown of multi-coloured flowers appliqué at neckline and hem. For Miss Pamela Fisher a picture frock of white satin faille with a thick ruche of satin and silver leaves for her shoulders, with a train of white net needle-run with silver. For Mrs. Napper-Tandy a gown of yellow and gold brocade with a nice bodice inlet with a tucker of gold, a train from Brussels of lace and net displayed on gold cloth from Worth of Paris and Hanover Street West, and for Mrs. Joan Hague an immortal kirtle flowered and trim as her gentlehood, woven in silk from the Barbary goats by woof and weft be the gunner's mate[14] on the frozen hill in Hewendon (can't spell it) Bucks.

[14] Petra, whose husband Denis Tegetmeier had been in the Artillery.

How are you, dear René—I do hope you are better. I'm sorry for not writing but I've not been feeling very lively. I could not help copying this out for you, it's astonishing—I have only *inserted* two words and *left out* three others and changed the sequence twice, that's about all I think. What a pity they don't write their leading article up to that standard—'needle-run with silver' is top-boy stuff, isn't it and O the names!

Did you see the picture of the conference between our chaps and Hitler. Something like this:

No—no good—sorry—too tighed to try—au revoir—Prudence sent some *heavenly books.*

To R.H., 2 April 1935   *Fort Hotel, Sidmouth*
... Prudence sent me Admiral Collingwood's letters. They *are* so *good* in places—poor old bugger. They kept him at sea for about ten years without leave watching the Frogs and Spaniards. He wasn't half fed up about it too—and tells some bloke at the Admiralty that he would have had six sons to carry on the honour of the family if they hadn't kept him away from home so long—We're the boys who make no noise.[15] The man who took the photographs at Ottery is insuduentally called Badcock —but I loathe coarse talk.

David quotes with delight Collingwood on the Cape St. Vincent show. After, 'when the Admiral first received information of a Spanish fleet of twenty-eight sail of the line ... making in all forty sail. We were fifteen ... he *determined to attack them*', David interjects 'Good old Belloc!'

To R.H., 15 April 1935   *Fort Hotel, Sidmouth*
... *Had lovely long long letter from Prudence* this morning and a nice pair of socks that fit and are the colour of a pale lioness, and two Trollope books I had not read, to wit *Doctor Thorne* and *The Vicar of Bullhampton.*

I'm waiting for the doctor to see me, he wanted to see me again—I went to him when I hit my napper—they may crime me for neglect of Brigade standing orders re wearing shrapnel helmets in the forward area—for all ranks. They cop you under this—same as self-inflicted wounds. By the way has Pte. G[ordian] Gill had his sentence (pending under Field Courts Martial) promulgated yet—poor bugger. (You reported to me some time back his serious crime of self-inflicted wound in hand, you remember.)[16]

[15] A soldiers' song, much too obscene to quote, which David would occasionally sing.
[16] David, head bent against the wind, had walked into a lamp-post. Earlier Eric Gill's son Gordian had broken his arm—from this arose David's picture *Carr's Splint*, now in the National Gallery of Canada, Ottawa.

The doctor been and say I'm all right but wants me to only smoke *ten* cigarettes a day—and have bath in *morning* instead of *night* and do some *physical jerks* each morning. O bugger bugger bugger and rest half an hour before dinner and lunch and only drink two gingies a day—He is nice but it's always the same stuff. *Doc:* 'Are you worried about any things?' *Am I worried me arse. Doctor:* 'What do you read—let me see—let me look—*The Nature of Belief*—Shakespeare—*Medieval Religion*—I shouldn't trouble the mind with anything disturbing you know. What do you read for light literature?' *Me:* 'Well—well—eh—eh—well —you know that's the bugger of it—well, I like *Alice in Wonderland* if I want to have a good laugh.' It *isn't half* embarrassing —the poor chap was trying to be good and useful and helpful— He's awfully nice. Anyway I suppose it's all right. He did all the old stuff, heart, blood, reflexes—everything—and said I am *absolutely as well as could be* by those tests. Dr., 'was I troubled with the old pornoes?' Me, says hold up! What's this—I say what's this—says only in the manner of all men—Humans Nature'— Dr. says Ah yes.

To R.H., 29 April 1935　　　　　　　　　*Fort Hotel, Sidmouth*
Hi hold up what's this I say speak up what is this says where is this so-called Hague's letter in retorts to your loving thoughts; *it is not come* is the retorts of this meagre chambermaid says where is this postman God damn his sole. Says here is this *Times* newspaper to get on with and a gralie fruge and a egg Christ what mores do you want. Says I know all about that which what does this meagre maid replie you know fuck-all about it, I've brought the *Telegraph* by mistakes—sorry sir.

. . . Met Kit Dawson on the Front here yesterday just before Prudence left[17] and I had him and his wife to dinner which was nice and I went to lunch with him today. He's now staying in Exeter until Saturday giving some lectures. I do like him. We talked a lot about Wales—he told me the first thing he ever

---

[17] It was on this occasion that, as they left Dawson, Prue, overcome in those few minutes by the width of his learning, remarked, 'My God, what a tiger!' 'Tiger' Dawson became established, but not to his face.

wrote was an essay on early Welsh stuff, Gododdin and Co. He told me about a newly discovered Chanson de Geste called the Song of William,[18] which he said is better than the Song of Roland in some ways.

Wednesday morning. On the beach and a soft lap lap lapping-in sea, with gulls sitting like halcyon birds sit. A bloody dog has just pist against the sea wall by me elbow. I say damn this animule. I had a p.c. from Prudence this morning from Avonwick—the place where my mother was—she went there from Totnes to see it again because she liked it so much—she saw a white stoat cleaning itself in the sun. O my how hard are departings. She has such a heavenly mind. (We decided that Part 7 [of *In Parenthesis*] is called definitely 'Poor Jenny is a-weeping on a bright summer day'.)

This can't be a long letter—because there is no time—did I tell you about Prudence giving me the *Heimskringla*—the Icelandic saga thing—Chronicle of the Kings of Norway, and how there is one nice thing in it about a dog who became King and was borne round by the Royal bodyguard and used to bark *three* words and speak *two*, rather like old Solly [Reginald Savage of the 'woofs']—but I believe I told you before. . . . It was jolly nice having Joan here for Easter—give my love to everyone at Pigotts.

After hearing of the birth of our second son, Richard, in June 1935, David wrote:

URGENT

13.06 hrs 6.35   *Sidmouth Post No. 2 Sap.*

To Mr. Hague O.C. Bearers (Child) AAA.OOO bloody ray AAA. received report (per field telephone) at above hour of successful dislodging action in area Pigotts–Hughenden salient. AAA O.C. Sidmouth details wishes to express profound satisfaction for endurance displayed by all ranks during the preliminary and very extended bombardment and no less for the

---

[18] This is *La Chancun de Willame*, first printed from the unique MS by the Chiswick Press in 1903.

dash and gallantry of the assaulting party AAA. You will kindly
forward a list of names for Special mention and distinction to
the proper quarter AAA And no hokey pokey. I am so pleased
I am overjoised I honest am and I send Joan lots and lots of love
and you too dear René. So it will be called Dick I understand.
Let me have some details when you've time. It's raining like hell
here and a great S.W. wind in from the sea. It was very nice
hearing your voice last evening. God bless you all.

Mr. O'Doule—not very funny after all—sorry but I found it
in the paper[19] and thought it would amuse you. Anyway lots of
love to you, Joan and Richard (unless it's somebody else).

The next letter is from Skipton in Yorkshire, where David was staying with the Christopher Dawsons, on his way north to Rock:

To R.H., 2 July 1935   *Hartlington Hall, Skipton*
On this day nineteen years ago I heard read by the Officer Com-
manding B Coy a document, a rescript from G.H.Q. announc-
ing the initial success of the first attack on his trenches on the
Somme. We were permitted to cheer. I can't tell you the gnaw-
ing thoughts as well up in your bosom at this memory. Dear
René it was nice to hear from you.

This is a *simply heavenly place. I do wish you were here.* It's
exactly like Capel in many ways—but more prosperous and less
instinct with the waste land feeling, but the general formation
of river, tree, hill slope, tumbled-stone-wall, sheep-thing—
remarkably similar—all private to young Kit D[awson]—very
nice. This house is solid, comfortable and Victorian and filled
tight as tight with books so that you don't know which to read
at all. So as usual you find yourself reading something you might
read anywhere—*The Listener* or Burke's Peerage. Here is a nice
Joyce bit I read this morning in the latter

> Two lions per pale crenellee for Bertie
> a trefoil slipped vert
> for Griffith

[19] A newspaper head-and-shoulders converted with pen and coloured inks
into O'Doule, a character in *The Private Opinions of a British Bluejacket*.

2nd and 3rd gules a chevron ermine
between three englishmen's heads in profile
Coupled at the neck and bearded proper
for Griffith of Penrhyn.

(No hokey pokey no words altered or transposed—the Bertie part is transposed from another coat.)

. . . So it's Richard Thomas Mary—not Richard Mary Thomas —Yes—I think it's better like the first, that is with Hague at the end. Do give my love to dear Joan. It's nice about the barrikin [Bass from Richard's godfather, Tom Burns] that's grand drink me health old cock—I expect you'll have the artillery and H.Q. and specialist details and all round pretty friendly-like. It soon leaks out when there's a drink on the tappee. Rather a shy-making word, that—but authentic enough. As, 'The Q.M.'s got some fine bonza cardigans on the tappee'.

I go to Rock on Monday July 8th. Kit and Valery go to London on that day. My route (Skipton cancelled, straight to Harrogate) be staff car Report at Railhead entrain at 11.38 at Harrogate for Alnmouth via Newcastle 13.51 hrs detrain at Alnmouth 3.29 sorry 15.29 hrs. Met be Corporal Mills in Mess-cart (mechanized).[20]

Late July 2nd. Bloody midnight in the old bilgee room down in kip. Ready to snore off.

Thought I would continue this letter to your old pall but damnation too tired. Just heard Kit put out his electric light. Poor Kit never sleeps without Sedormid & Co. and then hardly at all. . . . *Even* I seem a regular bruiser wid a fine swagger on me and a pipe in the hat of me compared with his health. I do wish he could be made well, he is so nice. Good night, René. I hope child Richard is well down damped down and under and all as peaceful as the heavenly regions. Some fucker has left a door open here—it's banging about like woof, like I don't know what. *July 3. Wed. 8 something a.m.* Wake up, thinks what of this

[20] 'In those days Helen [Sutherland] had a big Rolls and a rather depressed chauffeur called Mills'—Nicolete Gray in her Introduction to *The Helen Sutherland Collection* (London: The Arts Council, 1971), p. 18.

life? Is it all right? They bring you tea. I can see the top of a hill where I lie and some soft-wood plantation. Wonder what Hague is up to—perhaps pushing that brass thing in the Primus stove in and out down in the kitchen.

Late after lunch July 3rd. Went for a walk over the hills alone this morning and back under deep green places by the river and sat and shouted psalms in Welsh—I've got a Book of Common Prayer in English and Welsh which gives me great pleasure and you can learn a few words as you go along. Don't you think the sound of the words for Blessed V. Mary good—they are Fendigedig Fair Forwyn, pronounced roughly Vendigedig Vire (like i in fire) Vorwein.

We are going this afternoon to see a place called Grasswood, which is a tangled wood about the size of Mametz a mile or so square, very ancient and the site of British village and fortified hill—Dawson thinks post-Roman, perhaps the capital of Urien Rhedeg—who became the Uriens of M. Darthur. I should rather like to snore off the afternoon but I want to see this place. Did Tom talk about poor Henry John[21]—I hope he is not too upset by it all. Sorry you missed Harman—it was my fault for not remembering to tell you he has had to go away suddenly —it was because of that rush at the end that I forgot—I remembered as I waved my braces—then I thought you would phone before you went—so consoled myself by that. Prudence says you had a nice lap together and ate ham sandwiches in a bar —I do wish I could have seen you for longer—but there it is. Give my love to Joan and Petra and everyone at Pigotts. I meant to write about Trollope—yes I agree—I know it's *really* only second rate compared with the great human works—but I do enjoy it so for what it is—I seem to miss the point of Jane Austen—I must read another one sometime. I like Captain Merrivale in the Trollope [i.e. Capt. Marrable in *The Vicar of Bullhampton*]—he makes me laugh a lot.

[21] Son of Augustus John: a schoolfellow of Tom Burns, he had recently been drowned.

To H.J.G., 20 July 1935   *Rock*

... I've been reading Hopkins's letters—poor devil, he had a bloody time with the J's, that's evident. Been also reading a new *History of the Anglo-Saxons* by R. H. Hodgkin (Tutor at Queen's, Oxford, son of old Hodgkin, who did *Italy and her Invaders*, and father of young Tommy Hodgkin, whose portrait I did once that you liked)—a really beautifully done book, some lovely illustrations in it, and proper *maps*—and grand charts so you can see what was happening in Kent—Northumbria—Strathclyde—West Wales—Mercia at any given date—what one has always wanted. He's very pro-'Anglo-Saxon', but in a nice, affectionate, natural way; he obviously 'feels' a real 'thing' about that best Anglo-Saxon 'golden age' that produced the piety and particular art of the seventh-century Northumbrian kingdom, Anglo-Celtic Christianity, and then Bede & Co. But of course is too much of the Teutonic school to please me—but all the same, in a nice kind of way. It's a popularish book—I don't know what the experts will have to say of it. He is unable to be anything but a bit superior about the Welsh; it comes out in the oddest ways. But at *least* he admits that with the loss of the Island to the 'steady', prudent etc. Teutons, they in their hills wove, as he would say, a web of magic and imagination round the story of their defeat, which in turn gave to the world the Arthurian cycle. Which is indeed worth the loss of many islands and continents, seeing that nothing succeeds like failure, as Chesterton might say.

... I've been going through pretty good mental miseries too. It's *so* difficult to see any way through this maze of conflicting pressures and pulls and hold to one's 'General Line' as the Soviets say. I do think people have their own 'general line' somehow, and if they go seriously wide of it, it is pretty awful for them probably, although I suppose one can easily have a self-deceiving 'general line' so to say. I've always always as long as I can *ever* remember felt my business (however blindly) to be my work, and always knew that everything had got to go for that. I've always felt 'agnostic' about every other matter—though other people 'knew' about the legislature, the command of men, marriage, council, the whole realm of prudence and affairs. I've always known that I must be and am essentially a private soldier, in and out of the war, who with fear and trembling might *just* manage to learn to slope arms and *sometimes* remember to turn left on the command 'Left' and *just* have the physical strength to *not* fall out on the line of route perhaps: but that my *own* real life was that of judgement of the work to be made—line by line—to be unfettered when about that work, and that that was the *only* sphere *I knew* about, that my only contribution was that. Not indeed that it *was* a contribution, but that anyway perhaps it *might be*—or anyway that I was a fool *indeed* at all else. But now, since this curious illness that has deprived me (anyway for the time) of doing that work, I do find it *excruciatingly difficult* sometimes. I feel rather like a Lifeguardsman in a breastplate and spurs without a horse in a mine-crater in a gas attack. He might do the silliest things, mightn't he! And, having raised the question, I wonder what on earth he should do. It would be a good question in a military examination paper, for the staff. Dear Harman all this nonsense about myself.

To J.H., 2 August 1935   *Rock*

Wat is this scandal this red-haired Tom I deny it I challinge them I say I challindge them—which wat I say I deny it.[22] I am in bed, it is 11.35 p.m. I am sorry I meant to write sooner to thank you for your letter and dear René too. It is quite parkie here at nights. . . . *August Bank Holiday.* In a puffer going to see Conty [Constance] Sitwell and her daughter Anne in this palace at Barmoor. I have not been so well lately. *Lord!* it is depressing when you slip back again. Helen Ede comes for two days tomorrow and Prudence comes for a week on Friday. . . . I *do* hope she won't *hate* it and find the atmosphere difficult. There is no beer or rollicking, but I do hope it will be all right and not depress her

[22] Our son Richard was born with red hair. When David first went to Ditchling in 1921, with a dark-haired companion, the three Gill girls said one to another, 'I like the red-haired one best.' The red darkened to near-black with the years.

more or anything. . . . This puffer is going through nice rolling land with wheat and oat and barley fields shimmering like quiet sea, and black cattle and now the estuary of a small river, a good thing to see. I'm going to the Sitwells *on my own* for the day, so in puffer instead of car, and it's rather nice. Not so much Mills [the chauffeur] this and now Mills that and do be careful not to run down that bunny-rabbit and remember you must call at Mrs. Thing's and don't forget to take the other road and not to be later than 5.31 or 5.32 at the very latest.

August 7th Thursday. It was nice at the Sitwells yesterday. Helen Ede came this morning as arranged and I went to meet her. One of her first questions was 'How are René and Joan'. The Lord Tankerville of Chillingham and his new Swedish wife came to supper last night. He has only *one* subject—Social Credit—he talked for three hours about it. . . . I was *tired out* before he started and *dead* when he went. It's the Douglas scheme he cracks on about like anything. . . . I do find it a strain trying to think of so many things at once. I would like a Gingy and a good jocko meself—humans natchur. I had a catalogue of the Welsh painters exhibition—they have reproduced my drawing of Tommy Hodgkin—so glad you've heard from him—how does he sound, depressed or all right? Just had a nice letter from Nicolete [Gray] and a cheque for £16.16—she sold a picture of cattle I did at Pigotts to a Welsh schoolmaster from near Swansea—he came to see it—she said he was nice and Welsh, very silent, with a square face, and it was with reluctance that I sent his cheque to the bank, because it has on it 'Barclays Bank—Gorseinon Branch'. The nicest kind of Welsh place-name, nicer than Barclays Bank Crofton Park Branch, I must say.

Staying at Rock could be 'exciting and demanding', as Nicolete Gray observed,[23] and when Prudence Pelham visited there in August 1935 we received the following outburst—a highly coloured elaboration typical of that lovely rebel:

[23] Helen Sutherland's personality and influence, and the new world into which she introduced David at Rock Hall (and later at Cockley Moor), are described with close knowledge and yet with detachment by Nicolete Gray in her long Introduction to *The Helen Sutherland Collection*.

'Dearest René and Joan, It wouldn't half be a marvellous thing to see you both indeed. I am nigh to bursting. I feel criminal impulses of the worst kind welling up—Christ I could do with a spot of booze. May I really come next week? This is a house of "utter prevention" you know. I will ring you up on Tuesday or even Monday night.

'It has been *heavenly* seeing David and you do really get given the day off in a way—but you are *so* frightened of being late for lunch and the pub is just too far to swill in and be back by 12.30. Today has been an absolute joko of a bloody awful one. Start off late for breakfast. We are asked to make a wreath for Vera Moore, whose birthday it is. Sweat over wreath using flowers out of two pots on the table (which pots were specially arranged by Helen for other purposes) well bugger it all you can't think of everything—Plans to do a bunk to wit no appreesuation I am off.

'*Later.* Evening when everyone feels like cats on red-hot bricks—half the chaps waited in the library and the other half in the drawing room —each waiting for each—gong going to and fro before dinner. Helen was just *fuming*. It *was* awful and only cold rabbit to cheer you.

'There are many religious discussions mixed up with communism and good works. David leaps to doors and for coffee-cups. I have never seen him so agile.

'We sit by a small nice pond for a bit nearly every day and complain and are happy in turns—I do think it *awful* that David is to stay here so long. I'm sure it will make him ill.

'Too fed up to go on.

'It will be *lovely* to see you. I do wish you were both here because it really is screamingly funny and I haven't told you any of the nice things. In strength we might have reformed this house, but I doubt it! Love from   PRUDENCE'

To which David added a P.S.:

Christ there is not even a nice puzzy-cat to passe your frozen mutton to and it's raining like buggery.   D.

He wrote again after Prudence had gone:

To R.H., 24 August 1935   *Barmoor Castle,*
Lowick, Northumberland.

Well my china how the bloody hell are you.

I am writing this on Chathill railway station going to Barmoor Castle for the week-end. I did mean to thank you for your lovely letter before, which arrived when Prudence was with me. It was a nice letter. I do like it when a chap writes out in his own hand an apostolical writing—it made Paul live again. It would be rather nice to write a whole Gospel according to Taplow, wouldn't it. Do hope Prudence is still with you and that you are all having a *lovely time*, nise and plenty of laps. I do hope being here didn't make her miserable—she will have told you of some of the vicissitudes of this type of life, I expect. Poor Helen S. does get put out with the details of this so-called world. Just come to a station called Lucker—good job there is an L in it. O what a good job. Christ wat a temptation to alter the signs by night—well somehow I don't seem to be very fluent—what is this—I find I have no ideas—God damn summon up these immortal thoughts—you can't. I *would* like to see you.

Well here is Belford—next station Beal get out hop into car and up to Conty's to tea. I hope I have a nise time. Prudence liked the house and the chaps in it. She went over one day.

What of this Italians–Abyssinia war. Thinks what of it—it's going to be a horrible old nashti orl right. Beal coming up—get your kit ready old son. . . . Shall I go and fight for the Abyssinians—I still have my Royal Welsh tunic and cap.

. . . I hear croquet mallets without, do be reasonable. I have a huge four-poster bed, the first time I did ever lie in one. I feel like the King of France or rather like the Dauphin. . . . It does seem ages since I waved my braces at Prudence and you at St. Pancras Kings Cross or wherever it was.

Sunday 25 Aug. A bit more. The parson came to tea. Says I do not see you in Church—do you ever go—says no sir I'm R.C. What a mistake! He says to me before a crowded tea-table, 'What in your opinion is the essential difference between the C. of E. and yourselves?' *What a question.* I fair stumbled and spluttered and waved my pawkles—says hold up—what a question.

By December he was writing again from Sidmouth:

To R.H., 2 December 1935   *Fort Hotel, Sidmouth*

... Part 1 of my book was the *devil* to cope with and is very much cut down. Part 2, curiously enough, stands more entire. Part 6 has been more possible to deal with than I thought it might be—Part 4, the long part (60 pages), has been a bugger—I do hope it is something—I terribly want outside judgement. Sometimes when I read it it seems to have a shape, at other times it sounds awful balls and full of bad jokes and strained meanings. The real thing I'm afraid of is this business of Cockney speech. It's the very devil to try and make a *real enduring shape that won't be embarrassing* with the stuff—dropped h's and 'yers' and 'bloody' and all that are *so* difficult. And yet you've got to get across that form of speech somehow because so much of the feeling of the sentences depends on all that—How to make it not *realistic* is the bugger. I feel it's beyond my power—one would have to know a lot more about the construction of words and the origin of dialect I suppose to do it.

To R.H., Sat. evening 6 Dec. '35   *The Marina, Sidmouth*

In pub no paper but fly-leaf of book, to wit Borrow's *Wild Wales*—post going want you to get this Monday. Hope you are better. Hope sent-on letter from Prudence and T[ommy] H[odgkin] reached you—I remembered Longmans owed me money for the block I lent them for Gwen Greene's book [*The Prophet Child*, 1935] and asked Tom to send the cheque (a meagre £3.3) to you for you to come down next week-end or when you can. Hope you will not be offended. Christ what's this Uncle Pethybridge rattling his pockets for. But I think it would be good and help you get over your cold and I want to see you very seriously a great deal—I'm fed up in a type of way I may say and I want to discuss the possibility of printing this book in the spring. Unless we're all in the army. Phone me up if you can sometime. Still plastered up at side [after the removal of an abscess]. Looks as if Prudence won't be home for Christ knows how long now, don't it.

A few notes about *In Parenthesis*, dating from this time of its near-completion:

12.11.35. Which day's child is 'loving and giving' in the rhyme? Joan would know. Is it Wednesday's?

Does the accent come in Impera′trix so? I'm like some bloody barbarian trying to decipher one line of a Latin sheepskin in a year—bugger it. Don't half wish I had a clerk at me elbow to tell me things.

14.12.35. I do wish I could have written my stuff in those simple words [of French epic]—it does make my book seem flowery bollocks to a large extent. It's that verbosity that makes me hate it *so* in great tracts.

11.2.36. I do hope we can print my book in double columns[24]— I want it to be printed *just* as *you* want it so that you can at least print *one* book exactly according to *your* ideas of typography— I trust you about that—no frills—a slap-up no hokey-pokey printing. I'm re-writing my Preface for the *third* time—what a fucking sweat.

To R.H., St. David's Day, 1936   *Fort Hotel, Sidmouth*

They gave me leeks to eat today and put one in a vase on my table. I've finished my Preface and sent it to Harman because he wrote to me and said he wanted to read it. He will pass it on to Tom [Burns] to be typed. . . . Prudence was here with me last St. David's Day.

. . . I notice you use semi-colons in your letter to me—shall we start writing with great care and grammatical accuracy—shortly, and properly addressed. I think we might. Well my dear Friends I must lay aside my pen, for this present time; pray to excuse my writing of so much bollocks. I must in the future remember that

> Immodest words admit of no defence,
> For want of decency is want of sense.

Believe me to be your humble and affectionate friend,

WALTER DAVID MICHAEL JONES

---

[24] See above, p. 54.

Some years before, I believe in 1933, David had been elected to membership in the Seven & Five Society (seven painters, five sculptors), which included Ben and Winifred Nicholson, Frances Hodgkins, Barbara Hepworth, John Piper, John Skeaping, Christopher Wood, Cedric Morris, Henry Moore, Ivon Hitchens, Ceri Richards, and others from time to time. But David did not exhibit with them for more than three or four years.

To H.S.E., 3 April 1936   *Fort Hotel, Sidmouth*
. . . I have just received a communication from the Worshipful Company of 7 & 5 to the effect that I am not a member—having only registered 2 votes at the last election. What a pity I did not send in my dignified letter of resignation a year ago—but in a way it's much nicer to be hoofed out—certainly whatever happened I suppose my stuff would no longer 'go with' their particular goodness.

It has been said that membership in the Society was important to David's development as a painter, but I believe in that respect it had no influence on him whatsoever; though he might hail a passing vessel, he was always a lone navigator. A good many years later (1964) he wrote to Peter Levi:

It was *not* a group in the sense of holding certain theories or issuing manifestos—but just a few chaps who seemed to apprehend some kind of vitality in each other's works! But I suppose the dominant personality was Ben Nicholson, for whose work I had and still have a considerable regard, but he became more and more an apostle of the 'abstract' and in the end would tolerate no other work.

For some reason no letters from David to me or to any of the other three close friends have survived from the period between the spring of 1936 and the spring of 1938. He continued through this time to live mostly at Sidmouth, and to make longish visits to Rock, Pigotts, London (Glebe Place and Brockley). June 1937 saw the publication by Faber & Faber of *In Parenthesis*, and his mother died in the same year. He was in London at the end of that year, then again in Sidmouth:

[82]

To H.J.G., St. Valentine's Day, 1938   *Fort Hotel, Sidmouth*

I was glad to get your letter this morning—a very unexpected pleasure when I emerged from my room at about 10.45 and looked casually at the rack—it came by the second post and I'd already looked through a couple of bills and the *Times* in bed— I don't usually get letters by the second post.

What a heavenly thing of Donne's. I did like reading it. I remembered the bit about 'let the Spaniards in'—heavens, it's so crisp and nice. Well, so it's February already—I feel as though I had not been here very long; the time seems to rush by quicker and quicker, like the things in *Alice in Wonderland*. I respond to all you said in your letter—yes, it's all like that—it will be next year in a minute and so little done. I have not done any writing, because I decided I must try to draw again if I possibly could, but so far the result is not very reassuring. It still seems to tend to bring back my stuff more than other things, and consequently it is a very wearisome and slow job doing a bit when I can, and making not much headway, and I *only* know *one* way to draw and that is in a kind of fierce concentration.

The only times a drawing is good is when you nearly *break* yourself *turning the corner* from a muddle to a clarity, and it takes every *ounce* of nervous effort to be any good—so it is very difficult to proceed gingerly and soberly and stop when you know it will be probably fatal (I mean fatal because of bringing on some bloody recurrence of nerves) to go on and hope to recapture something next time, because for one thing you get so *bored* with working like that, and who can command inspiration? And yet I absolutely and definitely know there is *nothing* else I care about except this drawing business—*writing*, ah yes—*as much*—but after all, my equipment is that of a painter not a writer. My equipment as a writer is very severely limited by not being a scholar, and for the kind of writing I want to do you really do have to have so much *information* and know such a lot about *words* that I can't really believe I can do it except in a limited way—what I did in *I[n] P[arenthesis]* was really a special thing and very strictly within my limits, and by a series of accidents I think I just turned the corner—but O Mary! what a conjuring trick it was. But I may do some more—I'm sure I shall if I get weller and nothing awful happens and Mr. Chamberlain doesn't let Mr. Eden believe what Lord Hugh Cecil and Mr. Litvinoff tell him (or the other way round, whichever keeps things fairly quiet) and the old nerves don't come back and I get some nice peace and no bloody hokey pokey in general.

But anyway I want now to do some drawing—bugger, it's 10.30, the time I have to go down and drink whisky with Colonel Hastings. Well, it's his turn tonight; that means I can afford some of my own when I come back up here—when I will continue to write to you. I work now best in the evening from after dinner until about 1 a.m.—except for the hour down in the sitting room with Colonel Hastings. It is a nightly ritual and a reprimand if I don't appear—he is a pet anyway I wouldn't half like to be like that—which is rather as if I said I would like to be like Mae West or the Archbishop of York.

Back again from this drink, put on the electric heater, light a cigarette, pour out a whisky and water—I've stopped drinking soda altogether now and always take water, a simplification and less expensive (but oh dear *how* expensive whisky is, I *wish* I didn't have to drink it)—but what a lot I *smoke*, it's awful—I can't *tell* how many a day.

. . . I don't want to leave here unless it is necessary. It was so nice to get here in December after the rather unsatisfactory state I got myself into—I felt a lot better when I got away and alone. I don't mean I don't love being with and seeing my friends, *I wish I could be with them*, but if you get into a particular kind of state then it seems to me a type of solitude brings you to your own private senses in some way—at least, it does me, over some things. I think if I could only get not having the worse type of nerves and could work at painting or writing (Bugger—I did not know this had a drawing on the back—it is my leg. I drew it as a study for a thing I'm doing—bugger! I want it, but can't write this letter over again—well, I shall have to send it as it is and do my leg again if I want it) I should be quite happy alone always. At least I should not mind other types of unhappiness if

I could work properly, because it is all I really want to do, or ever have wanted to do (at least I want to do it so much more than anything else. It always comes back to that). It seems an innocent and proper enough desire. I hope They will let me do it. I mean They, God and Co.

... What was it like in Tom's car crash? I never can get the details of it or how bad it was or if the car was utterly wrecked or how frightened you all were or whatever.[25]

I'm awfully glad you sent some flowers to Prudence. In her last letter she sounded *so* unhappy, because she'd stopped sleeping again and found the psychologists so *hopeless* and *did* sound miserable—poor dear Prudence, it is horrible to think of her in Whitechapel hospital and not happy. What a real sod and bugger this neurosis is for this generation—it is our Black Death, all right.[26]

Dear Harman, I must go to bed now. I will write some more tomorrow. Goodnight.

Next day, Tuesday. What a silly, all-about-myself, pompous kind of letter this is—well—I'll send it—you are a trustworthy interpreter of moods and will forgive its disposition to self-interestedness, I hope. I have another *great* annoyance, and it is this, that now I've started trying to paint you can't do it by electric light, and as the *only* time of day when I feel more or less un-neurotic and with any energy is after dinner, I *can't* do what I see is necessary to this drawing, and in the daytime I can't bear to look at it because I've got little nervous energy and can only do casual things—like walk about or read a little. *Writing* does not present this difficulty. O bugger, they get you *whatever* you try to do.

[25] When the brakes of Tom Burns's little sports car failed as we turned (Tom, Harman and I) into the main Uxbridge road on our way to Pigotts, it was apparent that we would hit a brick wall opposite us, some twenty yards away. This we did. Harman remembers his great amusement when I got out of the damaged car and said, 'Now, *that's* the sort of accident I like—just time to make an act of contrition.'

[26] Prudence Pelham's nervous trouble was not, I believe, in any way similar to David's. She was under treatment for the first manifestations of the disease of the nerves, 'disseminated sclerosis' as we then called it, which was to bring about her death in 1952 at the age of forty-seven.

I hope Hitler and Musso and Schuschnigg arrange the affairs of Austria between themselves, otherwise these fools in England will say we must intervene to preserve the integrity of Austria or something.

To H.J.G., 31 May 1938   *Fort Hotel, Sidmouth*

Have only done one drawing after all and then started to take up again the writing I read to you when last I saw you, but have only done about 40 more pages. I don't know if any of it is any good. A very rambling affair—sometimes it all seems balls and sometimes I like it in places. But *I.P.* was chained to a sequence of events which made it always a straightforward affair, whereas this effort is, I fear, about 'ideas', the *one* thing I have always disliked in poetry—but now I see how chaps slip into it, because it seems that if you haven't got a kind of racial myth expressed in war to write about and don't know about our old friend 'love' and are not interested in 'making a story', it seems all you can do is to ramble on about the things you think about on the whole all the time, and that is what I think this is about.

It is about how everything turns into something else, and how you can never tell when a bonza is cropping up or the Holy Ghost is going to turn something inside out, and how everything is a balls-up and a kind of 'Praise' at the same time.

I see now why chaps write about 'separate' things in short poems—to wit, odes to nightingales and what not—but it seems to me that if you just talk about a lot of things as one thing follows on another, in the end you *may* have made a shape out of all of it. That is to say, that shape that all the mess makes in your mind.

David was more explicit later (see letters of 17 January and 11 April 1939) about this 'writing', the beginning of *The Book of Balaam's Ass*; and it will be apparent how true it is that the part printed in *The Sleeping Lord* is literally a fragment.

After his mother's death David no longer used his parents' home in Brockley as a base when he was in London; he was staying with Tom Burns in Chelsea when he wrote the following letter, soon after *In Parenthesis* had been awarded the Hawthornden Prize:

To H.S.E. and Helen Ede, 7 July 1938   *3 Glebe Place, Chelsea*

... I'm so glad you are glad about the old Hawthornden. I don't really think it is very much of an 'honour' you know—but it is decidedly nice to get £100. I was in sore need of it—must last long. ... I don't know if the Hawthornden will shove up the sales of book. Unfortunately, from the vulgar point of view, the Press have not been very helpful—the London papers practically said nothing. Just facetious remarks in the *Express* ['Something for His Locker', *Daily Express*, 25 June 1938] etc. Anyway, they are printing another 1,000 copies in hopes of new sales, René sweating on it to get it done in reasonable time.[27]

How awful the Press is—how appallingly they misrepresent me. No wonder political news is so appallingly inaccurate and mischievous. I mean if Musso or Chamberlain, or Hitler or Stalin, or anyone of importance is as misrepresented as a poor bloody writer—no wonder we get curious ideas about these chaps.

The next letter, from Rock, was written at the time of the Munich crisis:

To H.J.G., 24 September 1938   *Rock*

Your letter has just arrived—*what* a business—have we come to it at last—all these years something of this sort has haunted me (that you know—all my pictures etc., have been done with a pretty empty feeling in my tummy because of it) only I always vaguely hoped it might be averted (purely selfishly)—averted until I was, if possible, miraculously 'better' again and not the nervous wreck I am. It is so awful to be quite useless and only wait about, with the imagination going round and round—damnation. I *do* loathe it. It is so ignominious—it is awful to feel like an old woman in a panic when one needs to feel like a type of superman. I've known for *very* long that courage would soon be the only virtue worth possessing. I do thank you for

[27] The first impression, issued in June 1937, was of 1,500 copies.

writing. I wish now I'd written to you—I've wanted to all this last two weeks. I've thought of you *so* much, dear Harman.

. . . Been reading Lancelot Andrewes's sermons a bit. Lord, I wish I'd known him before—the tightest English I ever read— so, so good. But today could only read Pepys' Diary—just as dope, and bits of Evelyn—interesting to read together—what a pet world the buggers lived in without knowing it.

Yes, I heard Chamberlain's grand little speech on his first return. I did like that more than I can say. He is simply the real goods, there is no doubt about that—the only bright spot—But, Lord, what a weight the poor man has to carry, and hardly any bugger to give him proper support. (The *Times* have been all right, I think. Thought leading article for yesterday, 23rd, masterly and unanswerable.) You already know what I think about the Left—League [of Nations] and Co.—the 'idealisms' that have *terrified* one with their unrealities for years—and Chamberlain, I felt, from the beginning of his taking office, saw *real* issues and has struggled valiantly to *do* something—but I fear now, too late, perhaps—but perhaps in *any* case the German thing was set for this—I feel I don't know for certain about that —but I do know that on 'our' side the follies and dangerous un- true ideas have been contributing to a disaster. The infernal thing is that once there is a show-down no ideas matter much and one can't see any light at all as to what might happen. If one could one might not feel so wretched. Lord, *how* different all this is from 1914—but I suppose I personally must take into account that now I am a buggered-up neurotic and then I was an innocent uninformed boy . . . *bugger bugger bugger* I do wish everything was nicer. We are an unfortunate generation.

Old Bishop Turpin in the *Song of Roland* keeps on saying to chaps, 'Sirs, you are set for sorrow'. He would have a job to im- prove upon that statement if he were with us, I fear.

. . . My book seems already about the Zulu war.

That the innocence of the nineteen-year-old David survived at least his first two years in the army, can be seen in a couple of short pieces he wrote sometime around Christmas 1916. In one he looks back on his first year in Flanders and France, and in the second he asks rhetorically, *Is it worth it?* ('Now then, you, relieve that man on sentry-go! Late orlready!' The trench is still cold and wet; eyes still ache, and hands freeze. *But it's worth it!*) The enemy are not yet 'Jerry' or 'he', but 'the Boche' or 'the Hun'. It would be unfair to David to print these two pieces, but reference should be made to them, not only because they illustrate the illusions that comforted him, but even more because they show that his memory is at fault when, many years later, he says that his first attempt to write about the war was made at Hove in 1928. No doubt he dismissed these trifles as insignificant, but in fact they are both serious attempts at artistic composition, and in them can be recognized the seed from which his later writing was to grow to maturity; the links with history, the pale moon over the desolate valley, the battle in the hot sunshine—but written of in terms of the 'war-lords of Odin' and 'Europe prostrate 'neath the iron heel of the Teuton terror'.

To H.J.G., 17 January 1939   *Fort Hotel, Sidmouth*

. . . I'm trying to do my writing, but it's going a bit slow—but it usually does. Writing is odder than painting in some ways— one seems to stodge on and scratch out for hours and days and then sometimes, quite out of the blue, something breaks through that gives the thing a tolerable shape—but it seems jolly accidental. I *should* like to say how truly helped and pleased I am that you liked some of this new writing—because, as I said about *I.P.*, I was more helped by your understanding than by anyone else's. For one thing I believe we have an almost identical attitude to this 'word' business—it is a thing difficult to explain (impossible in fact) to chaps who haven't got it—or have it in some other way. I've got a miserable feeling that my new thing is not so 'tight' and 'made' as *I.P.* It tends to be descriptive in a way that bores me—also rhetorical—my chief fear and danger. I think this is because it is not so determined by factual happenings in which I was physically concerned, as *I.P.* was. This bloody difficulty of writing about 'ideas' and somehow making them concrete is a bugger to surmount—but I believe it can be done. The 'zone' part, of course, escapes that difficulty—and was consequently a bit easier to do. I'm immersed in my Absalom, Mass, part now[28]—It is a bugger to do and full of pitfalls—but one or two accidentally nice bits, perhaps, a line or so perhaps.

In the above David for once uses 'tight' to indicate approval, i.e. compact, well fitted together. (Applied to a painting it means for him forced, over-direct, lifeless, 'without recession'.) In the 'new writing' 'The Zone' is based upon the camp at Winnol Down near Winchester, from which the 15th R.W.F. marched to Southampton on 1 December 1915, to embark for France. It was written as the conclusion to *The Book of Balaam's Ass*. The central, Passchendaele, section is, like 'The Zone', based on facts, but on facts directly reported to and not experienced by the writer.

To H.S.E. and Helen Ede, 11 April 1939   Fort Hotel, Sidmouth
. . . I've had awful jitters about the international situation which has paralysed any creative effort. I am not only jittery but very angry. It is all such a conflict of *many wrongs* and all the English *moralizing* on the subject SICKENS me. All the old 1914 nonsense over again only much worse—but it is no use. I'm actually less bad about it now I think, although the situation in itself is very very very serious—I think they may find a way out yet— anyway, for a bit. It is sheer lunacy. I agree in a way it brings us all back to fundamentals. (Of course, living naked in a forest would bring one back to 'fundamentals' in some respects, but to do so would seem to me to be a regrettable thing in most respects.) I feel personally so sophisticated and decadent and ill a person, that, if there is a real showdown—I can't see what I would do. I wish I was young and knew *nothing* like I was in 1914. But neurotics have little place in this new and steel world. Various *illusions* seem to give courage to some blokes. Well, enough of this stuff. (I see this so-called Dictatorship v. 'Democcracy' business as largely an affair of the *sword* against *money*. It is more complicated than that, but that seems to me to be part of it, and very much at the root of it.)

About my new writing that I've been trying to do—it is rather difficult to say what it is *about*. It has not got very far—

[28] This is the first indication of the various Mass 'sequences', one of which is *The Kensington Mass* (1975).

about a third of *I.P.* I suppose so far—very slow—but still not slower than *I.P.* but MUCH more difficult to do, and may be all nonsense. It is rather disjointed and rambling and may have to be (if it ever appears) a kind of thing in sections with only the continuity of my own rambling mind to give it a kind of unity. Let me see—this is not public information—but I think it is really about how if you start saying in a kind of way how *bloody* everything is you end up in a kind of *praise—inevitably*—I mean a sort of Balaam business. Yes perhaps it will be called *The Book of Balaam*, or *Book of Balaam's Ass*. A spot of Job too! It started off by talking about how things are conditioned by other things —a person comes into a room for instance and all the disorder and deadness takes shape and life—but it has wandered into all kinds of things—got a lot more 'religious' than I anticipated in a way. I like bits of it—but whether it will achieve any unity remains to be seen. Anyway there it is. It is odd indeed how one fidgets away at these things that are too high for one. I feel if one had ten years of real peace it might come to something. But how strangely unconnected the life of the mind seems with the hard steel world—this contingent 'real' world, so called—yes well and real it is too, also.

. . . Dear Prudence got married *very sudden* the other day to a man called Guy Branch. I hope it will be nice and happy for her and make her weller than she has been—she's been ill so long with all my kind of neurasthenic stuff. I love her very very much and our friendship has meant everything to me. So naturally, however much this may be 'a good thing', I've naturally had a twisting, trying to get all the tangled delicate emotional bits and pieces tied up and sorted out. I only tell you this because of the intimate friendship we have and I wanted to tell you. *It is all private to you and Helen. I'm sure you'll understand that.*

These here human relationships are so heart-rending in a way. She is such a marvellous and unique, truly intelligent, and beautiful person. And I've been privileged indeed to have her friendship and kindness and affection. (I *leaned* on her in some obscure kind of way although we seldom spent time together—we were so very alike in a lot of ways, however incredible that sounds.)

So naturally a change in her life of so fundamental a character requires in me a readjustment. I can't talk about this in a letter—but I felt I would like to mention it to you as a friend. I'm sure you will keep it to yourselves.

I wish I could get back to painting but don't feel I shall unless we get a more settled world and my own mind also peacefuller. Painting is so curious—it is so 'totalitarian', and you DO have to be strong to do it, once you know the snags.

... I sent my book to Chamberlain and had a nice letter from him. Jelly [D'Aranyi] took it to him for me. It was kind of her.[29]

The opening part of *The Book of Balaam's Ass*, in which 'all the disorder and deadness takes shape and life', is based on the town of Sidmouth and David's deep affection for Prudence Pelham—thus:

> She's bright where she walks, she
> dignifies the spaces of the air and makes
> an ample scheme across the trivial shapes.
> She shakes the proud and rotten accidents.
> Small conveniences look shrunk, so that
> you hardly notice them.
>   Like when pale flanks turn to lace with agile stripes
> the separating grill

These lines, and his words about Prudence in the above letter, taken in conjunction with what he says about the uncompromising demands of his work, show the inevitability of his great sorrow over her marriage. Had David known her husband, however, he would not have used so bald a phrase as 'a man called Guy Branch'. He also exaggerates the suddenness of the marriage: Prudence had known Guy Branch, a friend of her brother John, since their school days. The worship she accorded him was his due.

To H.J.G., 24 April 1939   *Fort Hotel, Sidmouth*
... I'm reading the full edition of *Mein Kampf*, and it is *so*

[29] Although David kept a carefully written copy of his letter to Chamberlain presenting *In Parenthesis*, it would be unfair to print it here, for it shows that the rule of illusion was as effective in 1939 as it was in 1914; and in later years—indeed quite soon—David was to understand this. For Jelly D'Aranyi, whom David had met at Rock, see Nicolete Gray, *The Helen Sutherland Collection*, pp. 22–3.

different from the miserable cut-about edition I read previously. I am deeply impressed by it, it is amazingly interesting in all kinds of ways—but pretty terrifying too. God, he's *nearly* right —but this *hate* thing mars his whole thing, I feel. I mean it just misses getting over the frontier into the saint thing—he won't stand any nonsense or illusions or talk—but, having got so far, the conception of the world in terms of race-struggle (that's what it boils down to) will hardly do. But I do like a lot of what he says—only I must admit he sees the world as just going on *for ever* in this steel grip. Compared with his opponents he is grand, but compared with the saints he is bloody. And I think I mean also by saints—lovers, and all kinds of unifying makers. Anyway, I back him still against all this currish, leftish, money thing, even though I'm a miserable specimen and dependent upon it.

Fr. Martin D'Arcy, S.J., whose writings and conversation greatly influenced David, was at this time Master of Campion Hall, where David was staying when he wrote the next letter:

To H.J.G., 23 June 1939   *Campion Hall, Oxford*
. . . Over all that political stuff, I believe I've altered a bit—I feel less interested in it somehow at the moment. I feel I can't cope with it—that whatever one thinks or says makes no 'im-pression' and one's data is anyway so meagre. I'm feeling if I can't get back to my own 'art work', which is all I really care about, I don't know what I shall do. I also think all the time about Prudence but don't get any clearer about how to face up to it. O dear, this old romantic love, the only type I understand, does let you down. I do see why Lancelot ran 'wood mad' in the trackless forest for four years so that no man might know him is easily understandable, but all one does is to smoke cigarettes and drink an extra whisky or something.

Edwin Lutyens has been here, he built this place—a proper academic wag—nice and kind—but why do those types put up such a barrage of jokes, I wonder. Now Stanley Spencer is here, because there is an idea that he should do a wall-painting in the Lady Chapel. I've had an amazing time trying to 'keep the ring' between him and the J.'s. You can understand all that. I'll tell you all about it and lots more when I see you. I feel bewildered with the noise of contrary ideas and the infernal complexity of religion, sex, the structure of society, the arts and everything. All these chaps have bits of right ideas, and when you can see and sympathize with all the various apparently stark contradictory notions it is hard—hard enough to equate in one's own poor head, let alone explain.

For a number of accidental reasons, there is a gap in the correspondence as the war approaches and finally breaks out. David was mostly at the Fort Hotel, Sidmouth, during the first half of 1939, then in London at Glebe Place with Tom Burns, at Rock, and at Pigotts. He was at Pigotts when war was declared, and we can well remember the great excitement that possessed him and Bernard Wall. For hours on end, it seemed, they paced up and down the sitting room, talking, gesticulating, speculating—a very different David from the sadly introspective person seen in the preceding letters. Soon after the outbreak of war he returned to Glebe Place, and from Glebe Place to Sidmouth. Sidmouth was then to be his headquarters for the last time, until June 1940.

To H.J.G., 13 April 1940   *Fort Hotel, Sidmouth*

... During the last week I've not been so good, and can't seem to either paint or write—I suppose it's this gathering storm that makes concentration even more difficult. . . . Yes, old Jerry certainly did that job with astounding efficiency and dispatch. I *do* wish we could have effected a landing on his heels at Narvik—but one knows nothing, or very little, about what is possible and what is not. I was amused at old Churchill when he said 'They are very lively at these things' (to wit: Jerry getting his guns in position and all that). (In fact, I thought Churchill's Commons announcement rather good to read—there were some nice sentences in it. Of course, it's very much his cup of tea—but I thought there was a lot of unnecessary stuff also—all the first part was rather irritating, as far as I can remember. The old bugger is much best when he's just doing his professional 'report on operations' stuff, I mean. I wonder if he's more 'contemporary' about all that than he is generally speaking.)

Lord, what a *very important* book *Cumaean Gates* is! Published 1936, I see—and yet we never so much as heard about it! It seems to me that Mr. [W. F.] Jackson Knight is a rare bird— for one thing he knows what poetry is and what it is not—at least poetry in our sense. I am *most* grateful to you for giving it me. It is in every way exciting. The last chapter is full of things that hit the nail on the head.

I'm borrowing the Sixth *Aeneid* from a girl here to read. Of course, the Grail parallels interested me deeply and confirmed what I partly thought and was partly familiar with from previous reading. I must certainly read his other book *Vergil's Troy* [1932] (the magical protection of cities etc.). Every now and again as I read I felt confirmation of this or that, and of course it all bears very much on the thing I'm trying to write. Of course, I feel very acutely my lack of reading of all this classical stuff and most of all, as I've often said, my blockheaded inability to learn any language. It's an intolerable handicap. However, if there were one or two more Jackson Knights who combined real slap-up scholarship with a nose for the pattern and eternal correspondence of this with that, it would be jolly nice and helpful.

He's interesting about old Eliot—jolly good about him. (Awfully good about male and female principle, pp. 170-1.) He's an awfully good *writer*, too—there are some grand simply stated things, e.g. p. 170, 'when Juno and Venus pull one way very great havoc is done', and on p. 169, 'Vergil knew the cost of Empire; the cost in suffering, and the cost to conscience and to so many graceful things etc.', and of course the end bit of all that you read to me is *absolutely masterly*, and the final sentence about proper poets having 'to *know* and *say* what others could only *be*'—that's the thing in a nutshell—that's the cat's whiskers (I should not have thought it *possible* to express the truth about 'the artist' so exactly and with such simplicity)—it's incredible and very exhilarating. I can't think how he managed it. 3 bloodygreat cheers anyway for Jackson Knight and 2 Alleluias and a Heil.

The derivation of Pontifex Maximus and the original function of the Roman *Pontifices* on p. 102 is *fascinating*. I looked to see if he mentioned the Welsh Caer Troia and was *not* disappointed (p. 112). Well, one could go on—it's full of so much. Alas that we are treading this present Labyrinth so darkly. It's *so* hard to find any detachment within oneself and there's almost none outside in the people one meets.

I'm very glad you borrowed the *Heimskringla*—it's a great thing. My dear Prudence gave it me when I was doing *I.P.* What an odd world that Nordic thing was, an almost unrelieved rough-house. (I remember Prudence saying how Nazi it was—but it's more complicated than that.) I always remember how they *burnt everything* all the time. Terrifying lot of buggers. The account in *Hist. Harald Hardrada* (section 9) of Stamford Bridge fight from the 'other side' is interesting—as is all that Canute succession and relation to England I remember interested me. I'm writing this, rather unusually, in the afternoon, and keep on yawning with that dreadful afternoon fatigue that Sidmouth is renowned for!

. . . God knows, of course, what the next days and weeks will bring—it's on the move now undoubtedly—I wonder what the old Dux will do? It would be a nasty how-de-you-do if he butted in.[30] Is Douglas W[oodruff] still in Italy? Wonder what he will think of 'em. *Give my love to Tom* [Burns] . . . I've not heard at all from Prudence. I hope she's all right. I bet she's suffering agonies as this war develops, poor darling. There is a man mowing the cricket pitch, making that inimitable rattle and grass smell that England knows at this time of year and even in this year.

Postscripts: . . . I wonder if this war gets really serious whether I had better pretend I'm well and join one of these National Defence Companies. I've been wondering about it. It's all I could do.

Sunday. Just going to post this. Hear we've done some stuff at Narvik—hope it's O.K. in a big way. Lord! what a war of giants it is. I see poor old Martindale [Fr. C. C. Martindale, S.J.] is in Denmark. I hope they treat him all right.

---

[30] Mussolini declared war on 10 July 1940, and his contemptible invasion of France followed ten days later.

Stop Press. Started a watercolour today that so far looks more hopeful. Let us pray.

To H.J.G., 16 May 1940   *Fort Hotel, Sidmouth*

I wonder very much how you are. I hope you got my letter written before I went to hospital. I returned to the hotel yesterday. Feel very weak and curious, but suppose that is natural. It was curious getting that thing [appendicitis] suddenly. Can't write much, because of simply feeling too limp, but just wanted to say hallo and send you my love. I suppose you are terribly busy with all this rapid spread of this momentous struggle, about which it's no use talking at this time. I had a wireless earphone thing over my bed in hospital, so for the first time in my life listened rather a lot to it, and how curiously and uncannily the past seemed to come again to me—what with the smell of hospital and the white iron bedstead, and the nurses fussing, and the news of pressure along that familiar tract of battle, Namur, Liège, Tirlemont, Louvain. (The announcer's careful determination to say these words in as Frog a manner as he could manage made it in a subtle kind of way obviously 1940 and not 1914—I felt that very much.)

... The daughter of my doctor here lent me a translation of Virgil, which I've been reading. Somewhat disappointed—but of course translations are translations. I was interested in the Fourth Eclogue—I was ignorant of the precise place in Virgil where Our Lord is said to be prophesied—(teste David cum Sibylla)—I see it is in that Eclogue. ... I liked it when [General W. E.] Ironside in addressing the men returned from Norway spoke of the enemy as 'those people'. I was always delighted when chaps in the last war said, for instance, 'Some of his people are at so and so'. I don't know why it should please me.

1940—1946

Sometime between 18 and 30 June 1940 David left Sidmouth for the last time, and returned to London. He writes to Harman Grisewood on the first of those dates from Sidmouth, and to Tom Burns on the second from London. There is a change in the tone of his writing once he is back in London. He still swears about 'the general buggeration', but he is not so overwhelmingly oppressed. He sees more friends and has many things to occupy his mind; he is more active and can even paint again. This period saw the start of the watercolour, now in the Tate Gallery, which was ultimately called *Aphrodite in Aulis* (1941), a picture with which he was, on the whole, well satisfied. 'I'm doing a picture of Phryne the hetaira', he writes to Tom on 30 June 1940, 'and the sum of all beauty, who showed her splendours to the Court (at least her counsel did) and so impressed them that they said she was innocent.'

Tom Burns had gone to Madrid, to work in the British Embassy there, and David was left in temporary charge of the house at Glebe Place, until it could be disposed of. Later he went to Harman and Margaret Grisewood, close at hand at 61 King's Road, while still keeping a room at Glebe Place, and still later to other friends. He was much concerned with his father, who since his mother's death had been living alone in Brockley. From time to time he went to stay at Pigotts, it might be for a few days or for several weeks. I saw him myself but seldom, when I was on leave from the R.A.F. and before I went overseas in 1942.

To T.F.B., 30 June 1940   *3 Glebe Place*

Thank you so much for your letter. I wish I'd written sooner but you know what it is. I'm still here and all is well. Ann [Bowes-Lyon] came a few days ago as she was changing from night to day duty. Mike R[ichey] is home on leave and looks like a young lion with a blue anchor tattooed on his vast and hairy forearm—he's just the same—he took his slicer yesterday. I've been to Brockley and am hoping to see Harman this evening.

H. isn't so bad but pretty fed up and hard worked. I may go to Pigotts for a bit. Or perhaps to Helen's, but I still feel with the Blitz in the air (very much in the *air*!) I feel very doubtful about moving far. I've been writing some of my stuff and leading the usual quiet sort of existence. I see Bernard [Wall] a good bit, and go to dinner with Douglas and Mia [Woodruff] and Fr. [James] Brodrick, which was nice, and of course I see dear Harman whenever possible. So all goes smoothly as to our private lives.

. . . I bet it is *bloody* hot in Spain. I think about you a lot and wonder how you are liking it all. It's weird to think of you there. Rum when chaps are away doing something quite different and all *looks* the same—the room—etc. as if you might walk in any moment and say—'Come on, Dai, let's have a pint—I'm absolutely dying for a quick one'. . . . The *Tiger* [Christopher Dawson] is expected in London tomorrow. I hope to see him—wonder how he is, he's only coming up for a day or so—I believe he's better in health now a bit. Charles E[vans] got married this week. I see in tonight's *Evening Standard* that the sweet Veronica Fraser is getting married on Monday to old Phipps's son (Ambassador Phipps, I mean). She hasn't half got nice eyes, *apart from* anything else.

I think I must have my first whisky and water today—will do so, forthwith, and drink to your dear health and all. Very bad news from Prudence—she's got a kind of paralysis down one side—but I don't know any *details*. Guy has had a rough time and once reported missing, but *all right actually*. God, what a business it all is. I *can't* get any news from her—I heard this from Baba R[othschild] and Joan also, to whom she managed to write. Alack. I do hope it's not as bloody as it sounds, poor sweet Prudence. She suffers like one of those types of mystic in a way.

Ann looked jolly nice I thought in her tight-fitting tailored blue coat and black tie and white collar, which I had not seen her in before. She complained that they had put too much padding in the shoulders, but I rather liked it. Paul [Richey] came and took the car. We looked high and low for some documents to do with petrol or something—but could find nothing—anyway he's got it, I mean the car. Eric [Gill] is still in bed. René has gone to Bisley to do a course of firing, because he is such a good shot, it turns out! The sweet Margaret B[ailey] has left London again for a bit. She is a heavenly person, indeed she is. Christ, must do the blackout.

Aug. 6th. Oh damn damn. I lost this letter and only just found it again—you will think I am never going to write—I had a lot to say, too. I saw Ann last Sat. at Mike R.'s, he was going back on Sunday. Today I've been to Veronica's wedding—extra grand, with naval ratings to pull the car down Warwick Street. Veronica looked heavenly. Ronnie K[nox] said the Mass and Vincent [Turner, later Fr., S.J.] officiated at the marriage ceremony. Douglas and Mia and Co. were there, and had a nice time afterwards: a nice wet of bubbly at Tite St. and lunch with Helen As[quith]. Old Belloc looks so much aged, I was quite surprised. Not seen him for some years.

Have at last heard from Prudence. She is coming to London this week to a hospital for nervous diseases, and is very pleased that I am here and that I can go and see her—she sounds pretty bad but tremendously brave and vigorous of mind and spirit in spite of all. I hope she will get all right—as it is a paralysis caused by the shock of the war strain and is therefore of nervous origin. I feel it may get right again—not I imagine like an organic thing quite, but bloody awful. She is bloody angry about it, which is so nice, I mean angry rather than sorrowful, but that also, no doubt —but you know what I mean—her spirit is of the Gods and no mistake.

Aug. 11th. Been to see Prudence, she is in hospital in London. She was cheerful but is temporarily paralysed down one side—as I said—it was heavenly seeing her. Guy O.K. so far.

14 Aug. I've just heard that Guy is missing, isn't it *too* awful— poor poor poor Prudence. I was going to the hospital to see her but they asked me not to go for a few days, I will let you know more as I hear anything or see her—O bugger bugger bugger. With very much love. God bless you a lot. Sorry to inflict all this nasty news on you. I do hope *you* are not cast down. I'm all right and quite cheerful mostly for some unaccountable reason. *Now 15th.* Just been to Mass of the Assumption at Westminster.

To T.F.B., 28 August 1940   *3 Glebe Place*

... I wish I had written oftener—I feel bad about that—but I've not seemed to be able to. A fairly strained time in a way—nothing dramatic or decisive or anything but a strain at least for blokes like me. So far all is as usual—no outward difference, except those wailing sirens at odd times day or night, sometimes long spaces with nothing and then a rapid succession of raids and raid-warnings. *So far*, as far as our district is concerned, it is raid-warnings and distant bumps and all that. People seem quite unconcerned—a little jumpy, in an amused kind of way, when a car changing gear (or whatever it is) sounds like the beginning of a raid signal! The weather is fine as late summer turns into autumn. London looks very beautiful as it always is at this time of year. We've had a bit of a return of flea-plague—but not on the scale of 1938—but bloody annoying, they are curious insects —not fleas at all really—I wonder what they are?—they don't bite at all events, but it is an embarrassment. I've had a bout of influenza—and got up for the first time yesterday, feel pretty weak—it was curious lying in bed sweating, with medicine bottles, and flowers and all, at night listening to those 'things that go bump in the night'—not heard by myself since 1918. That low whine and dull thud away in the distance reminded me of my first shell in Xmas 1915.

I don't think the human race will ever get adjusted to 'explosions'. They are bad for the human mechanism, and just as the tube-lift gives one a nasty feeling in the stomach—directly assaults the central nervous system, so does the explosive—it is entirely independent of 'danger' really—though of course associated with danger and damage—I suppose it is partly the 'power' thing (like thunder gives people a turn) in that it displays a power out-of-proportion with the frailty of flesh and blood, I suppose—indeed, is all fear that—yes, I suppose we are afraid of that against which we seem to have no adequate armour or offensive weapon—all very elementary really. Now I'm wandering in my usual way. Yes, I see dear Harman pretty frequently—as often as he can—he's jolly tied up of course and uncertain these days. I mean uncertain of his fixtures because of his work. I've not been allowed to see Prudence. I had hoped I might be some help—just possibly—but of course no one could be—anyway I understand from her nurse (a nice Welsh girl with a lovely face and a lovelier voice from Meirionydd, what the English call Merionethshire, she says the word with exquisite perfection) that P. is *really* a *little* better and I trust her statement more or less. I trust I may be allowed to call within measurable time. P. thinks Guy may have been picked up by an 'E' boat or rescued on the coast of France. Pray God this is so. She asked after you when I last saw her, just before the bad news.[31]

. . . As I write the balloon barrage is very high in the sky as though the battlements of London were in heaven (as I devoutly hope they may be). . . . My father still is patient and happy in Brockley—he spends a certain amount of time in a neighbour's dugout, when need is—not that anything has happened there, but they get a good bit of gunfire I think, being near the barrage-belt. He is just as ever. Confident and content. I suppose because he lives interiorly and truly like old man Enoch 'with God', it's amazing—I wish I knew how it was done.

I wish I knew what to advise you. No—I don't think at all that your wishes are 'uncontemporary' (that was a nasty one and most unjustified!). *I think you ought to do whatever you bloody well feel inclined to do*, and, sweet Tom, don't let it get you down. It is difficult for *anyone* else to know a person's mind. Anyway it is not a *moral* question. But it would seem that *if* you can be of *use* in *any* place, stay put. We've all got ourselves to think about—and by doing what we can best do and *most want* to do, ourselves, we best do what is best for the jolly old 'community' in the end. I'm sure of that. . . . I don't think you ought to think about what you say about other chaps in Europe and the whole world having such an awful time—if one starts comparing the miseries of others with one's own relatively happy lot there is no

[31] Guy Branch, a pilot in 601 Squadron of the Royal Auxiliary Air Force, was lost over the Channel; his body was washed ashore on the Normandy coast and buried by the French. After the war Prudence went over with Mike Richey to look for the grave, and she cut a stone for him: *Ad lucem.*

end to it, and one would tend to just *try* and have a bloody time so as not to feel one was more fortunate than some—people do that quite a lot. It is always a danger, and inhibits one sometimes from achievement and enjoyment—*I know about that in a kind of way.* One sees it operating in a crude and obvious way when chaps won't enjoy this or that because Aunt so and so has cancer, or when chaps say 'It is awful that I should put back this nice whisky when you think of poor Fr. Snooks saying matins in his cold chapel, etc.' Well, as G.K. said, 'Why should *salt* suffer?' . . . I think you were somewhere near it when you say (in your more personal postscript to me) about this 'love' thing being 'above and beyond or below and beside' —I mean it's *all* those *four* things at once—it's on a different plane. I mean one *might* take the line, because of some inner compulsion, and say in *any* given circumstances, 'Hell, bugger them all, for me, I will be as near Miss X as I bloody well can be, even if she is nasty and completely indifferent—empires can crash and the lands be waste—let the buggers get on with it—I must be near this nice girl—I can do no other, come what will'. I still don't think the question is a moral one (I mean except that everything is!). That is what I like so much about the Morte Darthur actually. It is a collection of instances of chaps putting that before this and this before that, according to their several natures and impulsions—there is no trite 'loved I not honour more' (that's a more recent notion) for honour itself moves with the object of worship—everyone instinctively understands this (except a certain kind of textbook theologian or, lower down, a person who has made *absolute* some *relative* scale of values that is of some particular society, e.g. club rules etc.). There is no answer to this question. It is the crux of all behaviour. What is sauce for the gosling is by no means sauce for the gander, and truly when we've tried like hell to make the 'right decision', 'ofttimes we do what seemeth for the best, but it turneth out for the worst'. *Don't I know it!*—it is about all I do know for certain!

. . . It is singularly odd, that business of how we've all lived for nearly a year without the least idea what to do for the best as far as our private lives are concerned—of course I feel this appallingly—because I'm so absolutely, by one accident and another, an onlooker, damned odd—it's a wonder one does not feel worse than one does really—but it is a bugger how one can't decide the simplest thing because of it all. I wish I'd been able to do more work, because if one can't be of use in the machinery of the thing one literally ought to get on with one's own stuff—but here of course Rosy [T.F.B.'s personification of neurosis] steps in. Did I tell you Charles Evans's wife gave him for a wedding present that darkish marchish picture of Sidmouth—it looks nice framed and it has arrived safe and sound at Soddens—£22 net, *I* thank you! Jesus, this money thing that's what really worries me—I can't see how I can *get any more ever*! and not even back works to sell now if anyone wanted them. It really is a jamb or will be pretty soon. Must now drink a Haig. *So* glad about your Black and White. What a joy. A great flight of pigeons have gone across the window—like the sacred doves of Aphrodite (I think a lot about girls) at the temple at Askalon.

... It is bloody annoying when those fucking sirens go just when you want to go somewhere, or get away from somewhere. Sometimes the buses stop and sometimes they don't—it seems to depend on the temperament of the drivers etc. Eric is a bit better I hear.[32] René is O.K. and Joan also. I meant to go to Pigotts for Petra's birthday—but did not make it. Helen S[utherland] sent me £6 the other day. She is all right and wants me to go up there[33]—I suppose it would be a good idea in a way —but again it is so bloody hard to know and I don't like leaving my papa in London with all this bollocks on. 'O that I had the wings of a dove,' as David sings, 'and could fly away and be at rest.'

I've been reading Dionysius on the Divine Names—it's the cat's whiskers, I think. Three cheers for Denis and the Greek mind. Funny buggers the human animals. What a mix-up, Churchill, St. Thomas, Joyce, Musso, Miss Ann Bowes-Lyon,

[32] Eric Gill died on 17 November 1940.
[33] i.e. Cockley Moor, in Matterdale, above Ullswater, Cumberland, where she had moved, from Rock, in 1939.

Miss Olivia Greene, the Lady Prudence Branch, Adolf, Mike Richey, Jacky Cross, Mr. Stanley Morison, Dr. Charley Burns, the Slogger [E. I. Watkin],[34] the Crafty Hague, the Tiger, His Eminence, P.P., Stanley Baldwin, Major Bloody Attlee, Julius Caesar, John the Baptist, Fr. John Baptist Reeves, O.P.—*the bride of Christ is patchy*. Aphrodite and Ares with the god of the philosopher, in comes Pascal, and the Revd. Martin D'Arcy (God bless him), and ——— ——— burns the contraceptive, and Mrs. ——— hides the Summa under unwashed linen and Mr. Wells.

To T.F.B., 4 September 1940   *3 Glebe Place*

This is only a short letter because I want to catch the post to say that everything is O.K. here and everyone all right and cheerful. It is *bloody* hot—absolutely like old Port Said today. I crept round to the pub and the sweat rolled down and I sweat only *very* occasionally. I visit the pub by the river twice a day and talk to (or rather am talked to by) old Vyse (the potter). Occasionally, more likely on Sunday, Harman comes to the pub, and sometimes Margaret. Bernard W[all] comes here very often, most days in fact, for an hour or two according to what he's up to. We get raid-warnings a good bit at any old time in the 24 hours—one has got quite used to the sound of the old sirens, occasional bumps, and 'noises off' etc. It is a bloody curious type of war. This tit-for-tat bombing & Co. It is odd in many ways—everything goes on as normal except that if one makes an appointment it may get put out if there is a warning—but of course you can always *walk* anywhere during a raid-warning.

Last Sunday Harman and I walked along the Embankment during one, waiting for Mass to start (they tend not to commence Mass if there is a raid-warning), and H. had a few words with a kind of old air-warden woman attached to the church—he, Harman, saying how absurd it was, that Mass was supposed to be at 11 o'clock and how it buggered-up one's whole morning for no purpose, and she citing a document of H.H. the Cardinal saying that Mass was not to start before the 'All Clear' went—it

[34] For long a close friend of Christopher Dawson, Watkin's nickname—in private circulation—was very much *lucus a non lucendo*.

was bloody funny. I think the worst part of it is that chaps tend
to have sleepless nights—because sometimes they last for hours—
with nothing happening—just the burr of a plane and perhaps
an occasional bump—near or far. You ask in one of your letters
if it is like the Front line or the Reserve, well, neither, *not by a
long chalk!* More like a place of billet some miles behind the line
in the last war, where one was liable to be bombed by airplanes
especially at night and where one was continually being dis-
turbed by 'warnings'—more like that really.

Postscript. Still trying to do my picture of Phryne—hope it gets
done. I've made her into a nice girl—it is an interesting picture
to do.

To T.F.B., 14 September 1940   *3 Glebe Place*

. . . Harman and Margaret are cooking supper and I'm upstairs
listening to a record of the 'Reproaches' by the old Sistine choir.
There is a raid on and shrapnel bursts very high up and a good
way off. It is a funny world and no mistake. It would be nice if
you were here, I only mean the more chaps of roughly the same
kind of general reaction (Rosy and winds-up of various personal
sorts apart). It has something to do with 'comfort' or 'safety
first'; (that is, of course, cut across by the chaps who fear being
caught underground and those who fear most the nakedness of
above ground). Also one does not mind at all perhaps for some
hours and then, in identical circumstances, one suddenly minds
a great deal and would like like *anything* some completely in-
vulnerable hole to go to. To me it is all a kind of resuscitation,
under vastly different and weird circumstances, of the last war—
all very different in every way except this reaction of different
temperaments—there is a 'social' thing in it too—the 'upper
classes' and the 'lower classes' (God damn the inadequacy of
those loathsome terms) react on the whole and generally speaking rather differently—or pretend to. Here the 'economic'
thing tells. I think 'position', 'backing', 'authority', 'habit of
rule'—'do this and he doeth it'—'fetch me a whisky and soda'
affect, very profoundly, the 'kind' of 'bravery' and the very

subtle differences of reaction. I feel it in *my own self*—being neither flesh, fowl, or red herring, socially—but by having become by one accident or another 'supernumerary, attached, pending allocation to unit' (as the military jargon goes) to the upper classes—yet with my roots among the lower orders (of whom I have *great fear* and whose reactions I *hate*, but for whom I feel a deep *understanding* at the same time). I feel *quite different* in morale, for instance, when I am with Harman, for instance, from when I am trying to disentangle the reaction of the suburbs, servants, etc. That is why the excellent anonymity of the army is so good. Rosy herself resides a lot in the complex maladjustments of the social order, I feel pretty certain of that—there are a million gradations—but some of us are caught and transfixed in a more obvious fashion between the 'ruled' and the 'rulers'. I've thought a lot about this and I am certain that it is true, and profoundly affects the whole struggle. It is absurd to say that Winston (for instance) *can* have the same reaction to the dropping bombs as the people in the Surrey Docks, and between those two extremes there are a million gradations—all mainly of an 'economic' nature at root. Death, mutilation, deprivation of every sort comes with a singular disparity on the 'rich' and 'poor'. The very nature of their fear is of a subtly different character. I see this very clearly. That is really what this war is about, a good bit. There are truly a *million* and *ten million* variations and seeming contradictions in this, but it becomes increasingly clear to me, as in peace so in war, the Ritz and the Doss House, so far from being united in death, face death with utterly other emotions. And that is one of the basic problems of our age. The cat is creeping (rather than leaping) out of the bag. They are knocking at the door and tapping at the floor.

Thursday 18th Sept. What a lot of balls the old whiskies tell— anyway I'm sober now.

. . . The bastards have got the church in Cheyne Row and killed some chaps in the crypt, I understand, our church, and they have bracketed all these streets here and there with bombs. Yet to the eye the place looks untouched still. They put a small incendiary at the corner (where there used to be that lamentable restaurant we had breakfast in once) but little damage. The dislocation of this is pretty trying—one can't get anything I mean, posts etc. all very up-buggered—telephone and all that. If I could fix my father I might go to Pigotts—but really I want to stay with H. and M. [Grisewood] for a bit if they wish it too . . . H. and M. and I went to see my father in a taxi because we *could not* get him on phone. *Pretty bad* bombing down there. The R.C. church that I used to go to when at home had one right in the middle, and the next house but one to my father's got it also, and some of his ceilings are down—but he was amazingly cheerful and refused to move.

A chap came to Glebe with a note from you to see if he would take it, but he would not because of there being (*Oct. 4*) no protection of any sort. He seemed surprised that I had a room there —perhaps you forgot to tell him about that. . . . Harman is on duty tonight and Margaret is away at her mother's in the country, so I am in solitary state [at 61 King's Road, Chelsea]. The guns are pooping off and the windows are shaking but I've only heard one bomb and it's very comfortable and I'm drinking Haig—but soon that too will be impossible because of the lack of money. I am hoping to remove the pictures from Glebe to Pigotts—by a van if possible—I think one ought to do that if possible—it would be infuriating if they were destroyed—but I never know quite what to do about it. H. and I are *very* puzzled about all this air war in *every* respect—it seems to have *no shape*, nothing is followed up—one would have thought it would have been much more effective. The bloody thing has been going on for weeks now and has been bloody awful in places—and horrible in many ways but *ineffective* and none of the *obvious* things hit, really—more a nuisance than anything else (the real horror is the East End, but there again it is the houses of the poor, apparently, not the possible objectives that have got hit. Of course this must be so unless the planes could really come very low. Intense artillery bombardment in the last war was sufficient to show how difficult it is to really hit *the* target)—it is all very extraordinary, and quite incomprehensible, *staggering* number of churches hit—must be entirely accidental but it is most curious, and hospitals also—one noticed the church thing very much going from here to see my papa. By the way (and apart from the war) poor old Caldey Abbey has been burnt down—a pure accident—I'm sorry—but it was a bloody building however.

Today news of Chamberlain's retirement, poor old C. I still think him by far the most tolerable of the bunch and a most admirable character. (Sudden *huge* barking of A.A. guns—about like the Western Front for a minute.) Now it is quiet as the tomb again.

. . . Had I money I would like to take it [Glebe Place] all over all myself—but that is not possible for financial reasons. I would like to hang on to my room if it is possible—I'm anxious about my father.

After a good deal more indecisive talk about Glebe Place and possible plans, David continues:

I've written this part of this letter three times. Supposing that I did go to Pigotts for a bit—it would really not solve anything for long—because I'm not getting any money at all now and have only a tiny bit that I'm living on, which will soon exhaust itself—in fact I am at last coming perhaps face to face with bedrock 'economics'!

Oct. 10th. There being no further use for my kind of activities—bugger it all. However that's all beside the point—and only just flows from the pen as I write. I think we are in for a very long war, and all notions of standing up to intensive air attack—and then all well—is really not true—it will be a slow hammering—and pretty grisly—the winter is going to be a real bugger, the bombing-war of attrition. . . . Prudence, I hear, is in the country again, so I suppose her paralysis is a bit better. I've not heard directly from her however—not from anyone, one lives entirely isolated now. Bernard [Wall] came to see me one day—he has taken Barbara and the children to Oxford, he has to be in London part of the time himself apparently—but not seen him lately because, in the evening, it is such a sod getting about—

what with one thing and another. Well dear Tom goodbye for now. God bless you.

—All written with a lot of Haig so forgive it. Said all that before, and that, sorry. I fear this screed will convey nothing to you but uncertainty and muddle but that is perhaps unavoidable—don't allow it to depress you. *Perfectio artis consistit in judicando*, ah! ah! —and the virtue of Prudence is to command, but the Art of Doing just now is a bit of a sod.

At this period David suffered more, I believe, from financial worries than at any other time. Helen Sutherland, who had helped him in more ways than one since before the war, was sending him a certain amount each month; Jim Ede was indefatigable in arranging for help, and a generous contributor himself. The same may be said of other friends. He may still have been receiving a small sum weekly from the Artists' Benevolent Institution (something like 25/-). Kenneth Clark at the National Gallery had organized a fund for the assistance of David and other artists. *In Parenthesis* brought him a little. He sold an occasional picture. What worried him was not so much the absolute lack of money as the uncertainty of its arrival. One way or another he could not, with such friends, ever be destitute; but reliance on their help was, if not an embarrassment, a constant reminder of his insecurity.

To T.F.B., 29 January 1941   *3 Glebe Place*

My father has continued ill and I've been going to see him continuously—that's all been a *great strain* and no one knows quite what to do about it—*money* is the great problem—and money problem is increasingly awful—no one seems to have any, and everyone wildly clamouring for debts unpaid. I can't get the bloody agents to shell out—poor sods, their clients aren't paying them.

... At last I've got someone temporarily to tidy up and do a bit of cooking—but *she* is about 100 years old, a Norman peasant, I think—and takes about 5 hours to make a bed and 12 hours to get breakfast and when you feel awful with this flu, all that made it seem like a loony-bin! However—it's all right I suppose really and I suppose will straighten out.

Poor Prudence is pretty knocked up with all this war thing—it is terrible to see her distress about Guy. . . . The old house at Brockley has had an incendiary bomb in the front garden and some of the windows blown in and all the water-pipes burst in the cold—all during my father's stay in the nursing home—he's jolly unhappy about that, otherwise he is very cheerful, as ever, only getting, like all of us, pretty concerned about the pennies. Old Dr. Fothergill whom you used to have to talk to over the phone in the days of my greatest 'Rosy' has been hit, but he's getting better, a ceiling fell on his arm and hurt it—otherwise a rather 'miraculous' escape. He rather enjoys all the war-stuff I think, rushing round at night and seeing to chaps and putting out fires—how marvellous chaps are—especially old chaps—he's over sixty. Makes me feel a most useless kind of fool. Mia W[oodruff] is in terrific form—absolutely her cup of tea it seems, this affair of coping, raids & Co. Douglas, I like more and more—he is so humble underneath that somewhat forbidding exterior that I used to dislike a lot.

The Tiger growls low on Boars Hill, I'm told. Young Barny Wall is in Oxford, bloody fed up too—*which applies to a lot of chaps!* Helen S. sends me £6 a month—God knows what I should do without that.

The next letter is from Onslow Square, where David was staying in the house of Arthur and Daphne Pollen:

To T.F.B., 21 June 1941   *57 Onslow Square*
If you can forgive this appalling delay and negligence—it is truly awful. I *did* write letter No. 2 but I can't find it now and so write another one. The awful thing is that Rosy has attacked me again. Nothing to do with the war—at all—just because I've been trying hard to work again. I had completed my picture of 'Phryne' and completed the *Four Queens find Lancelot sleeping* and started another of the Morte Darthur set and this bloody old Rosy attacked me just in the old way. I was *astounded* and don't quite know what to do. I *really* thought I was rid of all that. The awful thing is that if I could only *do* this set of Morte

Darthur pictures the *Tate* would *buy the lot*[35]—it is *too* awful.

I miss Harman appallingly—they have gone to live at Richmond, found a house and settled down there . . . but I'm jolly sorry for the *complete* break-up of all the old Chelsea thing. *I can hardly bear it.* I do miss seeing Harman and calling in on them, more than I can say, but I see that marriage *must* do this, I suppose, *in the end.* . . . I get on well with Arthur Pollen, he is very sweet and nice. The awful thing is that he is going to give up this house and try to live in the country with his wife, if they can find a house—so I shall have to move again, I expect—God knows where! I still drink whisky if I can get it—at night—it seems the only thing. This damned sleeplessness has returned. It seems so *maddening* that all I want to do and care about is to paint and that that is the *one* thing that makes me really *ill.* What a fate. . . . It is *absurd.* I don't much fancy going to see old Woods again—this is no time for *another ten* years of 'masterly inactivity'. . . . I have taken to the old game of making my own cigarettes, as tobacco is easier to get than cigarettes. I've seen Prudence once or twice—on her *rare* visits to London. She is about the same, I think. Better in health, I thought she was—she rides a lot and so perhaps is just physically better. *Loathes* being in Sussex of course.

. . . Did you see my letter in the *Times* for 30th May—about King Charles's statue. Arthur signed it also.

P.S. Sunday morning—wrote this letter late last night—fear it is a depressing one—but better send it straight away or it will never be sent. Very warm today. Just got news of the Russo-German war. Well I'm blowed!—not that it is a surprise, of course.

---

[35] A number of David's watercolours were, in fact, acquired by the Tate Gallery about this time: *The Chapel in the Park* (Rock, 1932), bought from the Redfern Gallery in 1940; *The Terrace* (Hove, 1929), given by the Contemporary Art Society; *Guenever* (1940), bought directly from David; *The Four Queens* (1941), also bought directly from David. Only the last two were of immediate financial assistance to him. Other works, for example the 'Phryne' or *Aphrodite in Aulis* of 1941, went to the Tate much later, in 1976, after his death.

In October 1941 David moved into lodgings at 12 Sheffield Terrace, off Church Street, Kensington, where he at first took his meals. He was fortunate in that he had a number of friends close at hand, including Louis Bussell, Bernard Wall, Basil and Nicolete Gray, and, of course, Harman and Margaret Grisewood. David dined at least once a week at the Grays', and they and other friends were able to help him, particularly when he found that he had to supply his own rations.

When at Sheffield Terrace David would go to Mass at the Carmelite church in Church Street (later destroyed by bombs). This, with memories of St. Cuthbert's, Fr. John O'Connor's church in Bradford, provided the first scene for the series of poems grouped around *The Kensington Mass*, and for the idea behind the picture that was first known to some, at least, as 'The Kensington Mass' and later as *A latere dextro*. (The move to Harrow in 1947 brought a change of scene, in the picture, to the Church of Our Lady and St. Thomas of Canterbury in Harrow.) Church Street and the Carmelites also prompted a number of well-known drawings of torus-necked girls.

To H.J.G., 17 October 1941   *12 Sheffield Terrace*

... I had to register for Industrial Service today (they said I would be called up for an interview in due course. I wonder what bloody thing one will have to do). I ought to have done so last Saturday and only found out about it by the merest accident—as I never hear the wireless and never see a paper to speak of now. I've not yet managed to get the *Times*. They sent me a complicated bit of paper about what to do.

No 'bloody thing' resulted. His doctor gave him a certificate, dated 20 November 1941, which stated:

'In 1932 he had a nervous breakdown and developed symptoms of mental depression—a depressive psychosis. The condition was severe. The course has been marked by improvement with relapses.

'He has been unfit for consecutive work in his own profession for nearly ten years. He is unstable, and under stress of duty would relapse.

'He is, in my opinion, quite unfit for routine service in a military or in a civil capacity.'

To T.F.B., All Souls Day 1941   *12 Sheffield Terrace*

Thank you so much for your wire, it was jolly nice of you to remember my birthday. . . . Prudence suddenly turned up the other day. She's much the same—cursing the Welshmen of her valley like anything !!! She's not well, but retains all her vitality and determination, and, as a matter of fact, I *thought* she *looked* better, in spite of the bloody time she has had—I suppose it is the natural well-making effect (in a kind of way) of merely living in the mountains instead of in old Spengler's 'megalopolis'. I was delighted to meet George Reavey and his wife, they live quite near here, really 'near' even from my immobile point of view, in fact here [*sketch map*] is a graph of their nearness—jolly nice. There is no need to explain when, where, we habitually meet [the pub halfway between the two]. . . . It was nice seeing him also to talk again about all the old stuff, Joyce, Eliot, the Frogs, the arts of Form—the plastics and the graphics. Prudence says he looks like an opera singer, and of course he does.

I've just written an article for the *Tablet*,[36] it's in this week (Nov. 1st)—I suppose you will see it in due time. I am afraid it is rather a *pompous* piece. I was driven to it because of the things written about the arts and the Church by John Rothenstein and Dom Wilfrid Upson etc. in the summer, only being slow in uttering, I've only just written it. I saw old Douglas [Woodruff] the other night, with Dai Mathew and Chris Hollis & Co—it's awfully difficult to talk to Douglas because there are always other chaps there and the conversation becomes more or less jocular back-chat of a mostly Roman Catholic type. . . .

I'm trying to write my book [*The Book of Balaam's Ass*] *again* now, and have found a typist in Ken. High St. who can type. We had an air-raid warning the other night for the first time for many months. It was funny to hear the familiar sound.

I don't know quite how long I shall stay here. It is so bloody small and dark, I mean the room. My father is about the same. I go on a bus to see him about once a week . . . send him a picture p.c. if you have time, he wouldn't half be pleased. James Jones, Oaklawn Nursing Home, 27 Laurie Park Rd., Sydenham S.E.

---

[36] 'Religion and the Muses', included in *Epoch and Artist*, pp. 97–106.

Hague is getting his commission [in the R.A.F.]—I do hope
he will like it. I saw him the other day which was a great joy,
and Joan also.

The Speaight is now at the BBC. He's giving Harman and
Margaret a dinner at Claridge's tomorrow night—he's a bloody
amusing bloke, the way he does these 'grand' things at this hour
of the day.

At this time David had begun digging up the endless supply of gold
bricks from Spengler which were later to be incorporated in his
writings:

To H.J.G., 26 February 1942   *12 Sheffield Terrace*
... I've been immersed in Spengler, I'm battling with him.
I've not measured him up yet! (if I may say so without appalling
presumption). He's *so right*, and, as I think, also *so wrong*. But I
can't really tell quite where, or what, it is. I believe it resides in
that Jackson Knight thing—he has liquidated *Juno*. It is a male
thought-world entirely. Now that won't do—I mean it's far
more complicated than that. But I've driven up much more to
what it's all about—and I'm jolly certain that chaps who just
talk about 'O yes, that's Spengler's idea' just know very little
about it, or probably have never really sweated on the stuff. But
still I'm pretty undecided what I do think about it nevertheless. A lot of it one just reads as if one were reading one's own
exact thoughts for the past twenty years put down by someone
who could think clearly and who had the power of expression
and elucidation. One just recognizes the 'truth', but it is far
other with other large tracts of it. So far I've only been able to
ascertain that what I disagree with, and resent, is his insensitivity
and scorn at certain important junctures, his schoolmaster's
laying-down-the-law tendency, his cheapness and brutality and
inhumanity, and something very like bluster when he really is
on a sore-ish point. Such expressions as 'Who cares if they do go
under'—that will not do. It's odd, really, because he shows such
enormous sympathy and understanding of greatness in both
religion and art no less than in political and military achievement. Perhaps it just is this German jack-boot thing—only one

has got to be so careful about finding an easy explanation—and that is a very easy one.

He's worse in his less good aspects. In this little *Hour of Decision* book [1934] than in the *Decline of the West*, because it's much more, in a way, 'propagandist', not quite propagandist, but more with an immediate purpose, less concerned with an analysis of history than with hinting as to how chaps had better behave now and in the future if they are to be worth anything! Nevertheless it is enormously interesting and full of true things, astonishingly acute intuitions, and undeniable facts, also damned funny—if one happens to sympathize. He's jolly outspoken about the state of Germany at the date of his writing it, 1932. He is very interesting about the National Socialist thing, although without mentioning it by name. . . . I would very much like to know how he really went down with the chaps in power before he died. . . . He regards the whole World Revolutionary thing from 1780 or so onwards as calamitous (though 'inevitable') to Western man (and compares it to the age between the Gracchi and Caesar at some length, both in this book and in *D. of the W.*) and consequently thinks that building up a 'new' strong ruling class by, even at this late hour, conserving what is left of the 'healthy', 'strong', 'instinctive' (as opposed to 'intellectual') 'aristocratic' elements, can any country survive. He is very doubtful about how this can be accomplished in England, and in fact is doubtful if it can be done anywhere with success. If not, he thinks (but I am *grossly* simplifying) that the future of the West is done, and the coloured races will, after a long or short period, 'rule' instead. (He is *particularly* fearful of a double impact coming from the 'white' revolution of the proletariat and the 'coloured' uprising joining forces (without meaning to) to destroy the West. I think he's pretty good as to this—but it's involved, but very interesting, to me, very probable, especially in view of events.)

Of course, he regards the West as *culturally* exhausted, as we know it is, anyhow, but thinks that 'honour' & Co. and 'necessity' demand that chaps should, so to say, have 'the will' to see this last phase through, like 'men' (what ho!), and in any

case if 'A' does not do so, 'B' or 'C' or 'D' or 'X' will. It is
rather at these junctures that he gets cheap and a little sixth-
form, I feel, develops a kind of 'cant' about the nobility of
'beasts of prey' and starts to bluster a bit, which I find very
tedious, and not at all a mirror of 'honour'. But it's mostly,
again, the *way* he expresses it that one jibs at—*not* the thesis. I
think he lacks the *humour* of true disinterestedness. I think perhaps that's what it is. Both the humour of a cockney in a mined
trench, or the humour of a Chinese Ming, Wang, Wong, Tung
(or whatever it is) Waley-poem, and certainly the humour of
calling the Fall the Happy Fault! But I've not got down, yet,
by any means, to what I think about it. But I do wish we
(René, Eric, Tom, Tiger, Douglas, you, me, and all our mates)
had thrashed some of this stuff out—instead of the far less
penetrating authors that have been so studied for all these years.
I'd love to be able to talk to Eric about all this—but perhaps he
would not have made much of it—I don't know.

I find I have no soap and it's early closing day, and anyway
no one awfully pleased to go and get anything for one. So I
tried washing with some camphorated oil first, then hot water,
toothpaste and talcum powder—it worked quite well—*hands*, I
mean, don't think this camphorated oil would be good on face,
or balls, for that matter!

To T.F.B., 15 March 1942   *12 Sheffield Terrace*

. . . Been trying to get on with my book. Been reading Tacitus,
partly to do with that. He's jolly interesting. Considering how
relatively early he was in the Roman Empire, it's interesting that
he speaks as though the whole show was long past its peak, and
that only luck and divisions among the enemies of Rome could
save the situation.

Well, Tom, I must post this quick, or it will suffer the fate of
other of my letters to you, that have got written and never sent,
by being left half-finished in my pockets or mixed up with *The
Book of Balaam's Ass*.

To T.F.B., 16 May 1942   *12 Sheffield Terrace*

. . . I thought of you in Spain very much the other day, because they cleaned the El Greco *Christ and the Money-changers* at the Nat[ional] Gal[lery] and put it on show all by itself—it's an absolute corker now it's cleaned—(it was just a yellow drab mess before) but now it's an absolute knock-out—talk about 'super-realism'—it looked about twice as 'real' as the people walking about in front of it—I've *never* seen anything like it—for power and beauty—not for many years. It restores one's belief in the human race—for a bit! I wrote to Ken Clark and asked him to keep it on for an extra week and he very kindly did so.

I was reading 'Anna Livia' again the other day and suddenly remembered that I suppose you often have walked by 'manzina-hurries off bachelor's walk'. When I go and ask the landlady for my soap ration I always think of Joyce's 'Throw us your hudson soap for the honour of Clane . . . ah, and don't forget the reckitts I loaned you'.

It is astonishing how he has that permanent quality of pro-viding 'quotations'—like *Hamlet*—when you're familiar with a little bit of him.

Yes, it must be odd for you to be seeing those square-heads sitting about the place. Helen S[utherland] has been in London this week—had dinner with her and Teddy H[odgkin] at a place in Charlotte Street—forget the name—but had some kid—you know, kid of the goat I mean. I'd never eaten it before—it was jolly nice—had an awfully *genuine* taste—and very tender and special. With vague aroma of 'goat'—I now see why blind old man Isaac in the O.T. approved of the 'savoury meat' of the kids that bitch Rebecca provided for him—what a lovely story that is! . . .

Prudence is much the same. Went to the zoo with her the other day, which was nice, we had a nice time—but it's a lousy place compared with what it was—few animals comparatively and probably most of the staff doing more essential things—so not quite so well kept. Do you remember how I used to phone you up from the Lion House and you could hear the lions roar your end of the phone when you were at Sheed & Ward and I was 'sketching the animals'—that's a hell of a time ago.

I saw my father yesterday—he asked after you. He's not too good—but very cheerful and happy—his patience is amazing....[37] Just read a thing in the concluding chapter of Collingwood's *Roman Britain* which I find appropriate, 'The conflicts are too complex, the issues too obscure, the cross-currents too numerous, the decisions too local, to make possible the appreciation of any single formula to their solution; and it is at least reassuring sometimes to remember that, if we found such a formula, we should unquestionably be wrong. Uno itinere non potest perveniri ad tam grande secretum'—jolly nice to end a book of great learning and sweat like that.

Two anniversaries were never forgotten in correspondence with David: Trafalgar Day, 21 October 1805, and Admiral Howe's four-day battle that ended on 1 June 1794:

To H.J.G., The Glorious First of June, 1942   12 Sheffield Terrace
... I saw Tiger Dawson a few days ago, had dinner with him in what Tom used to call the 'Mausoleum' in Queen's Gate Terrace—I must say it is a gloomy place. The Tiger had just had tea with the Archbishop of Canterbury, the Bishop of London and Arthur Cardinal Hinsley, and Miss B[arbara] Ward—what an astonishing party. It was heavenly seeing the old Tiger again and he was not so bad, and sent you a lot of love. He was very funny in his own way. A bit severe and frightening in the way deep learning is apt to be—but by chattering about this and that and all the odds and ends I could think of, I drew from him some remarks which I was pleased to hear. O dear, it's nice to talk to someone whose brain is the right *kind*—that's what one sighs for—the disagreements don't matter—but the *temper*—the *kind*—the *sort* of thing that a chap regards as *significant*—that's what one wants—and that is hard to come by.

He'd read Powys's *Owain Glyn Dwr* (of course! what's he

[37] David's father died the following year, 1943.

not read?) and we chuckled together about the things in it, and we discussed a bit the resurgence of cruelty, torture, police-state & Co.—agreed that historically it's a very complex subject indeed—I mean *vis-à-vis* the Christian Church etc. He said he found that Catholics, in his experience, since he became a Catholic, were getting far more, not less, 'institutional' (in the bad sense) and mechanical, so to say. That the age of von Hugel, the 'belief' in the Holy Ghost, in the subtlety of where truth re-sides etc. seemed far away—and a belief in effecting things by organization and formulas etc. etc. (among Catholics) growing rather than lessening. In short, that 'propaganda' is universally dominant in the Church as outside it, and once you yield *interiorly* to the propagandist attitude you're sunk. We talked about how that one of the 'condemned propositions' of Luther was 'that the burning of heretics is offensive to the Spirit'—well, that the burning of heretics *is* offensive to the Spirit is obviously true—condemnation or no condemnation. Yet rather than make this admission they go in for all kinds of beatings about the bush to justify the papal absurdity—all of which is a pity and *quite* irrelevant to the truth of the Catholic religion.

I saw Prudence the other day. She looked very unwell indeed, I think, but was cheerful and just as ever. She was very worried about Stanmer and the general mess they're making of the place.[38] It must be pretty heart-rending.

To T.F.B., 28 June 1942   *12 Sheffield Terrace*

... I like your photograph—jolly nice to have it. It's rather a joke, you look like a native of the country and the bit of land-scape behind all looks very typical—jolly nice-looking friend, I must say, jolly nice. Having a photograph of you taken recently makes your existence seem more real or something. I feel I could see you getting up and walking off in that dry sun-lit landscape and drinking out of those glasses. I've got no news and this is only a short note to thank you for writing and for the

[38] Stanmer, the Chichester home, between Brighton and Lewes, had been taken over by troops. It now belongs to the University of Sussex.

phot. Had dinner with Charles [Burns] at Harman's a couple of weeks back which was nice. C. is just the same. Going to have dinner with Vladimir and Diana tonight—and Manya [Harari] on Monday, so the old connections keep up more or less. Chaps are arguing and stamping about a bit at the moment. I hope to see Joan [Hague] on Thursday. She's coming up to see Prudence and me—not seen her for a long while. Prudence is pretty ill really, that damned paralysis just keeps on coming back in different parts of her body. It is amazing how cheerfully she takes it—but it is awful, you know.

Just read Mark Twain's *Huckleberry Finn*—I missed it when I was young—it's damned funny and very interesting as giving various accidental glimpses into America of the middle last century—very interesting. Also just read Cecil Chesterton's *History of the United States*—which is a most awfully good book, and very illuminating. I knew so little about American history really. He wrote much better, with more restraint, than old G.K. did—but there is a definite family resemblance in style, none the less, but he's harder-headed and not so flowery and so better. . . . It's a complicated thing when one goes into it—this American set-up—quite unlike anything else, clearly. That Southern states 'civilization' seemed to have something to it, and clearly North and South have produced *individuals* of quite remarkable 'character', 'principle', and *aspiration* particularly, and I see that there were elements of what you might call a 'culture' (at a pinch)—not of course a Spenglerian 'culture' but using the word in the more common sense, but always a colonial culture. I wonder what would have happened had it remained almost entirely of the blood of the early settlers, as it did until the huge middle-European etc. immigrations of the latter part of the last century. But *all through* it seems to me that 'aspirations', some admirable, some deluded, some pathetic, have dominated it.

In the next letter, to Harman, David has been quoting from *The Dream of the Rood*—the lines (39-41) reproduced in *The Anathemata*, facing p. 240—and continues:

To H.J.G., 8 August 1942   *12 Sheffield Terrace*

... It's glorious, and so is it all, when the Cross speaks about the *weight* of the hero and how the hero and the wood were bound together. It is a loss to the world that this great northern conception of the crucifixion has never *really* been expressed in plastic art—I feel—certainly there is immense nobility in the early gothic crucifixions—but neither the regal, priestly, ones of the Byzantine tradition or influence, nor yet the 'franciscan' 'suffering' 'human' ones express the hero, the 'gwledig' of the people 'strang and stiðmod' and 'modig on manigra gesyhðe'— do they, really. (There is a last-century Welsh Methodist hymn with a heavenly tune, called 'March on, Jesus, victorious, girt with thy glittering sword' which in a more sentimental and cheap way has a bit of the idea—but not really—it's too much 'Onward, Christian soldiers', of course.

To H.S.E., 27 March 1943   *12 Sheffield Terrace*

... I've just bought a large map of North Wales and pinned it to the wall. It looks like a great beast stretched out—that arm of the Llyn peninsula—strange how any map is so convincing and real—and how one can never make up a map. Well, not strange at all really, because it is reality. I enjoyed Mrs. Winnicott's talk about the erosion and the stalactites etc. Incredibly 'romantic' these exact scientific things are, and the more factual so much the more moving. I always think it strange that old man Darwin moaned in late life that he could no longer appreciate poetry because of his long and devoted service to the facts of material science—God damn it it ought to be the reverse—I've only just tumbled to the simple scientific fact that 'water' is the womb of all life—and of the simplest organisms—well that thrilled me no end—no wonder baptism is by water. . . . You mention in your letter the last five years (ten really). Well, if you don't wish to mention my illness—then it is a blank—except for this book which I am slowly and torturously struggling with and God knows when that will reach fruition. . . . Well of course *I.P.* was largely *completed* during the ill years—but a lot done before, and I sometimes wonder if doing *I.P.* and painting at the same time helped to make me ill. I did *60* paintings in the summer before I got ill, 1932.

To H.S.E., 3 July 1943   *12 Sheffield Terrace*

... I went to a lecture with my old friend and old master Mr. Hartrick the other night, given by the artist [T.B.] Hennell, on Blake, with lantern slides and then I saw what you have so often said about the enhancement (and enchantment) given to some pictures by the size on the screen.

I've always reckoned I 'liked' Blake, but my God!—that size and with that luminosity they fair bowl you over—absolutely terrific. A certain tightness which, sometimes, to me, mars Blake all disappears and the freedom of them becomes really overwhelming. I was very glad I went. The lecturer was good and informative also—but it was those enormous great shapes that really startled one. That one called *Cain* with the distraught Eve and Adam and the dead Abel etc. really looked unbelievable in its power.

To H.S.E., 19 August 1943   *12 Sheffield Terrace*

... and when you say you owe me a debt in the realm of ideas etc.—I can only return the compliment—It is rather strange this business of what chaps 'give' other chaps in the realm of ideas, appreciation and so—because when one looks back over a long period it is damned hard to know who gave which what. I often think about that in relation to different chaps, and it's clearly very complex, and I would not mind betting that half or more than half the theories which pass for 'history' of art or persons (or nations) is hopelessly at sea when they say glibly 'so and so influenced so and so and that produced such and such'— the *inner* history may have been often as not the other way round, or anyhow a very tangled and chancy affair of *mutual* influences. I feel, of myself particularly, that I owe *everything* almost to a series of chaps without whom I would have been a really bloody awful artist, and more than that, often chaps with quite wrong ideas influence one for the good in this 'art' business. It is jolly tricky.

Very likely I should never have developed *any* of such life as exists in the 1930 period but for a combination of accidents, both in life and thought—and the depth of badness as an artist of which I am capable is easily proved by a glance at earlier work—and that much earlier thing I got from old Hartrick was only usable after I had been through the Eric thing. (I mean no disparagement of the Eric thing—but 'got through it' in the sense that I could 'use' it for my own purposes.) I'm sure it's a point chaps don't much see—it's a long up and down process, at least with blokes like me. The only thing I know (or think I know) for certain is that what I want a painting to be did become clear, *in direction*, up at Capel and on Caldey, and that the 1932 group got nearest to what I had in mind—but a *very long way from the goal*. (I suppose that may partly explain my complete crash—I was conscious for some long time before it came that I was straining every nerve to do something more than I had power to do.) Whether I ever now shall be able to pick it up or continue remains to be seen.

To T.F.B., 25 September 1943   *12 Sheffield Terrace*

. . . I've just read a most admirable little book about the stage by Graham Greene in that series [Britain in Pictures] that Dai Mathew's seamen book [*The British Seaman*] is in. (Speaking of seamen—how true what you say in your letter: yes—the navy people are almost always O.K.—I suppose partly because our navy is our most authentic thing—they have 'Being' in some way—real—but the profession of the sea itself, apart from our tradition may have something to do with it—it's a very interesting thing. I wonder if old Mike [Richey] will turn up soon—his father seemed to think perhaps he might get leave soon—I hope so.) G. G. is a most lucid and concise writer for that sort of résumé, it's *awfully* good, I thought. He seems to know a hell of a lot about the stage, in fact it's surprising what a lot chaps do know one way and another! He reckons Dryden determined the whole shape, so to say, of subsequent stage craft etc. He does not think much of Congreve apparently. I do hope you are O.K. and got back safe and sound. No news really. Write when you get a chance. Give my love to Eliz. G[ully] when you happen to meet her: I'll give your love to the chaps. Saw a report in *Times* of a bull escaping down the Madrid underground and causing some excitement—so I suppose you'll hear about that when you get back. Sounds damned terrifying. What a shock it would be at a London terminus! It was nice seeing Joan again—I *must* try and get down to Pigotts for a few days before it really gets winter. What a joke meeting Mervyn Peake—I do see him by accident in the street sometimes, I must say it is phenomenal the way you met almost everybody you know on that short visit— quite extraordinary. I think you will enjoy that little book with bits from the Romantics. Old Grigson seems to have really made a most remarkable collection [*The Romantics* (1942)]: just right, it seemed to me.

There is a nice thing on the title-page of a life of Charles James Fox I've been reading—Fox said in a letter: 'One owes something to one's friends, something to one's station in life and something to one's country'—jolly nice and jolly true to his period, isn't it. Hell of a good chap old Fox. I've got a very clear idea of the bull-fighting since your admirable and clear description—Harman and Margaret and I each enjoyed that so much. I look forward to going down to Richmond to see them so much. When I can. It has made *all* the difference to these years of war being able to go and talk with Harman there and crack a few jokes and it's such a heavenly house and situation altogether. I missed them terribly when they left Chelsea. That marked a real stage in the war and the temper of the war—it is strange how often a change in the world, or national, or outer, or whatever, situation, corresponds with a change in some quite personal, domestic, intimate, or whatever, situation. I've so often noticed that. That's what the Tiger means I expect when he says your leaving Sheed & Ward marked a change in cosmic things! —what a jocko. I wish you were here with some nice Haig and a lot of *soda*—I've definitely come to the conclusion that it's no damn use *whatever* without soda in spite of all that the Picts and Scots say.

Although he did like his whisky in those days, David's consumption was a mere drop to that of some of his friends. No one, I believe, ever saw him more than mellowed by whisky, and I would wager that he never knew what a hangover was like.

As the war went on, however, he was finding it increasingly difficult to survive. Towards the end of 1944 he wrote to Jim Ede saying that 'during the last years' he had been spending about £6 a week—an amount for which he apologizes. It was, in fact, a reasonable sum for a frugal bachelor living in London: a skilled artisan in the country, say a compositor in a printing office, would earn rather less in those days. It was about this time that Jim Ede arranged for a number of friends to pay sums of money into David's bank. Some, or most of them, did so anonymously, and Jim himself was among the anonymous subscribers. His identity had to be revealed, however, when he suggested that a subscriber of, say, £50 a year might receive one of David's pictures in return for three or four years' subscription. This is presumably the 'scheme' David refers to in the following letter:

To T.F.B., 19 November 1944   *12 Sheffield Terrace*

Lord, what a damned disgrace it is for me not to have written for so long. I hope you got my wire sent a few days back. I did get your letter in August and thank you very very much for it and for what you say. It is most awfully good of you to go on helping with that quid a week for the time being. What a *bloody* curse all this financial thing is, it freezes everything—even thinking about it, let alone talking about it. (Jim's scheme is of tremendous help—he is an astonishing chap.)

Well, dear Tom, I'm sure I sound damned casual but I do appreciate all you've done. I am so delighted that you are happy—so delighted. I do send love to you both.

About the pictures: the ones that belong to you are: Can't give titles because never having been exhibited they have not got titles, or if they have I can't remember them. But they are (1) the picture of sea from the terrace at Hove with a bit of green wicker chair showing.

(2) Garden at Brockley with big tree in summer and cat walking on wall.

(3) Door of little room at Pigotts with cattle outside, and flowers etc.

(4) The portrait of Prudence.

(5) The illustration to the *Satin Slipper*.

At the present moment they are in the following places: No. 1 is in the vault of the C.E.M.A. (Belgrave Sq.). 2 and 3 are at [57] Onslow Square. 4 (Prudence) is on tour with a C.E.M.A. exhibition, now at Harrogate. 5 is at the moment with me here, because the glass is broken, not by a bomb but by a workman, and I am getting it re-glazed.

As to the present monetary worth, I should say (1) £40, (2) £30, (3) £40, (4) I don't regard for sale—I should like to some day exchange another one with you for it if it can be done, (5) £30.

These prices are merely to give some idea of the rough worth by dealers' standards, as far as I can guess.

When the Michael Sadler collection was sold up at the Leicester Galleries they got somewhat higher prices for some (for example the *Terrace* one ((No. 1)) selling *from* a gallery would probably be £45 now)—but these are the minimum that my watercolours seem to be on our old friend the dealers' current market.

What a bore all this is.

Well, how are you? I had a letter from Elizabeth Gully saying she was home from Spain. No news—absolutely none. See old Harman mostly each week, thank God for that. About the only person I can talk to with any real agreement in any intimate way. He is O.K. but tired you know and overworked.

I went to Pigotts in July for a week's visit and stayed 2½ months! Very nice seeing them all. All much the same there. Poor René [a mistaken adjective!] has left Sicily and gone God knows where—the Far East, I suppose—Joan very fed up, but very brave, and well on the whole. She is developing into a more and more solid and marvellous character. Does half the work of all Pigotts. Michael, and your godson, Richard, are *jolly* nice boys, both at Ampleforth now.

My lunch has just come in on tray. Must eat it.

Sorry about protracted nature of the writing I'm doing—but quite imposs. to publish it in bits: just have to wait till it's finished. It's a fearsome job—may be all balls—but I don't think it all is.

Went to a long lecture by old Eliot about Virgil the other day: bloody good. I miss Bernard [Wall] very much, he's gone to Italy.

Sicily seems a most remarkable place from René's account—remnants of real civilization still lingering, as no doubt in Spain —they have a big thing in Sicily about the Roland and Oliver legend, which is interesting, and also the Trojan War.

Am having dinner on Wednesday with the Speaight, he's been to Paris. Everybody seems to have been to Paris. Saw Graham Greene in the street the other day—not seen him for ages and ages, not since we used to see him before the war. I'm having lunch with him one day this week, I think.

Bloody awful letter this is—sorry. Anyway it sends you a lot of love and I think of you a *great* deal—it's *so* difficult to write— nothing *really* of consequence to say that can be said properly— have to be reserved for when we meet—I wonder when that will be?

Been reading, for relaxation, the life and letters of Millais —damned different world from anything we've been used to —jolly interesting to me, so close yet very far. Well I am determined to post this, excessively *stupid and insufficient* as it is, or it will share the fate of many other unsent letters! Please forgive this ungrateful and long delay and please write and say you've got it. And very much love to you always and to you both. Keep safe. God bless you. Much love.   DAI
Prudence walked in one day last week quite out of the blue and unexpectedly—she happened to be in London. She was not so bad and just the same and asked how you were.

As for the removal of those bloody pictures to the country— I suppose it could be accomplished—Pigotts is the only place I can think of. Saw Paul Richey the other day—he's gone to Brussels. Mike [Richey] also I saw, he's gone East.

To H.J.G., 4 July 1945   *12 Sheffield Terrace*

... I had dinner with Jackson Knight on Saturday at the Paddington Hotel where he was staying, and had a most interesting talk with him and plucked up sufficient something to read to him a bit of my writing—it happened to happen naturally and it seemed not a bad idea to see how another kind of chap from us altogether took it. He seemed to like it quite a good bit and it was amusing to notice what he liked particularly. These chaps are awfully interested in the metre thing, aren't they?—and on what you contrive with vowels and consonants and all that (things you don't know you've done except that it seemed the only way to do it to make it tolerable and to say what you meant). But chiefly I was pleased because (I only read him a little, of course) he seemed amiably disposed to the classical network and seemed to think it *worked* O.K. His interpolated remarks were nice and very interesting, and he's jolly nice because he's got a free kind of mind, and although a 'don' most certainly jolly different from them—not that, when I come to think of it, I know much about dons. He's so passionately interested in his subject, that that alone is grand.

I was pretty embarrassed about having to pronounce various Latin and Greek names and words, but he was helpful about that. I expect the pronunciation was torture to his ears occasionally, nevertheless. He was pretty emphatic that I should say, e.g. Dēmētēr with all the *e*'s very long, and that I ought to say lōrī-ca (accent on *i*) and not lo-rica, and one or two other things, but I'll tell you about all that when we meet. It raises various points. (I mean it seems clear to me that there cannot be a *regularization* of the pronunciation in my case, because some of the words and phrases I have acquired from the ecclesiastical thing, as soft *c* etc., and others are more or less Englished as familiar *names*, e.g. Lucius Aelius Sejanus (though that one *is* jolly attractive I must say said 'correctly'), and a lot else and others again are technical terms or derived from purely classical etc., and I suppose it is only in the latter two cases that I ought, with advantage, to use the modern-scholarship pronunciation if I can.[39] However, dealt with in Preface, I think. I wish you had been there, you would *love* to talk to him. He's packed full of just the kind of thing you like. You *must* meet him properly, some day.

He's done a work on Homer and he'd been seeing Eliot that day about it being published—Fabers are doing it—it should be grand.[40]

He thought *Anathemata was* the accurate title for my thing in more ways than one, which I was pleased to have his opinion about, because, apart from the two meanings—ana-thema and anathē-ma—both of which are meant to be conveyed by the subject matter, he thought that the meaning 'things *laid* up to the Gods' also would mean, in the case of this stuff of mine, the stuff laid up in the mind of the author—put aside and brought out, so that in a sort of way *any* writing of this sort could be called the anathemata of the person concerned.

. . . I'm sorry to bother you, but *would* you feel at all inclined to lend *both* the pictures, the Caldey one and the animal [*Agag*], for a *short* time to a small (and select!) exhibition of paintings which the British Council are sending to Paris in order to show the inhabitants of Newcastle what coal is really like. I would not suggest that this borrowing of your two should be done, were it not that I've got to try and find a few *good* pictures if poss. for *two* exhibitions at the same time—the other is a Tate exhibition going to Brussels and Amsterdam. O the Kultur Putsch. I wish there were some hard money in it, I must say.

To H.J.G., 5 July 1945   *12 Sheffield Terrace*

. . . I suppose by reason of the change of climate, I have just been down to the polling booth to vote for the first time in my life, except when I voted in Ireland in 1918 in order to get off parade for a few hours. I *nearly* did not vote in the end (but a Labour supporter, thinking to persuade me of the iniquity of the

[39] There were occasions when David deliberately falsified accent or quantity, but some unconscious mistakes can be heard in his own recorded readings.

[40] W. F. Jackson Knight died before he finished this book, *Many-minded Homer*, which was edited after his death by John Christie and published by Allen & Unwin (1968).

5. ENCLOSURE (Pigotts) 1931. Oil on canvas, 24 × 30 in. *Private collection*

6. SIDMOUTH 1940. Watercolour, 19¼ × 24 in. *Arts Council of Wales*

Conservative candidate, said: 'Why, he has a *dreadful* record, he voted *against* sanctions on Italy, *against* intervention in Spain, and *for* Chamberlain right through'. That piece of gratuitously offered information hardly had the desired effect)—as I *cannot express* the contempt I have for *all* these bloody politicians because of the false, cheap, claptrap that has been quite unnecessarily let loose throughout the whole of the so-called 'campaign'. I do believe it is all seriously a great mistake, even tactically—because I find the disquiet voiced by all sorts and conditions of men. Well, we shall see.

1946—1947

The end of the war brought with it the end of a well-defined period in David's life. He had been in a poor state, it will be remembered, in Sidmouth (mostly) in the months before and during the war. After he went back to London in 1940 he led a more active and vigorous life for some years, saw many friends and made new acquaintances. He did a great deal of painting and a great deal of writing, working chiefly in the quarry from which *The Anathemata* was to be extracted. His own small shelter at 12 Sheffield Terrace was always a necessity to him, and a comfort, but at the same time his isolation there forced him in upon himself—as had happened at Sidmouth—and provided a lurking place for 'Rosy'. In the late summer of 1946, while he was staying with Helen Sutherland at Cockley Moor,[41] Rosy emerged and attacked with all her attendant demons.

'Miss Sutherland was very kind,' David later told a friend, Colin Hughes, 'but no one could really know what it was like unless they had been through it. The main symptom was being frightened. The Bible often mentions men's knees knocking together; it was really like that; it was worse when I was at home; Freud really had it right, this father/mother relationship.' Hughes's memory of their 1973 conversation is not necessarily verbatim; but 'frightened' should be read in the light of Blake's remark (often quoted by David), to the effect, 'Do you, sir, paint in fear and trembling?'

David remained at Sheffield Terrace for a time; then, in 1947,

[41] Kathleen Raine writes of Cockley Moor, and of David's staying there, in her autobiography, *The Land Unknown* (1975), pp. 128–39.

through the good offices of Dr. Charles Burns, he went to Bowden House, a private nursing home whose director was Dr. Crichton Miller, at Harrow-on-the-Hill. His treatment was under the direction of Dr. Stevenson ('Bill' at times in the letters). To both these doctors he was immensely grateful. There was an almost immediate and, it would appear, a permanent improvement.

When David first went to Bowden House he said that he hoped the doctors would not try to make him 'an ordinary person'. Dr. Stevenson evidently understood the extraordinary nature of David's genius and saw that there could be no hope for him if he could not apply it in practice. The nerve specialist who had treated him in 1933 had suggested that if David's work, whether painting or writing, brought on his trouble, he should abstain from it (the 'masterly inactivity' to which David refers above, p. 112). Dr. Stevenson understood what David meant when he spoke of the difficulties that present themselves to the artist in this 'age of steel', and made David himself see that they could be solved only by a frontal attack. After a first period of rest and gentle recreation, he was ordered to paint. He obeyed, and he won. Of the pictures he showed at the Redfern Gallery in 1948, 24 were painted in 1947 and 1948, and they included the *Vexilla Regis*, painted in Bowden House, which he valued, I believe, more highly than any other (cf. the letter of 28 August 1949 to Mrs. Ede).

Two letters, written to Harman Grisewood in the summer after his breakdown, are a record of the period at Bowden House:

To H.J.G., 16 July 1947   *Bowden House*

I was very *delighted* to get your letter. This is the first letter I've written to *anyone* for about two or three months, and is only to send you and Marged all my love and greetings. I shall have a lot to tell you some time, I think, but won't *try* just at the moment. The *theory* of all this psychotherapy is *of the greatest interest possible*, but of course takes time to assimilate and make bear fruit to oneself, as it were. Anyway, I've been better able to read a bit, and been better in myself, on the whole. In any case I can truthfully say that the *principles* of the business seem to me highly illuminating—and it is *something* to feel that. The doctor here I like exceedingly, and I think he is more than ordinarily able at his job—so it seems to me—but of all that later.

The other patients and the staff are all exceedingly nice. Unfortunately, I've had a sharp return of that fibrositis the last few days and have to go to bed again—it is a *beast* of a thing—but they've treated it and helped to shift it vastly quicker than when I had it before, though it's still painful. They did all the different physical tests when I first came in, and it seems that there is *nothing* wrong at all physically, except that my tonsils are not too good, and they *can* be a contributory cause of neurosis etc.— So they may have to be dealt with later on.

I've thought of *you both a very great deal* and wondered very much how you were and whether or no you had finally shaken the dust of the BBC from your feet,[42] and how it all felt. I can well believe that it must seem strange.

... I've been reading *Pickwick Papers* and Kipling's *Jungle Book* (second part) and the *Travels* of Mungo Park (excellent book—do you know it?) and some of Freud's *Totem and Taboo.* (The latter with much more understanding than when I had a go at it some months ago.) Damn these beastly little bits of note-paper—I've no foolscap, and feel cramped and odd writing on this stuff. *So* glad you liked the thing in *The Changing World.*[43] I've done some gardening here, you'll be astonished to hear, and play ball with people—very odd (a rather nice very large heavy ball—like a football—they call the game 'medicine ball'—jolly embarrassing term). All part of the set-up, you know. I *hope* it all really does something *constructive* in the end.

... Just had to do a jolly odd thing (for me): lie on a grassy bank with my back exposed naked to the sun as a part means of shifting this fibrositis. What we are induced to do!

[42] See Harman Grisewood, *One Thing at a Time*, pp. 157-64. He rejoined the BBC at the end of 1947.

[43] The essay 'Art and Democracy', written 1942-3 and reprinted in *Epoch and Artist*, pp. 85-96. It appeared in the Summer 1947 issue of the magazine edited by Bernard Wall and Manya Harari, for which see the former's *Headlong into Change*, pp. 167-91. David drew the cover for the 'England' issue, which is reproduced in Manya Harari's posthumous *Memoirs 1906-1969* (1972), facing p. 241.

To H.J.G., 24 August 1947   *Bowden House*

... Well, I'm still here. No, *no moustache nor golf.* I've not done any more gardening or anything unexpected—except I've played Badmington [a spelling we cannot lose]—*rather* nice game. Something nice about *very light* rackets and projectiles combined with the violence and agility asked of the players. I have to try and paint now. I paint trees from my window. It's part of the curative game, as, *in their judgement,* I've now reached a period when I *must* paint, because they maintain that my *major* conflict displays itself in relation to painting and that it *must* be fought out in that terrain—that's not the whole story—but a very important part of it, *whatever* the inclinations, results, difficulties, feelings etc. etc. I've not *written* anything yet—but I'm *supposed* to get down to that also, to wit, Book.

I have ups and downs, and can't say much to elucidate very coherently the progress of the treatment—but they appear to be confident in the progress, and certainly in some directions at least there has been real progress. All being well, I'll be better able to tell you about it later on. It's a long job.

... They don't look with much favour on my returning to live at Sheffield Terrace, but what precise alternatives I don't know yet. ... All this is costing an ocean of money, but there was no alternative. If all goes as is hoped, it will (as they say) be money well spent. I've more or less given up seriously reading the papers—I feel I know it all (I, Teiresias, have foresuffered all). I heard Churchill's broadcast—curiously pathetic—a waft back to the war period and a genuine note. He's a real person and not a bit of a person (I don't feel he *really* understands either the nature of the social revolution or our precise point now on the chart of history. But he *is* a *relief.*) ...

P.S. It is incredible the proportion of Scottish blood here, both on Staff and quite a bit among patients. Crichton Miller is of course a Scot, and so is Dr. Stevenson, who treats me. Also, as I say, others of the staff are. Perhaps the serious *ethical* thing plus other things about Scots has something to do with a tendency to become doctors. The scientific mind but with a *serious* service-to-humanity thing also—Charlie B[urns] has it also. It's interesting that so many of the Burns antecedents were ministers of the Presbyterian Church—let us consider old Tom also with ref. to this, and indeed the man in black, George of the Society [i.e. Fr. George Burns, S.J., another brother]. You tend to become a kind of 'senior boy' after being here a bit—quite a bit of the school thing here in a quite nice kind of way. A tentative implicit idea that as a patient himself improves he can be of some slight assistance perhaps to other patients. The housekeeper is however pure Welsh from Montgomery, and is very disappointed that I can't speak Welsh. We occasionally hold sessions together on the Welsh character and the alien English. I provide the history and she the contemporary scene.

After leaving Bowden House later in 1947 David saw Dr. Stevenson regularly, once a week, for some time. At about this time he summed up the artist's position in a note (8 October 1947), now unfortunately fragmentary, for the doctor. The thesis and idiom will be familiar to readers of *Epoch and Artist*, but here the application is to a particular individual—as, indeed, it is in the poem which opens *The Sleeping Lord*, 'A, a, a, Domine Deus'.

It is difficult to see how the peculiar qualities that characterize the art of painting can continue to co-exist with a civilization such as our own is, or is becoming. (The root trouble about a materialistic conception lies here—if things are thought of as simply utile—as for instance a radiator or a gas-fire or an electric bulb—then a kind of conflict arises in the mind of the artist with regard to them, and he tends to go to earlier forms of light and heat, as candle and wood-fire, when he is expressing the universal concepts of fire and light. This in turn creates a kind of loss of touch with the contemporary world—his world, after all —and a kind of invalidity pervades his symbols—it sets up a strain. However unconscious, it produces a neurosis. Previous ages did not know this tension.) A painting is a *sign* in the sense that a sacrament is a sign—an effective sign. In a civilization as fundamentally alien to sign and symbol (that is, valid symbol, i.e. . . .

David often speaks of the tension which arises when the artist has to accommodate himself to modern civilization. He is an outcast in the wilderness, a scapegoat. He has to serve the world but he does not belong to it, and does not understand it. In his own case there was another form of estrangement. He felt that he had no defined social position; he had moved away from the social level of his childhood and felt an alien in the supposedly higher levels—an impostor, he says at times—in which there was much that he admired: not wealth, but an assured standing, based on an aristocracy of birth and tradition. He speaks of this later, and includes the revealing sentence, 'Rosy [i.e. neurosis] resides a lot in the complex maladjustments of the social order'. This is more true of his earlier than of his later years. As time went on, he was more at home in that climate; he understood that his own character and talents placed him outside any social classification; small things—tone of voice, pronunciation of certain words, trifling habits—that at first were deliberate, became habitual and unaffected.

The passages that follow are taken from similarly fragmentary notes written for the doctor at this time. David is arguing, quite rightly, to my mind, that to say that in his breakdown he was trying to escape from some sexual fear or other uncertainty was to leave the problem untouched; and I believe that he made his doctors understand this.

I do not question the findings [of the doctors] at all about my fear etc. with regard to sex—but I do emphatically say that over and beyond those symptoms of imbalance in my own make-up, there is the concept of 'not marriage' as a perfectly rational desire in order to pursue what appears to this or that person to be a greater good. Here it seems to me the whole of history bears witness. This is not 'celibacy for its own sake'—that no one has ever maintained—at least only certain sects like the Manichees. But to reject the obvious 'good' of marriage for some other 'good' is a principle which is universally admitted in civilized tradition. I have always felt this very strongly and question if it is wholly owing to the aforesaid escapist thing in me. I should like also to mention that I feel that the 'contemporary situation' has a real bearing here—it seems to me (and I have all my life been aware of it) that at the breakdown of a culture (bringing great abnormality at all levels and very great divergence of standards of every sort, and economic pressure—all detrimental to mating and normal marriage even for tough and resilient persons) many people who otherwise in a normal world would get married, quite logically avoid doing so if they feel they have some vital work to do, because the conditions of their time make it virtually impossible for them to marry and bring up a family without at the same time prostituting (or something like it) the work they do. A Catholic at all events cannot marry except with the primary intention of building up a family. Rightly or wrongly, I have *always* known or felt this not to be my job— from my teens I have had this in mind. This *may* be a 'rationalization' of my inhibitions and fears of sex, but, discounting those, the attitude seems to me to be completely defensible and reasonable.

I think the two views are probably far nearer than appears at first sight, but I do think there is a bit to clear up, and I think perhaps psychology as such is less concerned than are religion and metaphysics with hierarchies of perfection. What may be an admirable and salutary thing at one level may be unsatisfactory at another level. Whatever our psychic make-up, we all desire perfection, even at the expense of great misery.—This gets one into difficulties . . . 'Why do you want the moon when you have the stars?'

. . . Jesus Xt and women. Luther's idea. Not possible for theological reasons. Our Lord only known to us intelligibly in a theological and mythological manner. No offence as far as I am concerned, but might have queered the pitch with some Catholics.

. . . The difficulty of the painting business. E.g. last picture [*Vexilla Regis*]—idea of 'impenitent thief' very slight ingredient —one of many half-suggestions. Painting odd in that one is led partly by what evolves as the painting evolves, this form suggesting that form—happiness comes when the forms assume significance with regard to this juxtaposition to each other—even though the original 'idea' was somewhat different. The consequent extreme difficulty of 'talking about' or explaining a painting. The happiest ones seem to make themselves. I get into a muddle because I am really after the felicity of forms and their technical contrivance, but tend to get bogged down with a most complex 'literary' and 'literal' symbolism at times. Subject is *everything* in one sense and nothing in *another*.

Have been worried from time to time about possible effect of analysis on the peculiar balance of ingredients in my painting. Hard to say where I stand at this moment, because to my mind my happiest and best work was just prior to my illness, in 1932. Then later the two Morte Darthur compositions [i.e. the *Guenever*, 1940, and *Four Queens*, 1941]—successful and authentic in another way, as also the *Aphrodite Pandemos* [i.e. *Aphrodite in Aulis*, 1941]—considered not psychologically balanced. Since then done little or nothing that seemed to me really to *get there*.

Since being here this new beginning—I like some of them quite genuinely—but *must* admit that I can't yet see it as *authentic* (i.e. not yet as much 'me' as my pre-breakdown work) and sure of direction or as pleasurable as the 1932 ones. But feel as yet too close to it to judge properly. . . .

Another note of the time concerning the *Vexilla Regis*:

Further notes on elements in this tree picture. The horses were introduced partly and perhaps mainly as far as my conscious mind was concerned to attempt to break the rigidity and immobility of the design and get a lateral flowing movement across and also to indicate a series of distances and give recession.

This picture, in my view, exemplifies unsolved dilemmas in a rather acute manner. The Aphrodite picture, on the other hand, does in my view, and on the whole, resolve them. The balance between form and content and many extremes of conception are satisfactorily maintained—that is why I like it.

His more general notes continue:

If I sometimes seem ungratefully doubtful about results of treatment, it is only because I feel in some moods that in spite of all the very great knowledge and penetration that psychology is able to bring to bear—yet as the whole height and depth of man is concerned it is so extremely elusive a matter—it seems almost like trying to extract a deep and very small splinter with a large pen-knife or whatever is the proper metaphor.

The will, not the intellect, buoyed up by the idea—will it last?

Occasionally I have felt that the urgent and imperative demand for an answer, coupled perhaps with a slight suggestion that such-and-such must be so, has caused me to admit something which was only a half-truth. Even under narcosis I felt this a bit.

I have learned to see that psychotherapy is on more valid and solid ground than I had perhaps supposed, not that I doubted its ability or its principle so much as that I feared it might prove very inadequate—by lack of precision—rather like extracting a tooth with a pair of carpenter's forceps that would not even go into the mouth. That in some particulars in my own case the experience was indeed like pouring acid on an etching plate— there was the pattern quite clear. I see how intimately the physical states and feelings are linked with the hidden psychological states. I see that *everything* one does is conditioned by one's psychopathology. I see that unless and until unconscious and subconscious are subjugated to or in harmony with the conscious will, a conflict and the symptoms of a conflict are bound to be present. I have learned that at least in the case of the phobias that assaulted me when drawing, a knowledge of these causes and a conscious effort based on that knowledge can and does beat down the fears—mitigate them or even remove them, and that painting can even become far from being the chief occasion of fear, the chief release from tension.

It was a wonderful achievement on the part of the doctors to make David understand that the will could be 'buoyed up' by the 'idea' and that painting could provide a 'relief from tension'. If one looks through reproductions of his many 1932 pictures and of later paintings, one sees how right David is when he says that the introduction of the 'literary' element—which means also religious, historical, metaphysical, mythological—raised the further problem of retaining the freedom and authentic abstract form of his earlier work: he had to make a spoon or spoil a horn. Interesting, too, that he used the psychologists as he used the writers, thinkers, poets, that he consulted or made use of in his writing: he took from them and adapted to his own purposes, and expressed in his own idiom, just what he needed and no more.

To continue with his own notes:

I feel I have perhaps been more successful in benefiting from the treatment in the realm of drawing—of concepts—than in ordinary affairs—though there, too, I see an improvement and a vast difference, of course, from when I came to Bowden House. But I seem to be able to apply what I've learned more readily in drawing than in what are called 'practical affairs'. But that remains to be seen, rather. But I understand far better the ramifications of the sexual impulse and how the fear of assuming the 'father figure' position works in the most unexpected conjunctions, and I see how all my life I've avoided such a position in innumerable and subtle ways.

Before coming here the only alleviation I knew of was the neurologists' 'masterly inactivity'. When I was previously ill, 1933, a sea voyage did temporarily produce a cessation of my symptoms for some years, but I now see that like the imposers of the Danegeld the unconscious demands a higher and higher blackmail—less and less activity as a price, so that the *only* way is to beat the unconscious in open war. I still find certain applications of this very obscure and hard to achieve, and I see that a great faith is required—but I see that this is, in principle, the correct and only way.

I see how one repeats the pattern of one's life in a striking way. I always had an inkling that this was so, but rather regarded it as a superstition, but I now see why this must be so. I feel I have still a very great deal to learn about how to *utilize* the principles I have been taught here, and that is perhaps where my chief anxiety now lies.

I still find it a problem why God should have left man without a means of scientifically understanding the unconscious until the study of recent years, except that the prevalence of disorders tends to bring a way of dealing with those disorders in the terms of any given period, I suppose—but that is not a wholly satisfactory solution.

A last fragment of such notes from the Bowden House period:

? Xtianity the religion of extroverts. True that man's faith fluctuates but chart of the ups and downs of psychoneurosis and the chart of that fluctuation of faith, not at all necessarily the same, in my opinion.

III

COUNTERATTACK, ENTRENCHMENT 1947—1964

*

Harrow (Northwick Lodge)

It was the David who left Bowden House towards the end of 1947 and moved to Northwick Lodge in Harrow-on-the-Hill (and later, in 1964, to the Monksdene Hotel in another part of Harrow) who became known to many younger friends; and I believe that they would agree with me that in spite of his ever-increasing dissatisfaction with the world in which he lived, in spite of his entrenchment in his own small fortress, of his exasperation as he sought to pack more and more into both his written and his plastic work, of his indecisions, of his increasing fastidiousness, of his immobility (increasing, not unnaturally, with age, as many of us already know or will learn later), of at least one new emotional disturbance—in spite of all these he held his own and never sank back into helplessness.

Of this his industry is surely proof. The letters he wrote between 1947 and his death in 1974 amount to well over a million words; he painted some of his most elaborate pictures and a large number of curiously wrought (in the old sense of the adverb) inscriptions; he completed the long and intricate fabric of *The Anathemata*, the pieces brought together in *The Sleeping Lord*, the earnestly didactic essays collected in *Epoch and Artist*. And it should be remembered that what was printed was but a small proportion of what was written, perhaps one-twentieth. Any person who looks at the surviving MSS will be astonished at the endless repetitions and re-draftings. A passage will be written out again and again and again, with perhaps one or two verbal changes. It is as though a man were competing in the long jump and were constantly returning to the starting point of his run because, as he was about to take off, he found that he had missed his step. This is not difficult to understand in the composition of a poem: but it seems quite extraordinary in the writing of a letter—particularly a letter for the writing of which there was no real necessity—or of a purely factual paragraph. For example, there are half a dozen different versions of the note at the head of the extract in *The Sleeping Lord* from *The Book of Balaam's Ass*, any one of which would have served as well as the version printed. There are six, seven, eight, nine, drafts of a letter acknowledging, and speaking at great length about matters connected with, a book of no importance or value, sent to him by the writer; and no amount of time or trouble is too much for David when he is dealing with a book or question that shows acuteness of understanding.

Those who met David during this period are in some ways to be envied by those who had known him for many years, even though his younger friends may envy what the older generation had gained from earlier friendships. To the younger, David spoke with the authority of his years, and he must have been seen by them as a teacher. I do not mean that his older friends did not learn from him—many of them owe to him all that they know of certain matters—but he generally spoke or wrote to them as sharers of an old hoard of knowledge and enquiry. At the same time, his younger friends very often brought to him exact or specialized knowledge that his older friends lacked—in many fields, languages, archaeology, pre-history, linguistics, literary and military history.

In this respect, Northwick Lodge was an ideal centre for him. It is (or was, for it has been pulled down) a large block of a house on Peterborough Hill, about halfway to the flat top of Harrow Hill which is in the middle of Harrow School. The house was owned by Mr. Carlile, who had been a Harrow housemaster, and in it lodged a number of young professional men or students and several Harrow masters; also, at one time, a number of American servicemen. It was accessible to serious visitors but inaccessible to chance interruption. David's room was large enough; the window afforded the view he needed, with trees, playing fields and what was still more or less open country. He was alone and yet with company. He was friendly with, and benefited from the society of, some of the masters.

Though he was without vanity, David did, I believe, enjoy the increasing respect he commanded. And one of the reasons he enjoyed that respect was that it helped him to carry out what he regarded with almost evangelistic fervour, unwilling though he might have been so to express it, as the poet's mission. It should be remembered that when he spoke of the 'gratuitousness' of the arts, he was speaking simply of the nature of the artefact as such. It is also part of a particular man's work and life, and that life is directed towards a particular and well-defined end. David took very seriously, in practice, the parable of the talents, as is apparent in the notes quoted above (pp. 135–41) which he wrote for his doctors at Bowden House.

At Northwick Lodge Stanley Honeyman is—or perhaps, in view of his present age, one should say was—a typical, if also special, example of the great refreshment David received from youth. In 1949 or so, Stanley was one of David's fellow lodgers.

'I should have been studying', says Stanley,[1] 'and David should have been working, and we spent our evenings talking. I would talk with him until about ten or eleven, and then he would get back to his work. I'd just come out of the army and I think that that was in itself a common ground, because David never got out of the trenches, and we had this common bond—different wars but the same army. I was twenty-three, and David had a tremendous knack with the young.

'At that time I knew nothing about him, but one day I was sitting in the large drawing room overlooking the garden, and I happened to be looking at a book about Seurat—a painter I liked very much—at a reproduction of *Une Baignade*, the one that is in the Tate. I can remember it as if it was still yesterday: David came into the room. He was then fifty-four, and to see a young man just out of the army looking at such a picture interested him vastly. We sat down together and agreed that this thing had a special sort of coolness and marvellous quality. After that I spent hours up in his room looking at pictures.' Pictures, the army, the Roman army, military history, whatever the subject, Stanley never left David without the feeling that he had said something that nobody else in the world would have said in that particular way. 'It's a staggering feeling: very often you might almost miss it, for it was delivered in such an unusual way—but this man: something damn silly like Manchester United beating some Welsh football team, and he would say, "Yes . . ." and come in from the side with some fascinating comment completely different from anyone else's— some totally unexpected gloss—lateral: lateral thinking in the true sense of the word.'

It was this ability to relate one thing to another that David admired in other writers and thinkers (even if some extravagance had to be overlooked), in Jackson Knight, for example, and (so seductively and at the same time infuriatingly) in Spengler. Relationships, of shapes, colours, ideas, memories, traditions, were the basis of his poetry and painting. Hence his fondness for lists. I mean such things as the following, taken from one of the MSS associated with *The Kensington Mass* and its kindred pieces:

. . . corbels, hangings, sacristy lizards, the master of the robes, gold-sticks, gildings, beadsmen, commissionaires, carriers, run-

---

[1] I take what follows from a conversation of 1978, kindly noted for me by Peter Orr, another, even younger, friend to whom David was later to be indebted in many small and greater matters.

ners, exorcists, signallers, door-keepers, auxiliaries, bell-ringers, Knights of the Sacred Head, Moreen Jane Roper's Grail gon-falcon, sea-scouts, and she-guides, ambo mouldings, aumbries, the Carrara toe of the Prince of the Apostles, Hyacinth, Joy and Fay at prayer in echelon, daughters of the Mayor of the Sacred Palace and Mayor Molyneux himself, obscure almost everything for Mr. Tod, kneeling six pine pens back from the carmine baize reserve . . . General Gandolf himself late of this parish and all his men drowned at Passchendaele in a very dark sea.

This playing with words and names, from history, liturgy, war, brings out another point, rightly emphasized by Stanley Honeyman in the conversation referred to above—David's great sense of fun. If everything might be, and often was, described as a 'monumental bug-geration'—or, In Parenthetically, a monumental bollux-up every time —it was also a 'colossal jocko'. So it was that disgust with modern technology was tempered by delight in sheer speed. Later, David would dine with the Honeymans in Chelsea and Stanley would drive him back to Harrow in a fast car. 'He'd adore going fast; we used to roar down Western Avenue and he'd say, My God! I know one night we got from Chelsea to Monksdene in eleven minutes, and David thought it enormous fun.'

Various accidents reduce the number of letters to his friends that can be drawn upon for the first years at Northwick Lodge—the pernicious ease of the telephone often made it unnecessary to write; some letters were lost in normal domestic economy ('I *know* I left it on the dresser') and others, unhappily, in moves from one place to another.

One important letter has survived, however, about the picture *Vexilla Regis*, painted at Bowden House and among those shown in the large exhibition at the Redfern Gallery in May–June 1948.[2] That David was later very much more satisfied with that picture than the notes quoted above perhaps indicate, is shown by the 'prohibitive' price (the adjective is his) he placed on it—£500. *Vexilla Regis*, now in Kettle's Yard, Cambridge, was later bought by Jim Ede's mother, to whom David writes about it in 1949:

---

[2] This was to be his last exhibition of pictures for sale. Many were sold; but it was a long time before he could collect the money—and that at a time when he was most in need of it.

To Mrs. Ede, 28 August 1949   *Northwick Lodge*

... Anyway, I'm glad the picture [*Vexilla Regis*] did arrive safely. There was no need to send me the cheque yet—after all, you might not have liked the picture after looking at it a bit! I do hope you did not send it feeling that it must be sent at once. Of *course* the remainder can wait until it is convenient to you. I'm awfully sorry it's such a lot of money—it has no relation with the ordinary price of the picture—it was only that I put that large price on it because it was, to me personally, and for special reasons, a picture that I did not intend to sell in the ordinary way, except for that sum—but I did not really think anyone would require it at that price—as it is, I am exceedingly pleased that you should have decided to buy it and that Jim will some day posssess it. Another person had to see it again first before I could have it sent to you because I had promised them the first refusal of it, but it so happened that they decided they could not have it. So all was well and I was able to send it for your approval. I'm most awfully glad you like it—because not always when one sees a reproduction does one like the original —sometimes it disappoints one. But I *do* think, in this case, the reproduction is a very feeble rendering of the actual picture. You have perfectly understood, in a remarkable way, much of the content behind the form of the picture. Yes, Rev[elation] 22:2 ['. . . on both sides of the river was the tree of life . . .'] certainly comes into it, though the *main* jumping-off ground was, I think, a Latin hymn we sing as part of the Good Friday liturgy in the Roman rite. Two hymns, in fact, one starting *Vexilla Regis prodeunt*, 'Forth come the standards of the King' (written I think about the 5th century I think in Gaul),[3] a very ancient processional hymn, in which are many allusions to the tree and the Cross, and to the Cross as a tree etc., and the other starting: *Crux fidelis inter omnes, arbor una nobilis*. This is a rather long hymn and in various of its verses deals with the Cross as a Tree in concise and very noble and moving language—really

[3] The traditional date for the first singing of Fortunatus's hymn is 19 November 569.

very grand. The robin you ask about: well there is that thing about the robin getting his red breast from the red drops from the Tree of the Cross. The general idea of the picture was also associated, in my mind, with the collapse of the Roman world. The three trees as it were left standing on Calvary—the various bits and pieces of classical ruins dotting the landscape—also older things, such as the stone henge or 'druidic' circle a little to the right of the right-hand tree in the distance and then the Welsh hills more to the right again, the rushing ponies are, *more or less*, the horses of the Roman cavalry, turned to grass and gone wild and off to the hills. (This idea, probably in turn, comes from something in Malory's *Morte Darthur* when right at the end, after the death of Guenevere and the break-up of the Round Table, Lancelot and other knights let their armed horses free to roam where they will—for the riders have now finished with tournaments, display etc. and gone off to be hermits and the like.) The leopard's pelt and the trumpet in the left-hand bottom corner are supposed to be the instrument and insignia of a Roman *bucinator* or trumpeter, as though the owner of them had been part of the guard on Calvary—that sort of idea. The tree on the left of the main tree is, as it were, the tree of the 'good thief', it grows firmly in the ground and the pelican has made her nest and feeds her young in its branches—Our Lord is likened to a pelican in her piety in one of the Latin hymns of Thomas Aquinas. The tree on the right is that of the other thief, it is partly tree and partly triumphal column and partly imperial standard—a power symbol, it is not rooted to the ground but is part supported by wedges. St. Augustine's remark that 'empire is great robbery' influenced me here. It is *not* meant to be *bad* in itself but in some senses proud and self-sufficient. Nevertheless it is shadowed by the spreading central Tree and the dove, in fact, hovers over this tree of the truculent robber for somehow or other he is 'redeemed' too! I think that is about all. I should like to make plain that none of this symbolism is meant to be at all rigid, but very fluid—I merely write down a few of the mixed ideas *that got into* this picture as you were kind enough to ask. A Church dignitary once said to Lord Tennyson, with reference to a certain poem 'Do these figures symbolize Faith, Hope and Charity?' to which Tennyson replied 'They do and they don't and I don't like being tied down!' or words to that effect.

It's very like that in painting or any work of art, I think. So many confluent ideas are involved in a single image. It so happens that in this picture I have been able to 'list' some of the ideas of the content for you. (It would be far less possible to do so in most of my pictures of course—at least far less easy—this picture is after all somewhat of an 'illustration' as well as a picture. Not that it was deliberately so—it came like that.)—But they were less explicitly intended than perhaps it sounds, when written down, and there is much other stuff besides. It interested me about your straight fir tree outside your window, because actually, of the trees which started me off on this picture, one was a pine and the other a fir (the other, I believe, a chestnut). They were outside my bedroom window in the nursing home when I was jolly ill for seven months—I did a number of drawings of those trees and then in the end did this complicated picture, very much influenced by the previous drawings, though quite different. The picture went through many vicissitudes, and suffered much alteration and was nearly torn up more than once. The psychiatrist, under whose care I was, *made* me go on, so that it was produced under rather special circumstances. (In a sense my doctor could be said to have been a 'part-producer' I feel.)

Well, you must be weary of this epistle, but I felt, as you asked about it, you might like to know these few facts. I do hope you go on liking it. I wonder what dear Jim will think of it. I owe so much to him in so many ways. I was delighted to see him looking, I thought, far better I thought than when last I saw him—and, as you say, Helen also looks far better than last year. They are a marvellous pair. I do hope they have a nice time in the North.

A couple of other things relating to the picture: the nails with their ribbons were suggested by the Paschal Candle which, in Catholic churches, is lit during the Easter season. It is a very large candle and always decorated with flowers etc., and in the middle of it are inserted five separate grains of incense usually in little gilt containers, arranged in diamond formation, and although the actual history of this custom is very obscure, they are now taken to signify the Five Wounds of Our Lord. You mention also a Madonna, but I don't think there is one in this picture. The little female winged figure in the wood to the left, such as might be over a fountain—the guardian figure of the sacred well —that sort of notion—I think that was my idea of it. Well, again, thank you so *very very much*, and forgive this horrible writing of mine, and the length of it. If there is anything else you would wish to know, ask me, and, if I can, I'll tell you, and I am sorry about bothering you with wires.

P.S. Also of course the Yggdrasil of Northern mythology, the great tree with its roots far in the earth and its flowers in heaven no doubt comes into the picture—for all these things are one thing in some sense.

Though we have few letters from these years, there is a message of 1952 on the fly-leaf of a copy of Admiral Sir W. M. James's *The Durable Moment: Horatio Nelson* (1948):

Happy birthday for Joan from David, Feb. 1st 1952. Dearest Joan, Think you might like bits of this, anyway letter from young tar beginning toward the foot of page 293 makes the book worth having, but it is a most interesting book all through, I thought. May be however you or René (to whom much love) have already read it, as it's been out for some while. I've been not well since just before Xmas, hence I never acknowledged your nice card, or Mary's. Love to her and Petra and everybody. I do hope you are well.   DAI

Remove this horrible so-called 'jacket' I left it on as a protection in post.   D.

The centre of David's life at this time was the completion of *The Anathemata*. On 6 September 1951 he writes to Jim Ede that he is in the final stages of correcting the typescript; and there is a note on 1 October 1951 of luncheon with T. S. Eliot: 'took him my MS of *Anathemata*'.

To H.J.G., 5 August 1952   *Northwick Lodge*

... I've not yet got the positively last corrections [for *The Anathemata*] from Faber. It was nice seeing Tom E[liot]—he's a jolly nice bloke and I like him more the more I see of him. How he manages to be the great poet he is and do all the other things he does—business at F's, going about the world etc.—passes my comprehension. This great *capability* combined with an artist's sensitivity and battering of the senses—it's remarkable. He must have *great* strength and balance to an unusual degree. I *think* he once said he had *some* Scots ancestry and the Scots are very *able* people. Exactly the opposite from the Welsh, I feel.

... I do hope they review the *Ana.* properly. I don't see it having many sales and I see every reason why chaps should find it a bit of a putting-off book in various ways. But it would be at least something by way of encouragement if at least a few blokes reviewed it, even if they blasted it.

A letter of later in the same month reports:

To H.J.G., August 1952   *Northwick Lodge*

... All is now settled about book except the 16 odd pages with final corrections that should arrive in a day or so. The 'secret date' of its publication is October 24, the Feast of St. Raphael (never thought much about him. I understand his name means 'the medicine of God'). The illustrations will consist of the seven inscriptions, the unicorn engraving, and the Arthur and Merlin picture that I borrowed the photo of from Joan and René. I should have *liked* two more, including the Polyhymnia drawing, but this was found to be impossible and would have put up the price even more, so there it is. I was disappointed that I did not pull off the Lamb and Flag picture[4]—we had it photographed but it looks an *awful bore*—just *would not* come to life without the colour. It *so* often happens that when you do a thing *specially* it will *not* come off. However, after all, my *original* plan was to have inscriptions only. But I think the Merlin picture is a good

[4] Cf. the picture called 'The Victim', published as the tailpiece to *In Parenthesis* in its original 1937 edition.

idea as it gives the right twist to that 'Mabinog's Liturgy' section.

... Yes, I *did* see Tom E.'s hat 'crying Stetson!' (I wish he'd write another poem as good as *The Waste Land*). Yes, he has a Merlin thing most certainly and somewhat unexpectedly.

The Anathemata was published as promised at the end of October 1952.

In conversation and correspondence with David (both, it is true, irregular at this time) he never spoke to me of the reception of his work. I was astonished, therefore, to find from his correspondence with his other friends how much importance he attached, for example, to reviews; but it soon became clear to me that this was not due to any vanity or self-esteem, but entirely to his conviction of the poet's mission, that his work is both a private and a public worship. He was, therefore, most anxious to know that he was understood, and would (as many of his other correspondents will confirm) take great pains to explain himself, and would be immensely grateful when a friend or stranger found some key to what the poet feared might remain a puzzle—even if the key was not, at times, a very good fit.

To H.S.E., 17 December 1952   *Northwick Lodge*

... I've been (between ourselves) somewhat cast down over its [*The Anathemata's*] reception. True, there have been two or three good reviews, Kathleen Raine's [in *The New Statesman*, 22 November 1952] in particular. But so far on the whole there has been only a dim response in some quarters. Not that one wants praise, but one does, I think, hope for consideration and analysis and an understanding of the nature of the work from certain kinds of people, at all events. The *Times Lit. Sup.* [14 November 1952] was quite all right up to a point, but, I think I can say without conceit, not adequate. It stressed the 'difficulties' of the work and its 'obscurities'; it was quite sympathetic and complimentary and, I think, meant well, but the *impression conveyed* was that the work, though interesting, was too involved in a specialized kind of 'learning' to convey much to the average reader. (It would have been a good review, say, for *The Spectator*, but for the *Lit. Sup.* it was not sufficient,

[154]

in my opinion. I had hoped they might, for instance, face up to some of the problems stated in the Preface, because Preface and text present quite separate matters for discussion.) I had rather counted on the *Lit. Sup.* doing something more helpful than this. I had not expected much of other papers because the standard of literary criticism is now *very low indeed*. The *Yorkshire Post* gave it a *very good* review [28 November 1952], very appreciative and *to the point*, and *Time and Tide* [29 November 1952] gave it a most enthusiastic and perceptive reception [by Emyr Humphreys] of reasonable length. There have not been any other reviews at all as yet. Bobby Speaight wrote a thing about it in *The Tablet* [29 November 1952] and that was also nice, and he made some points worth making. Harman has written a *very* good thing on it for the *Dublin Review* [no. 458, 1952]. I wish he could have written it for a more widely read magazine, as what he says is interesting in all sorts of ways, quite apart from my stuff. . . .

And again dear Jim, I should like to say how much I was *comforted* and delighted by your liking it and liking it in the *right sort of way*. It is not *'learning'* that is required (*I am not* 'learned', I only root about among stuff that scholars write in order to *verify* things I'm *attached to*, to check up on this and that. Actually if it comes to 'scholarship' I'm an absolute dud. As you know I have very few 'accomplishments' and practically no 'education' in the accepted sense of that word. I try to write by the same process as I paint. The two arts seem to me to present just the same problems as to 'matter' and 'form')—it only requires a kind of human thing, a bit of hard thought, a humour, a response to what we call 'poetry'—i.e. language at a heightened tension—a sense of form and shape, an exact and evocative use of *each* word. You have a sense of *all* that in you, so I felt that, *given time*, you might like it. I know it's a bit of a bugger on the surface; but underneath it's pretty straightforward really, compared with most modern 'personal experience' and 'psychological' kinds of poetry. I tried very hard to make a lucid, impersonal statement with regard to those things which have made us *all*—of this island. Even its 'Welsh' stuff is not there because I happen to be in part Welsh, but because the Welsh mythological element is an *integral* part of our tradition. Nor indeed is even the 'Catholic' element there because I happen to be a Catholic, but rather because historically speaking (and leaving aside the truth or the untruth of the Christian religion) it is the Catholic thing which has determined so much of our history and conditioned the thought of us *all*. Again, the seafaring thing is not there because my grandfather happened to be a mast and blockmaker (Eb. Bradshaw) but because one *cannot begin* to consider Britain without being straight away involved in the sea and all the sea meant both in the domain of fact and in our whole poetic tradition. (Though, needless to say, these three facts: my being a Catholic, in part Welsh and linked from childhood with the 'Pool of London' world, through my mother, made it possible for me to write these things. But the things written of are not personal to me, but are the inheritance of us all. That's the point I wish to stress.) In a sense *The Ana.* is the least 'idiosyncratic' or 'obscure' of writings *as far as data* is concerned at all events. Now one would expect professional literary critics etc. to see all this straight away, wouldn't one? Some of them of course do, but I hoped they would jump to it more brightly. I am very grateful to Kathleen Raine for her understanding review, and as the *New Statesman* has a wide sale, it may do some good. . . .

P.S. I have some very sad news, dear Prudence (Prudence Pelham that was) died. I have only quite recently got the news, though it happened a little back. It was a great shock to me, as she meant a very great deal to me, though I had not seen her for some while. I felt I should tell you, as I remember coming with her to Elm Row [Hampstead]. She was of the rarest possible nobility of mind and like no one else at all.

During these years Prudence and David had been to some degree cut off from one another, the latter suffering from temperamental immobility and the former from recurring attacks of disseminated sclerosis. David learnt of Prudence's death—as Lady Prudence Buhler[5] —when he was about to send her a copy of *The Anathemata*; a letter

[5] She had changed her name by deed-poll.

from her lawyers told him that she had remembered him in her will. It is consoling to know that Prudence's last years were made happy, happier than ever before, by the love and companionship of Robert Buhler. All her friends will recognize her when he writes, 'I had never met such an enchanting, intelligent, magical girl before, and fell *madly* in love with her . . . we had an idyllic life together, marred only by the overhanging awfulness of d. sclerosis, which Prudence bore bravely and stoically—and I did my best. But her magic overcame everything. . . . We often used to see David in Harrow. He would drag out drawings from under his bed—reluctantly—and Prudence always brought needle and cotton and sewed on his buttons.'

Quite a number of David's books, which went to the National Library of Wales after his death, were given to him by Prudence, sometimes her own copies passed on to him, and some have entertaining messages. Thus, inside Barbellion's *Diary of a Disappointed Man*: 'N.B. Don't let Mike [Richey] get at this, as it's unobtainable! D.J.'. *The Oxford Book of English Verse* (I presume he had lost his own copy): 'Prudence Pelham 1934, for David in the year of exile 1945 with much love'. Michael Ayrton's *British Drawings* (1946): 'Dearest Dai, this is just a Christmas card bec. I can't see you and don't know what you want. I found some smoked cod's roe for your breakfast-in-bed. Was sorry to hear you weren't well and doubly sorry not to see you. I'm just back from selling the farm and feel emptied out of that valley and every other! Happy Christmas, dear Dai, keep warm and best love to you from Prudence. See p. 46.'[6] R. H. Liddell Hart's *The Revolution in Warfare* (1946): 'Dai, with love from Prudence. Shall I mend your other sleeve or have you done it yourself?' Among other books Prudence gave him was *Finnegans Wake*, in May 1948.

To T. S. Eliot, 1 June 1953[7]   *Northwick Lodge*

Dear Tom, this is an accompanying note (that is to say I've delivered the drawings to David Bland) only re the illustration and tailpiece I've tried to do for your poem *On the Cultivation of Christmas Trees*. I like the poem very much, but it was a good while before I could find out how, if at all, to 'illustrate' it. I

---

[6] The reference is to Ayrton's praise of David's drawings as 'a symbol of the continuity of tradition . . . not that they are archaic, but in their lyrical, linear freedom'.

[7] No 'Glorious First' for T.S.E.

fear I've scarcely done so—all I've tried to do is to make a drawing that has, perhaps, some sort of *Heilige Nacht* feeling. The wounded stag seemed a way of perhaps combining the stags that feed on the hydromel that drops from Odin's Yggdrasil with the white hart that I mean as a symbol of Our Lord—and I was thinking of the psalm *Quemadmodum desiderat cervus ad fontes aquarum*—so he's by a stream and flowers have sprung up around him (because his blood fertilized the soil—rather as the wounds of Adonis made the anemones grow in Palestine). I didn't know how to manage the tree, because it *so happens* that I *don't like* conifers (perhaps because of their uncompromising rigidity)—and it's difficult to get away from conifers in the case of Christmas trees!

Well, I don't know at all if it will reproduce—but it's about all I can do. My sort of drawings are not very patient of reproduction even when I try to make them so.

The tailpiece is, as you see, from the *Communicantes et memoriam venerantes* prayer in the Canon of the Mass, where, by a bit of luck, Lucy has retained a place. As she was martyred in Sicily and is a very popular cult figure there (so I'm told) I thought that provided a chance to bring in Persephone and her flowers—it's line 18 of hymn 28 in the edition of the Orphic hymns edited by G. Hermann of Leipzig early in the last century. But I expect you know it well. The Alpha and Omega in the inscription are partly because of the penultimate line of your poem. Should you feel that neither the drawing nor the inscription sort quite with the feeling of the poem do not hesitate to reject them. For I know how maddening it is to have something linked with one's work that does not enhance but rather obscures the intention.

I do hope you are all right.

Let's know sometime if you approve or disapprove of the illustrations. Yours ever,   DAI

The list in the letter that follows, one of 'referees' that Harman Grisewood needed when he was arranging that David should receive a Civil List pension, gives David an opportunity to indulge himself in one of his own lists: 'The Barber to the King of France' is frequently inserting himself into the MSS that date from this period.

To H.J.G., 21 October[8] *1953*   *Northwick Lodge*

Herewith this beastly list for your perusal. It reads pretty embarrassingly. . . . Many thanks for all the trouble you've taken.[9] Barbara M. [the Countess of Moray] it so happened, came over to see me today, and I asked her if I might name her as one of the referees if necessary. She said she would be pleased. (In addition to T.S.E[liot], Bertie R[ead], K[enneth] C[lark] and yourself, the possible names are Barbara, Clarissa [Eden, *née* Spencer-Churchill], [Fr. Martin] D'Arcy, Philip James, John R[othenstein].) Six Dukes went a-fishing! We need only a legate a latere, the Mayor of the Sacred Palace, the barber to the King of France, the Exarch of Ravenna and the wife of the Vicar of Britain.

Glad you liked Desmond [Chute]'s review [of *The Anathemata*, in *Blackfriars*, October 1953]. Am very anxious and excited to hear about your meditations on 'the situation' re *poiesis*. I *nearly* asked you, a bit back, what K[enneth] C[lark] thought of *Ana.* but I felt for *certain* that his reactions would be as you say. I think also that B.R. [Herbert Read] found it much the same, 'obscure'. Objectively considered this change of attitude (or whatever it is) which has broken across the conception of what a work ought to be like (in our opinion) is interesting as reflecting all sorts of other corresponding changes or determinations, but subjectively, at least for you and me, it is wholly depressing and also somewhat maddening. But, as I've said in conversation, I do feel that what, for short, I'll call 'our attitude' is now something of a 'lost cause'. That's O.K. 'Lost causes' are almost always the right causes, but it does shake one a good bit and give one a feeling of peculiar isolation. The temptation is to feel that it is useless to proceed, of course. For undoubtedly one does seem to require a measure of appreciation or understanding from at least a certain number of people. I don't mean that one has not got this, but I do feel that the Front is in a very dicky

---

[8] Trafalgar Day, but, oddly, no mention of the fact.

[9] In connection with the Civil List pension, David, a couple of months later, writes of his earned income for the past year: 'As far as I can make out the sum is £307.2.7. This is professional earnings, exclusive of all expenses and one gift.'

state and liable to be overrun in most sectors. As for the reserves, well, where are they?

To W. H. Auden, 24 February 1954   *Northwick Lodge*

Dear Wystan Auden, Please forgive this note *being in pencil*, but my pen refuses to work and I wanted to write without delay (being a terrible delayer) to thank you for your letter sent on to me by Harman G.

I was actually going to write to you to thank you for doing that review in *Encounter* [February 1954]. Yes, I appreciated it *very greatly*, for a number of reasons, but chiefly because you, who are a poet, liked it and understood it, and bothered to write about it in an objective way. I do thank you very much.

I did have a few appreciatory reviews when it came out, such as Kathleen Raine's good one in *N[ew] S[tatesman]*, and there have been a number of others, but in a general sort of way the reception was—well, a kind of cautious reserve, or nothing at all. The *Sunday Times*, for example, which reviews most things, remained altogether silent.

It is interesting that you should ask, in your letter, about E[zra] P[ound]'s *Cantos* because Edwin Muir, in a review in the *Observer* a year or so ago [2 November 1952], appeared to take it for granted that the *Cantos* were largely responsible for my 'style' and, only yesterday, I received a magazine called *Nine* that Peter Russell edits, in which John Heath-Stubbs, in an appreciatory notice [Winter 1953-4], says that the form of *Anathemata* is so influenced by the Cantos as to 'amount to direct imitation'. Other reviewers have said something similar. But the fact is I must confess to having not read the *Cantos* until after *The Anathemata* had gone to the publishers.

This is a pretty disgraceful admission on my part, but it happens to be true. It only goes to show how jolly tricky the business of 'derivation' and 'influences' etc. is in works. The same thing happens in the visual arts—art critics tend always to suppose some *direct* influence which, on examination, often happens not to be true. *Indirectly* of course anything can happen—but then that's only the *Zeitgeist* (if that's the right word). Not that it matters very much either way. But I think chaps should be awfully wary of emphatic assertions without being quite sure that such and such is the case. I'm not surprised when the, so to say, laity do this, but when those who practise an art do so it does surprise me a bit, because experience should teach 'em otherwise.

You are *quite* right, all sorts of similarities—sometimes quite astonishing similarities—are arrived at by different artists by diverse routes. After all, the same thing happens in the field of scientific experiment, and it is not difficult to see why.

However, I'm far from trying to say that I'm not indebted obliquely, in some ways, to E.P. (more in his earlier prose writings—things he said, I mean—not really his poetry at all) but greatly more to that stupendous old Joyce—*Lux perpetua luceat ei.* But what person of my generation could not be? That I take for granted, just as I take it for granted that all painters of the same generation were 'indebted' to the post-Impressionist movement.

But even in the case of Joyce the matter can be tricky when it comes to citing explicit examples. For here again it has been said that *In Parenthesis* owed a great deal to *Ulysses*; but I had not read *Ulysses* when *In Parenthesis* was nearing completion in 1932 (it was begun in 1927 or '28); for a number of reasons the Preface and notes were not written till 1936 but the text was virtually finished by 1933. I had read, and had read to me, *Anna Livia Plurabelle* in *c.* 1930, so any *direct* Joycean influence is likely to have come, not from *Ulysses*, but from *Anna Livia*. Sorry to crack on about this stuff, but I thought it might be of interest to you as casting further light on the *general* question of 'influences' in all the arts. As I say, I have found parallel instances in painting etc., and I expect you have too. One way and another these parallels are very interesting, but I don't think surprising. I found a most remarkable one the other day in an old copy of a magazine called *Wales* that Keidrych Rhys used to publish. In it [Summer 1938] was a short review of *In Parenthesis* by Vernon Watkins and he happens to call attention to a passage on p. 77 of *In Paren.* about the gunfire of the Ypres salient being heard from a more southern sector of the line, and the words quoted are: 'was always the dull toil of The Salient—troubling—like somebody else's war', and the reviewer compares it with two lines of a poem by Wilfred Owen:

> Northward, incessantly, the flickering gunnery rumbles
> Far off, like a dull rumour of some other war.

Well, I had not read Wilfred Owen's poem ['Exposure'] at the time of writing *In Paren*. Yet it does look like a water-tight example of downright plagiarism. The explanation here however is fairly simple and derives from the same experiential data and the same response of two people to those experiences. Actually hundreds of men might have made equivalent statements, for, time and time again, one heard it said, 'That's up Ypres way —nothing to do with us.'

Well, enough of this. I really am jolly pleased that you like *The Anathemata* and thank you again for what you wrote about it. Would you like me to send you a list of the corrections? There are a good few of them and one or two are important.[10] I'm *terribly* bad at noting mistakes in proofs however hard I try. And this particular book was a bit of a business in the way of proof-correcting. Moreover printers' readers don't seem to be anything like as good as they were.

I do hope we are able to meet in July all being well. As far as I know I shall be here. I never go anywhere. Either you can come here or we can meet at Harman G's. He's a wonderful person and has been a constant stay to me in appreciation, help and criticism over the work on *The Anathemata* as he was also with regard to *In Paren*. He's a person of the most acute and balanced perceptions, and *really* cares about the making of works, and that in spite of the fact that he's constantly hard occupied with administrative affairs, and that over a long period of years.

You know that anthology you made years ago with John Garrett, *The Poet's Tongue* [1935]—well, that has been one of my constant companions, it is a jolly good anthology and manages to have in it all the things that the school of Quiller-Couch, Walter Raleigh & Co. Ltd. manage to leave out!

[10] A good many of the corrections noted were made in the second edition of *The Anathemata*, 1955.

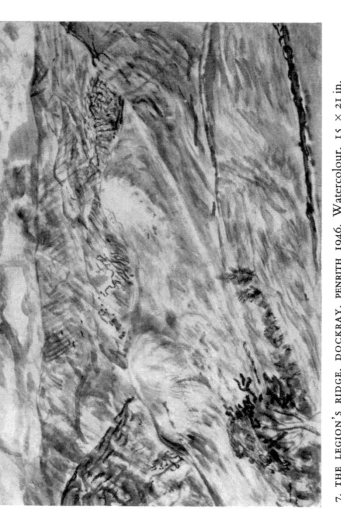

7. THE LEGION'S RIDGE, DOCKRAY, PENRITH 1946. Watercolour, 15 × 21 in.
Anthony d'Offay Gallery

8. CHALICE WITH FLOWERS AND PEPPERPOT (Harrow) *c.* 1950.
Pencil, crayon, watercolour and gouache, 31 × 22¾ in. *Private collection*

Oh, by the way, I was interested that you mentioned St. John Perse's *Vents* in your review in *Encounter*, because that other poem of his, *Anabase*, with Tom Eliot's translation on the opposite page, pub. 1930, was, I should say (to revert to this question of influences)* a poem that made a pretty big impression on me when it was published—I see that I read it early in 1931. I must not weary you further. Again thanks and if you would like me to send the list of corrections, I'll send it along with pleasure. Yours very sincerely, DAVID JONES

Yes, 'the Notes'! Insoluble problem, but I think that it was the only thing to do, for reasons explained in Preface. But with regard to the full-pages of notes, perhaps I was wrong in having the illustrations between them and the text, but it looked so *beastly* typographically to have a whole page of notes facing a whole page of text—so I arranged the illustrations on purpose to cover 'em up.

Your analysis of the eight sections seems to me O.K., except Sect. IV, 'Redriff', which is really 'about' my English grandfather, Ebenezer Bradshaw, who was a master mast- and blockmaker at Redriff (Rotherhithe), hence all the stuff about Baltic timber, craftsmanship etc. He was *very* Protestant (he objected to oaths but when roused he used to say 'Not for the Pope o' Rome!', thence my line '... from the scarlet pontiff o' the West' (p. 119), and the 'boozed Murphy' (p. 119) was one of his

---

* Skelton and parts of Browning have, I know for certain, been quite a bit formative of my stuff. About Dante, well, no, because I can't read Italian and I've never found any translation held me. I remember staying at Laurence Binyon's house when he was working on his trans. of Dante, and he'd just got a letter from Ezra P[ound] saying how bloody good it was. But I somehow couldn't get on with it—might now p'r'aps but doubt it.[11] E.P.'s letter to Binyon was jolly amusing and delighted old Laurence a lot, I remember.

[11] On Dante, see below, pp. 239-41: that quarry, unhappily, blunted the prospector's drill.

Irish Catholic workmen who was given to drink and pinching wood). For the lines 3 to 9 on p. 121 see Colossians 2:14 and I Peter 2:24 [both 'fastening to the tree or cross' passages].

To H.S.E., 24 November 1954   *Northwick Lodge*
... The Douglas Cleverdon version of my *Anathemata* is being broadcast [repeated] on Friday evening Nov. 26th—this Friday. ... It's a peculiar thing. They sweated on it, but of course, from my point of view, it is all over-dramatized etc. etc. etc.— one or two bits not so bad—Dylan Thomas said his [prerecorded] bits beautifully and the Welsh women in Part VII are all right.

To H.J.G., 26 November 1955   *Northwick Lodge*
Thanks for the *Wild Wales* Introduction returned. Don't know about it being used in suggested collection [*Epoch and Artist*], because Dent's, I presume, will sooner or later want to use it whenever they produce a new edition of the book—if ever they do.[12] It was a bore their not using it according to plan in 1954— the centenary year [of Borrow's tour of Wales]. They paid me only £20, a wretched sum, but *just* acceptable providing they used it—otherwise a feeling of frustration added to the meagreness of the fee disgruntles one a bit. How interesting that your mother should have been a Borrovian. It was something to do with period, you know. I was *exactly* the right 'age-group' to get the Borrow bug. I doubt if it's worth your time reading the stuff now. ...

The letter continues, in connection with an examination by X-ray, etc., which showed no disorder:

Lord, what extraordinary things these really modern X-ray photographic contraptions are. I was hours on a flat, blanketed surface, and every now and again a chap came along and said, 'I'm now going to take another series of photos'. Which done, one was left for a while, during which time one could ponder on

[12] David's Introduction to George Borrow's *Wild Wales* was published in the new (Everyman's Library edition (1958) and reprinted in *Epoch and Artist*, pp. 66–82.

the beneficent gadget-world and consider for a millionth time the world of the 'utile' and the world of 'sign' without getting any nearer a solution. I'm still utterly stuck on that problem—I *can't* see how it works.

I've not seen you since I went to get my C.B.E. It was (for me) a rather peculiar experience. I'm *very* glad that I was able to go— it just fitted in between one unwellness and the next! and even the day before I didn't think I should make it. It was a rather peculiar feeling being in that set-up *totally* alone—I can't quite describe it, but it rather felt as though one had strayed by mistake into somebody else's party—I felt rather like a bloke in disguise and under an assumed name—not really—but a little like that—not frightening at all—not remotely embarrassing, but just a bit odd, but not 'odd' either in any mysterious sense —just the oddness of finding oneself suddenly in an unexpected setting. One has to wait a good while in anterooms, which gave opportunity to consider a bit the architecture etc. Interesting how, no matter how 'baroque' the motifs in English places, the whole has a decidedly prim and sedate feeling. It's very big, isn't it—I mean large—the rooms—I should like to see it with all the chandeliers (is that how it's spelt?) lit. The Winterhalters are pretty shocking, I must say. There was a Rubens, or a reputed Rubens, in one corridor along which we filed to get into the throne room—but if it's a Rubens (as it says on the frame) it's not up to scratch.

In the room of investiture there was a gallery at one end and a military orchestra, and at the, so to say, 'altar' end a dais and throne of sorts, and in front of this Her Majesty presents the various insignia. Along both sides of the room and also beneath the musicians' gallery the guests of the recipients sit in great numbers on seats in tiers, and the recipients, having received their awards (and having had them taken from them and put into a little box, which is handed back to them by an official) are then guided back into the body of the throne room to watch the remainder of the proceedings (it's awfully like a school prize-giving, actually), which were over by 12.30, so that the actual investiture took about 1½ hours. Not bad.

There chanced to be in my group receiving the C.B.E. three or four officers, artillery, I think, in blue uniforms—red facings —spurs—*very* tight trousers—it was strange how these pre-khaki uniforms, pre-1900 in feeling, lent to their wearers a look much more far back still—so that one had an illusion of embryo side-whiskers and a lock falling over the forehead, and remembered the passage of the Alma or even Torres Vedras. It shows how the *slightest* visual thing can change the whole feeling—they even looked twice as 'English' as the civilians in morning dress surrounding them—of course, perhaps they were!

I had $77 from *Poetry*, Chicago, for the published fragment 'The Wall' [November 1955]. It's a peculiar little magazine. I thought the fee generous, don't you?

I wonder if you heard my broadcast on the 22nd [November 1955, Third Programme] about the Roman roads.[13] I thought it sounded all right, better than I feared. I had a note from Ronnie K[nox]—I'd written to him because I was invited but could not go, to a luncheon in his honour re Bible—did you go?—and he mentioned that he and Katharine Asquith heard and approved the talk.

To H.J.G., 18 May 1956   *Northwick Lodge*

I told Truslove & Hanson to send you Lloyd's *Hist[ory] of Wales*. I hope it's arrived safely. I thought you ought to possess this work now that you have become a *cymrodor*, so please accept it from me as a token with my best love.

Lloyd belonged, of course, to a past period of historical scholarship. This work was first published in 1911, and then again (with a fresh introduction touching the Roman period) in 1939, but it remains the only available history of Wales to the English-speaking world, and indeed even if one knew Welsh there is nothing in that language which precisely takes the place of Lloyd's book. I see the old boy was at Lincoln in 1883 and got a first in Classical Moderations in that year and then a first in Modern History in 1885. I think you'll find it quite enjoyable to dip into. I'm not suggesting that you should sit down and read

[13] 'The Viae', published in *Epoch and Artist*, pp. 189–95.

it all. But there it is, for reference. And, as a matter of fact, I think he wrote well, holds the attention, is civilized and scholarly, and one can feel also a strong emotion held totally in check. I believe he was a friend of Prof. [T.F.] Tout—what a long time ago such names evoke.

... I'm hoping to dine with Stephen Spender and Auden and Eliz[abeth] Glenconner at the end of the month. I do hope I'm O.K. by then as I want to go, for I very much want to see Auden again (but I hope 'Catholicism' won't again be the favoured subject of conversation, as it was when we dined at Garrick, if you remember).

... I still want to hear about your meeting with those Bucerites and Zwinglians and Melanchthonians & Co. What a business this religious thing is! Jolly tricky. By the way, what Melanchthon actually said to Cranmer was: 'in the Church it is more proper to call a spade a spade than to throw ambiguous expressions before posterity'. I looked it up after our phone conversation.[14] You will remember that Cranmer had the idea of convening a kind of Protestant General Council to offset, so to say, the Council of Trent, which began its sessions I think about 1545 (Cranmer's first Prayer Book was 1549, wasn't it, and I think it was some drafts for that book which occasioned Melanchthon's remark) and I think the above quotation is found in part of some correspondence about that proposed Council, but I'm not sure. Good Stanley Morison also quotes it in his most admirable book called *English Prayer Books* [1943], which you and M[argaret] gave to me for Christmas 1943.

What I very much wonder now is whether I'm really orthodox at all with regard to a certain aspect of the O[ld] T[estament]. (In fact it's the Jews that are the difficulty. I don't mean in any prejudiced way, but I do find a literal acceptance (and its implications) of the Israelitish history very difficult. But I shall have to explain what I mean at another time. No room here.

[14] Telephone conversations on such topics could last for an hour or more, and David's habit of holding the mouthpiece well away from himself—for fear of 'germs'—could be very trying to his partner in the discussion. Harman was a nonpareil of patience on such occasions, as was, later, Stanley Honeyman.

But worrying.) I'm sure I should have been a Marcion heretic except that I loathe all his ascetical thing—it's very peculiar— you see, Origen again—*bloody good and enlightened* about a lot of stuff but *quite awful* about this body thing.

I listened to Ed[ward] Sackville-West + Ben[jamin] Britten's thing based on the *Odyssey*. You know how I *loathe* that music + rhetoric thing, as e.g. in various works of radio'd entertainment that need not here be named. Well, for once I thought it did come off. I suppose because of the real genius of Britten as a composer, and I thought Ed. S.W.'s words awfully good too. It was all of a piece and very moving in places. It did one good thing to me. It made me re-read the *Odyssey*. I have here handy only that translation of [E. V.] Rieu. It is *most* peculiar. It seems to be quite deliberately full of cliché and a special kind of comicness, as e.g. 'Penelope was taken aback' and Vulcan, when he finds Venus with Mars, is made to say 'The sight cuts me to the quick'. It's pretty full, in fact chock full, of this sort of thing, and I take it that it *must be done on purpose* (maybe his purpose is to strip the work altogether of anything but the most commonplace—to make the telling really low-brow—I see the point but think it a mistake). However the *Odyssey* is rather like the Mass in one respect, chaps can do what they will with it but it never destroys the terrific shape. I find, on re-acquaintance, that this intervention-of-the-Gods thing which people say is so unconvincing and unreal and unlike anything we can be expected to feel, is, on the contrary, *extraordinarily* like 'reality'. Also, I find all the things Pallas Athene does and says in relation to Telemachus and Odysseus and Penelope very close indeed to our Christian ideas about—well, the saints and guardian angels and Our Lady especially—not that *I* know anything about these things, but I refer to what spiritual writers say. I find it incredibly moving where Athene does a little bit to help and then withdraws and lets the chap himself do something. I find that terribly convincing. It must be *astounding* in the original. Do you remember the bit where Athene makes Penelope go to sleep and then washes the tears from her cheeks with a special cosmetic that Aphrodite herself used for special occasions, and then she makes her taller and more shining and whiter than 'newly sawn ivory'. This was all in order to give the suitors an extra twisting —it comes not long before the great battle in the hall. And again in that battle Athene doesn't help with her full power until the issue is all but decided, and then high on the roof-tree she 'raised her deadly aegis' and then it's all up with 'em. Woven with the extreme savagery (by which I mean that the cultural condition was savage in the sense that Welsh or Irish or Zulu tribal society was savage) but woven with this (often glossed over by chaps) savage and repellent state there occur all the time emotions and chance suggestions of such tenderness and civility and sophistication that it makes one jump—and weep also. I can't explain what I mean—and as I say I've only this strange old Rieu translation, and before it was that trans. by Butcher and Lang (?) or somebody I used to read—more or less imitation O.T. prose—I wonder what the Loeb edition trans. is like? If it were Latin one would want text and trans. side by side, but as I know *no Greek whatever* there would be no point in having text. No more bloody room. Much love.   DAVID

To H.J.G., 24 August 1956   *Northwick Lodge*
. . . The French priest [Père] Jean Mambrino, Bobby [Speaight]'s friend, came again yesterday and discussed the *Ana.* from 4 p.m. to 8 p.m., so I was a bit exhausted. But it's astonishing how much he gets inside the meaning of it all and, thank God, really *likes* the best bits, and with a little complicated exegesis on my part gets hold of even the more insular complexes of allusion.

I've been doing a lot of going through old works and have found a quite nice pre-Eric, pre-'the movement', pre-R.C., immediately post-war (1919) oil sketch of a bit of downs behind Brighton.[15] It's astounding to see it and *then* look at something done in 1924 in the full tide of Ditchling etc. I also found a little oil life-study done in a jolly nice old-fashioned atelier in Kennington near the Oval. I use the Frog term because it really was the only 'art class' I've known in England that had some-

[15] This, or the painting for which it was a sketch, survives, but was unhappily much knocked about during the war.

thing of the continental thing. One just walked in, gave a chap a bob or something, signed a register (I think), tried to get hold of an easel or at least a stool and started to paint, after saying 'good evening' all round. It was run by a chap called Fipp or Fripp, I *think*, and even in 1919 or 1914 it was already a bit of an anachronism—very unlike the Board of Education art school I was attending at Camberwell before and just after the war. I (and two other friends) used to go to this place as well because one could draw or paint there any old time: on Saturdays or in the summer evenings when the regulation art schools were in vacation. So I'm glad to have found one surviving little oil study from this almost Whistlerian world—coke stove—big dusty plaster cast of the Venus of Melos and the Dying Gaul in one corner, a pall of thick cigarette smoke and the smell of linseed oil. It may have been at one time a warehouse of some sort —I remember it had a big wooden lock-up door (with a smaller door in it—like a stable rather). We used to argue a lot—and we used to think we were going to be terrifically great artists! The model used to undress behind a torn bit of curtain hanging from a ramshackle bent curtain-rod, if I remember aright—and the heat from the coke stove was terrific—but it was also a bit draughty and must have been actually very chilly on one side for the model and roasting on the other. I wish I had gone there more. (There were some who seemed to have been going for years and years, laboriously doing excruciatingly bad drawings —but awfully nice chaps—very courteous—at least that's the sort of memory I have.) But I really went only to get work done when it was not possible to go to the regulation place. I must say we were pretty single-minded, we just did drawings and paintings all day, every day, except Sunday. Pity it was so largely a wasted effort.

There is a kind of lack of economy of effort and a *real incompetence* that seems to cling to *all* that art-school, art-student, world. One ought to have become *much* more *able*, I mean, even just technically, than one did. But it was jolly nice, though we thought we were the saddest of men.

To H.J.G., 1 September 1956   *Northwick Lodge*

Before I forget: that French Jesuit [Père Jean Mambrino] who came to see me has gone back to France and he asked me to tell you that you are remembered each day in the *memento* in his Mass—until further notice! Incidentally, he phoned me just before his departure to say he'd just written a letter to the *T.L.Sup.* re *The Ana.*—because he was annoyed with what the chap said about it in that 'Religious Writing' article in the 'Frontiers of Literature' sup[plement] [*T.L.S.*, 17 August 1956]. So that his letter *might* be in next week's issue—we shall see. I have no idea what he's said, of course, or anything, but that he's written.[16] Thank you for what you say about *Ana*. I'm *mightily relieved* that on reading it again, and in quieter circumstances, you feel it holds up. That is a *real* encouragement—and Lord knows one seems to need reassurance over this matter, or, at least I do, for I get weary of it being just noted and more or less written off as a-curious-attempt-in-the-manner-of and specially I get weary of its being thought or called 'subjective', 'personal' —a curious work in its own twilight and so on.—Well, must not go on like this—but you know what I mean. So especial thanks for telling what you think of it after this lapse of time— and it alarms me that it was out in 1952 and now it's '56 and I've done virtually *nothing* much since—yet always seem to be messing about with something.

I've got so irritated with the *Times* leaders etc. that yesterday (Friday) I got a copy of the *Manchester Guardian* and found that (on this present situation) [i.e. the Suez crisis] it was far more to my liking. Though it was comfortless enough and confirmed my apprehensions. My fear is that there is, in certain quarters, such a strong desire to be rid of the present ruler of the Two Lands that *any* old excuse would be used to send a mixed force of Frogs and us from Cyprus to the Zone. Enough! ... I've just read, strange to say, C. S. Lewis's short autobiographical book *Surprised by Joy* [1955]. I'll speak more of it another time. But I

[16] A typed copy of this letter was later sent to David; it was published in the *T.L.S.* on 5 October 1956.

was astounded how virtually *identical* were things he read and thought about as a child and young man (the Welsh element apart) with those which I read etc. It was quite peculiar—almost uncanny—to find item after item occurring (including picture-postcards of Lily Elsie and Zena Dare). I suppose the truth is that in this country *c.* 1900–1914 two persons belonging to the middle class of more or less the same bent—no matter how different the circumstances—would land on the same stuff generally—but that it should be identical (or nearly so) in detail is interesting, don't you think? From Everyman's Library, the Home Univ[ersity] Library, the Temple Classics and even going to Denny's bookshop in the Strand to get them, all is the same. And then Chesterton later and the *Dream of the Rood* and then Langland and so on. Of course after that it's all *quite different*, because Lewis was formally educated, public school, univ. etc., but in just those early years the similarity of taste is extraordinary.

To H.J.G., 15 February 1957   *Northwick Lodge*
. . . It is *very strange* that he [G. M. Hopkins] spoke without appreciation of Langland, isn't it. That's the *only* serious black mark I know of in G.M.H. (Yet I have an *inkling* why.) Apropos of which three prolonged and loud cheers for the Third Programme and Elizabeth Zeeman of Girton because of this most admirable programme of readings of *Piers Plowman* which started on Sunday evening. Superb. Moreover, though P.P. is *very very difficult to read*, I think, without *some* grounding in Middle English, yet when *said* by a speaker competent in pronouncing Middle English most of the difficulties disappear, and one understands it almost word for word, or, at least, as much as one would understand, say, a modern countryman from some part of England where the pronunciation still remained strongly local and yokel. Mrs. Zeeman explained in an admirable introductory talk that she had 'modernized' it only to the very slightest degree and only in rare places where some modification seemed essential. I *feared what this might mean*, but, in the event, the fears were groundless . . . it is so lovely to hear the sounds as they were intended—it's a glorious poem and no mistake.

Mrs. Zeeman said it was, in her view, the best *long* poem in English, and then spoilt that by saying until we come to *Paradise Lost*. Bugger that, why she has to drag in a work of totally different *goodnesses and badnesses* I don't know, and it confused the issue altogether to my mind. *You don't want* to be reminded of Milton *at all* when in the presence of Langland. The singing at Evensong at King's College is well enough but *you don't want* to be reminded of it when Fr. Martin Larkin stands in the place of Melchisedec and begins to croak out the Preface to the Canon. *You don't want* to be told, when you are looking at the Ravenna mosaic of Theodora and her suite, that plastic art knew nothing finer till you come to da Vinci. Dearest Harman, I don't feel I know the answer to *anything any more*, but I *do* know that you can't really see what's 'right' with Langland unless you can see what's 'wrong' with Milton.

To H.J.G., 12 August 1957   *Northwick Lodge*

. . . You no doubt saw Pound's letter a few weeks back [T.L.S., 26 July 1957] explaining the limitations of his 'influence' with regard to things of Tom E[liot]'s poems? It was, in part, a dislike of arguing the toss about this kind of thing that made me refrain from writing to the *Lit. Sup.* myself about that article on Joyce's *Letters*, with ref. to *In Paren.*[17] Actually it would be true in the literal sense to say that my acquaintance with the work of Joyce was barely existent when I was writing the first part of *In Paren.*, in 1927–28 or so, and that round about the early 1930s René read out to me some of *Anna Livia*—and my knowledge of Joyce was virtually confined to that for a *disgracefully* long time. Indeed, I *owned* no copy of *Anna Livia* till you gave me a copy in 1939—two years after *In Paren.* was published. So for the reviewer to say that *In Paren.* was an 'imitation' of Joyce is very, very absurd on all kinds of grounds. Yet it would be quite absurd also to deny that Joyce, however obliquely, exercised a pervasive influence (or however one likes to put it) over all of

[17] The reviewer of *Letters of James Joyce*, ed. Stuart Gilbert (1957), had spoken of David as 'one of the few effective imitators Joyce has had' (*T.L.S.*, 24 May 1957).

us, rather as Picasso in the plastic arts. 'Influence' is not quite the word either. It is rather that problems of an artistic nature which many, many artists find themselves faced with at such and such a time are being solved in a specially valid manner by a particular man who may be little more than a name to these other artists. Yet critics, a few years later, would most certainly speak in terms of direct 'influence' and 'imitation' and so on. Art critics are specially unsatisfactory about this matter of influences. They would be serving a much more useful purpose if they examined the nature of the problem facing *all* artists in *such and such a phase* or *set-up*, trying to discover how the different artists solved, or did not attempt to solve, the problems presented.

Of course, the other remark in the Joyce article about *In Paren.* showed *another kind* of disregard of the facts of the case. The reviewer said *In Paren.* was based on an early Welsh epic, the *Gododdin*, but that this did not intrude on the reader (this was said as a compliment). Well, the scholars will not allow one to call *Y Gododdin* an epic. They call it a series of lyric fragments. Secondly, I had finished writing the text of *In Parenthesis* before I had read the English trans. of *Gododdin*. The bits from it which precede each part being inserted along with the titles of the parts when I was writing the Preface in Sidmouth in 1936–7. Of *course* I had known for many, many years *about* the battle at Catraeth, and knew there was a poem in Old Welsh about it— but that was *all* I knew until I got, in an old copy of the Cymrodorion publication, the Edward Anwyl trans. in, I suppose, 1935 or so. I cannot now recall. Of course all this is of no consequence, but it does show how inaccurate critics are in their assertions. I should have thought that *if* a past literary source were to be sought for in *In Parenthesis*, the works of Malory would be perhaps most noticeable in that allusions to passages of Malory are pretty frequent in parts, I noticed when last I looked at it.

To H.J.G., 11 July 1958   *Northwick Lodge*

. . . *Forty-two years ago*, yesterday and today, I was engaged in the operation in Mametz Wood described in Part 7 of *In Parenthesis*. By this hour (the evening of the 11th July) I was comfortably in bed in a *very, very, very hot* tent, of some sort, ten miles, I suppose, from the scene of conflict. I can't remember much about that part of it or getting back there, except I do recall being in a motor ambulance. I was *very* tired and slept and dozed in a troubled sort of way rather, and after that I remember the hot tent—(It was really a large marquee, halfway between the Front and the Coastal Ports, a Casualty Clearing Station, I suppose, but out of the Forward Zone, for girls weren't allowed near the front in *that* war—I believe: at least, not in 1916)—and (not unnaturally) the voice, the very English, very upper-class patrician 'decuriate' voice of a nurse of some sort. (Sorry about this, I can't find the word—I thought there was a word 'equestrian' meaning not *any longer* to do with horses but from the *class* of *equites*, but the dictionary seems to think that now it can be used only in the horseman sense, whereas I had thought of it as a quite common English usage for noble or aristocratic. I have all sorts of delusions of this sort, I find, about words.) I remember I thought it was the nicest sound in the world. *Voices are extraordinary*, I *think*, they have almost limitless power to deject, repel, bore, or elevate, enchant, console, attract and all the rest. I can't recall that we've ever discussed this thing about voices (the quality etc. of). But that particular voice was special for me, for I'd not heard an English woman's voice then since the previous December (1915), so I suppose that having come straight out of the 'bloody wood where Agamemnon cried aloud' and gone to sleep (and, I expect, injected with some opiate) and coming-to in the hot marquee, and being asked, in cultivated English, how I felt, left an indelible mark on me, and, indeed, it may be, it may *well* be (or perhaps this is all rubbish and that *everybody has* exactly the same feeling about this voice thing? *ΚΛΑΡΙΣΣΑ* [Clarissa Eden] has a voice which is an exact example of what I mean), that that is why, in subsequent years, I've felt, to a rather exaggerated extent, the potency of hearing a certain sort of voice as if it were a *physical touch*—a healing thing it is almost, in a sense, or anyway jolly nice—it could, of course, be truly awful if turned on one in anger.

The letter that follows was occasioned by the emotional disturbance referred to earlier. (Even more distressing letters could be quoted.)

To H.J.G., 27 June 1959   *Northwick Lodge*

... I know what a lot presses upon you and I *do* think it most kind (and, characteristically, civilized) of you to find time to write to me about that affair of my emotions. I *know no one* can say *anything* really to help much, and I am aware (painfully) of how tedious, in a sense, is the incessant bringing up of these things of the heart, even to one's dearest friends. And *you* have *always,* over the long years, been *exceptionally* considerate in *never* boring other people with these sorts of troubles, and I've always greatly respected that in you. So, in some ways, I feel pretty unrestrained and ashamed for the way in which I've made my moan and sad complaint during these last few weeks, or whatever it is. But I know you will forgive me and I do so *enormously* appreciate your and Margaret's sympathy. I don't think it's going to get much better for *quite a long while.* I think you are probably right actually about the advantages of *some* sort of (at least temporary) 'retirement', but these things are so incredibly difficult to judge, in practice—what actually to do in a given case?—it's so appallingly hard to make decisions of what might be called, I suppose, a tactical, or even strategic, nature, when one has *no* real idea how the front runs, or what the objectives are or, indeed, what the war aims are!—but one knows only that one's own trenches appear to be overrun and that one is not much of a soldier in any case (cf. 'O my! I don't want to die, I want to go home'). I'm sorry for this rather ridiculous analogy, but all I'm trying to say is that my feelings are, in one sense, of exceptional confusion. They are not in the least confused deep inside me, for I know down to the last, small, detail *what* those things are that, in this present situation, so distress me (though I am surprised at the *intensity* and *ubiquitousness* of the distress), but, having said that, I have no notion of (as they say) 'what to do for the best', and I've no doubt that one may very well have made and will continue to make, just

[176]

precisely the wrong decisions, for after all the things that cause the distress are hardly patient of exposition. For example, I *know* that an involvement in 'Welshness' has an awful lot to do with my intrication with Elri [Valerie Price, later Mrs. Wynne-Williams]. I'm paying dearly for my doctrine of *signa*! She's the only Welsh woman I've ever met really, and it came about through those letters to the *Times* in such a 'fatalistic' and unplanned manner that perhaps I may be forgiven for mistakenly thinking that it *must* in *some way* be significant and not without meaning. Now I've got to try to accustom myself to the truth that it is, after all, perhaps, or probably, or certainly, just an accident and no more. This is what I *hate* and this is what makes me *weep* (for not only did I half expect her to marry this bloke [Michael Wynne-Williams], but, as you know, I've never wished for marriage in itself, *very far from it*). In *some* ways the whole situation is very unreal—but can't go into the matter further here. I've been *very* aware of this all the time, of course.

I can almost hear the laughter of the gods. I believe in the reality of 'Romantic Love'. I always have. I know it's quite different from the Christian sacramental thing of marriage, and quite distinct from the Classical thing—a legalistic thing, but still, even so, they did pray to *Venus Verticordia* to keep their hearts true to their spouses—and that's a thing a lot of bastards don't know who talk much of 'Venus'. People's *ignorance* is becoming a real and terrible menace to any dear and subtle relationship.

Sunday June 28th, after lunch. I went to Mass and heard the most appalling rubbish talked in the bloody sermon.

A good many years later Valerie Wynne-Williams gave her own account of their meeting: '. . . I had written some letters to the *Times* [e.g., 5 June 1958] with regard to Welsh affairs. Dafydd also contributed some letters. One of them [11 June 1958] is in *Epoch and Artist* [p. 54]. I later invited Dafydd to a Plaid Cymru party I was giving. He did not attend but telephoned and asked me to meet him at Northwick Lodge. Michael (whom I later married) went with me on my first visit to Harrow. Later Dafydd told me that he had expected a fifty-year-old blue-stocking. I was twenty-four at the time and anything but an intellectual, but we did share a deep and caring love of Wales. . . .'

It is a tribute both to Dr. Stevenson and to David's own determination and good sense that the story ended in a more real delight. The Princess, young, beautiful, charming, intelligent, married Prince Charming, lived happily ever after, and remained a solace to David until his death.[18]

To H.J.G., 18 February 1960   *Northwick Lodge*

When I phoned the other evening and, as Malory would say, 'made great dole out of measure' (for which I'm sorry) I meant to tell you (apart from asking you about Selene, Parthenos, etc.) that I had listened with interest to the broadcast produced by Christopher Sykes called 'K. of K.'. As I listened to the account of the dejection and consternation the news of Kitchener's 'death by water' caused to those at home (apart from the Government, who seem to have been somewhat relieved!) my mind went back to a communication trench somewhere in the La Bassée area, where I chanced to be when the news reached the legionaries on the Wall, so to say. And knowing your fondness for the contactual and the concrete, I thought it would amuse you (and possibly Christopher S. also) to hear about it—and we all need amusement these days!

I shall of necessity have to 'romance' quite a bit, because I can recall only a *mood* and vaguely an actual scene—*very dim.* But I seem to recall how a chap came from the rear up this communication trench towards our front trench, saying, seriously but rather excitedly, that 'K' had been drowned at sea, and a linesman (*if* it was a linesman) stopped what he was doing, for a brief moment, and said something to this effect: 'Oh, 'e 'as, 'as 'e. Well, roll on fuckin' Duration', and then

---

[18] I associate Valerie with a typical example of the readiness with which all David's friends ministered to him (it would be unkind, maybe, to say that he was lazy and spoilt—let us say 'constructively inactive' and 'joyfully served'). I was with David as he was boiling water to make tea: boiling it in a small saucepan. An awkward and ridiculous method, said Valerie. David made those mumblings, well known to his friends, through which one heard '. . . all so difficult . . . shops—impossible . . . *can't* get out . . .'. Valerie left the room and returned in a very few minutes with an excellent little tin kettle—welcomed as though it were the golden fleece.

resumed whatever he was engaged upon. . . . Actually it rather reminds me of that taxi-man who said to Margaret, of General Weygand, early in the last war, 'What's 'e got up his sleeve?— 'is bloody arm.' Do you remember?

P.S. One nice thing has happened, the Welsh Section of the Arts Council have written to me offering me a prize of £100 (if I would accept it!) for *Epoch and Artist*. Isn't that a jolly nice help, *totally* out of the blue. I *could* not have been more surprised or more gratified, especially just now.

To H.J.G., 12 March 1960   *Northwick Lodge*

. . . I'm struggling with my Tristan picture [*Tristan and Iseult*, 1962]. I've transferred it now on to another piece of paper— which is a ghastly operation—but I could not do what I wanted with it on the original paper, and I did not want to lose the feeling of it by making the endless alterations and adjustments which I wish to make. So there was no alternative but to transfer it. Now I can proceed in my accustomed manner with some sort of freedom. 'My accustomed manner' is not meant to sound grand—it means merely nothing more than that I can now erase and re-draw a hundred times if necessary.

The first one now becomes rather like the *natural scene* and the one I'm working on the actual 'art-work'—the offering is the same, but under another mode, as it were. Though that is a bit much by way of expression, but something of that sort. I don't know whether I shall pull it off—it's the hardest thing I've tried to do—I don't know why it is so. I think it is because I have to find out so many, many things in some detail about the ship and its tackle. For *my* kind of drawing one *either* has to have the object *in front of one*—as flowers or trinkets or what not, *or* one has to find out the principle by which things work, helped out by memories of the sea and odd sketches, plus photographs, and not least, talks with dear Mick [Richey], that great navigator. (Only all the bloody ropes are still worse and the picture is really only in its earliest stages in one way.) Don't know why I should inflict all this on you—perhaps it's to avoid getting on with the job!

After all the trouble that David took to get every detail right, so far as he could, including the exact disposition of the stars on St. Brigid's Day, 1 February, he deliberately (as he admits in another letter) allowed himself to show the timbers of the vessel outside the planking. Three cheers, in his own words, for the Lesbian rule (cf. Aristotle's *Nic. Ethics*, 1137b: 'the rule adapts itself to the shape of the stone—it is not rigid': a simile very dear to David).

To R.H., 9 April 1960   *Northwick Lodge*

It was a *great treat* to see you again, and Joan—thank you *very much* for coming. I was so glad to see Joan looking so *well and young*—as for *you*, of course, you look *exactly the same* as you did 30 years ago except less thin in the face. What awfully nice children Rosi(a?)lind—how *do* you spell it? Is it Rosalind?—and Robin are. I thought those sailing-vessel models most beautiful— how *does* he do it—and on so tiny a scale and looking absolutely convincing.—I suppose it's the 'innocent eye' again. I loved the great drawing of the great ship with its *incredible* number of sails! Again the innocent eye. They get the entire feeling without, of course, realizing it. So when he asked me to do the billowing sail I hardly knew what to do, because all I could do was introduce a kind of academic impressionism—and it is precisely *the absence of this quality* which made his drawing so good. It's an impossible problem. (When a child asks one to draw something one feels rather as though one were being asked, unwittingly, to teach them a really *bad* thing—it's an appallingly difficult problem and there ain't no answer to it either within our civilizational phase.) I'm sorry I had nothing to offer them but china tea and biscuits—not exactly exciting for either of them, I fear.[19]

Where did Rosalind get her auburn hair from? Either Joan or you must have a fairly close ancestor who had red hair, because, I seem to remember, in that book about nigrescence, that the

[19] The children adored it: very grown-up. Robin was enthralled by David's S.M.L.E. rifle, obtained by a friend in the War Office, with the firing pin removed. Rosalind gathered up, cleaned and restored to good order all David's prematurely discarded 'biro' pens, and received later a fine polychrome letter of thanks.

incidence of red hair is governed by redness of hair in some near ancestor—I forget how it works. I know it's getting less, along with the fair-heads. . . .

After several pages on the subject of the Goidels and the relation between the Welsh and Irish tales:

Sunday. Sorry about this boring letter—I meant to write you a proper one but got bogged down in these bloody theories about Celts.

It is now Sunday and I want to post this—tell me when you actually receive it—if you do. These sodding posts are the limit. I hope you do that thing for the *Twentieth Century Review* or whatever it's called—whatever you say will be worth while. But it's a bloody bore doing it at all—I well know that.

Can't get on at all with my picture [*Tristan and Iseult*]. Feel quite exhausted with the complications of it. What a long time ago it is when I did the bloody things about 20 times more quickly—but that will never return. Last year when I was seeing Elri (that's the Welsh form of Valerie) I felt quite young again though it was only a bloody pain all the time—but now I feel useless and agéd—I am reminded of old Fr. John Gray saying of poor Reggie Savage: 'The man was born to failure'—do you remember his saying that?—on the lawn outside the porch at Pigotts, looking towards the orchard.

I never thanked Joan (Siwan) for her most welcome gifts—*munera* of huge eggs. I've never seen such huge eggs—I've eaten four of them already—I like eggs best of all—well, and olives and lemon and sugar. I drink hot lemon and sugar in water every evening—about six lemons a day—because I must drink *something*—and whisky is impossible except in small quantities, for a number of excellent reasons.

Oh, and the flowers—I do thank Joan for the flowers—they look heavenly now I've put them into a thing on the table by the window. There don't seem to be any real flowers any longer. The sods one buys at the florists are bloody useless—God! what a civilization. One last thing about Celts: if you look at the map and turn it round so that the top is *East* and not *North* you'll see what the ancients meant when they said that 'Ireland is an island opposite northern Spain'—the chaps are finding increasing evidence for continuous direct communication by *thalassic routes* between Gaul and Ireland and Wales and the Isles (of Scotland) —we get so used to thinking of the Dover-Calais-Basle-Rome route (made worse by Belloc & Co.) that we forget that after the Angle and Saxon invasions the Western fringes still had direct contact by this route—so that St. David and St. Patrick and other Celtic saints went to Lerins off the south coast of France—and Lerins is believed to have had an ascetic tradition coming from the Thebaid in Egypt. That accounts for a lot. There are *other* aspects of this 'Celtic' thalassic imperium in later times which I can't go into here.

The picture of Aphrodite over the fireplace is called *The Leeshore*. In my heart of hearts I don't like that either—it's too *tight* and *fussed*. What I *want* to do is one full of all the complications and allusions but executed with the freedom and directness that used to be in my still-life and landscapes—that's what I want to do before I die.

The picture, which so far as I know has never been reproduced, represents the wounded Aphrodite—wounded in the thigh, and not, as in the *Iliad*, in the hand—lying down and looking out over the battlements of Troy, with ships of war on the broad Hellespont. To my mind, neither tight nor fussy but full of delight.

To R.H., the Glorious First of June 1960   *Northwick Lodge*
. . . Still trying to get into a proper shape that confounded *Dream of P[riva]te Clitus*. Surprising what an awful number of hold-ups one has in a thing, once one tries to really perfect it, as far as one can. Tom told me a very good Spanish proverb: 'The best is the enemy of the good.' Awfully true, isn't it, of anybody's best, even if it's a poor best only. Much love to Joan. (Please thank her especially for the eggs.) And you.   DAI
I'm calling those saffron-haired girls in the Urbs 'meretricious sirens'. I like always, if one gets a chance, to use an English word which gives a kind of back indication of its factual and bodily origin.

[182]

Very exciting about the possible Roman remains at Pigotts. I used always to fancy that somehow the Romans had been up there—I don't know why. In fact, in about 1940 in a discarded writing I wrote of a Jutish chieftain that 'he burned twelve Welshmen in Pigotts garth and had his oats in Speen',[20] it's strange.

I'm in rather a state about going up to N. Wales [Bangor] to get this doctorate—I don't know how to organize myself and it's all got mixed up with the other thing—I've still had no word from her [Valerie], and somehow I thought I should.

In the end David did not make the journey to receive his honorary degree from the University of Wales (University College, Bangor).[21] In a much later letter to Harman Grisewood (see pp. 211–12) he speaks of his feelings about 'going to places'—or rather, not going.

To H.J.G., 28 March 1961   *Northwick Lodge*

When I phoned you on Monday evening to give you a general situation report of things agreeable and otherwise, I forgot one thing that I especially wished to tell you. It was to say how much I've enjoyed—indeed, been most delighted by—that Gilgamesh Epic [trans. N. K. Sandars, 1960] which you gave me for my birthday. It's *marvellous*. I knew a bit about it long ago from my cousin Norman Daniel, who worked out in Meso-pot[amia] with the British Council. He, and also Richard Kehoe and others, have told me a bit about the Epic of Gilgamesh but I had *no* idea how truly astounding it is. It's got *everything* and is as fresh as the morning. All the whole hero thing in a way. It gave me a curious feeling—like seeing what was behind—oh, I don't know what, but classical stuff, Celtic stuff (very much that). And now on reading the long introduction, I find it mentions this—the Welsh and Irish hero-type and so on. The story of the Flood is, as you know, in it and it is that that chaps talk most about (I suppose because of the biblical Hebraic story of Noah. Actually this is altogether different in feeling and in

---

[20] This reappeared in *The Sleeping Lord*, p. 102.
[21] See my *A Commentary on* The Anathemata *of David Jones* (1977), p. 219.

content—*quite* different) but actually I found that the least interesting part, although it's awe-inspiring in its barbaric primitivity, yet it shows extraordinary and touching awareness of all sorts. A huge feeling of the tragedy of the human condition. I expect I may exaggerate—perhaps it's just coming on it fresh—for one never expects to come on a fresh thing now!

The translation seems to me *in every way admirable*—perfectly straight modern English, but not losing the *poiesis*. *What* a relief from that confounded attempt of [C. H.] Dodd & Co. and their New English Bible. But there again I mustn't be unfair, because there are, in the case of the *Epic of G.*, no other translations echoing in the mind. So, if N. K. Sandars, the translator,[22] played freely with the original text of the tablets, I should be none the wiser. But I have *the feeling* that it's pretty literal and it's *certainly* most awfully good. Thank you, dearest Harman, for sending it to me. It quite stimulated me, for a short while, anyhow!

To H.J.G., 9 October 1961   *Northwick Lodge*

... drawings of that sort with chaps in sun-helmets and moustaches and revolver-holsters, sitting on ammunition boxes etc., are one of the main memories I have of the innumerable papers and magazines which my father brought home from his office every week-end when I was a little boy. Interesting, these accidental early associations. One lived in a kind of Kipling-conditioned world without knowing it. I expect it had a disastrous effect on my artistic apperceptions—as is instanced in the decline from the bear that I did when I was seven to the rubbish I was doing when I was fourteen. It was A. S. Hartrick at Camberwell art school who *first* turned the tide *a bit*, and then, after the war, my contact with Eric and, of course, a little before that, with the 'Movement', i.e. the salutary effects of what is lumped together under the term 'post-impressionism'. It's rum to think back over all this, but your sending me the picture in the *Listener* raised all these thoughts.

[22] For David's meeting with Nancy Sandars, see below, p. 213.

I am now, dearest Harman, in a pretty big muddle inside my-self—I can't see my direction and I'm beginning to feel a lot older than I did only a couple of years back. But I'm certain that I owe a huge debt to influences and persons operating from round about the middle of the 1st World War and continuing until, well, I suppose the late 1930s. The Catholic Church, people such as *yourself* in particular, and Christopher D[awson] and Tom B[urns], etc. etc. etc. Joyce, of course, Tom E[liot] evidently, Spengler, [Maurice] de la Taille, von Hugel, *all* seemed to provide a kind of 'unity of indirect reference'[23] which seemed to tie-up with what little artistic perceptions one had by nature oneself, and gave edge and certainty and conviction to one's work. But of late years I seem to have lost this unity of purpose, or whatever it was, so it's been largely a matter of just 'going on' without much inward feeling. For one thing, I find (or think I find) such appallingly little comprehension among the many younger friends (for all their *kindness* and *goodness* to me) of the essential issues—we seem to be right back, in a kind of confused 'democratized' coarsened form to problems that in the 1930s you and I thought were solved, at least for our lifetime.

It's no use cracking on, I know, and I know that you, of all people, understand about all this and feel the immediate impact of it far more than I do, in my more or less 'Ivory Tower' exist-ence. But it does sap the well-spring and make one feel pretty helpless, if not bogus.

To H.J.G., 11 January 1962   *Northwick Lodge*

... I *had* to tell you about that Thackeray thing—'Well, sir, I think I know the time of day'. I laughed like anything when I heard it and I still chuckle over it. It has that absolute authen-ticity, hasn't it? It reminds me of things that some of my mother's relatives used to say, when I was a little tiny boy, at the turn of the century. I recall an old man who wore *always* a silk hat and who used to say, '*Don't* he put the butter on'—perhaps after

[23] The quoted phrase is taken from Bickford's *Certainty*, a book introduced by Donald Attwater to Capel-y-ffin. See Eric Gill's *The Necessity of Belief* (1936), p. 128, with a reference to Fr. Martin D'Arcy's *The Nature of Belief*.

listening to some sermon—he used to come in after church sometimes and have a whisky and soda out of one of those tumblers [*drawing*] (they seem to have disappeared) on a silver tray. My father never drank anything—but there was always whisky for these odd relatives. What a changed world it is. There was then a much more *unified culture*, I think, for all this bloody stuff about democracy, for as you know we were pretty poor, but the standard of living was, I think, pretty high in some respects—unless of course one was *really* poor, and then it was *awful*, no doubt. But even for them nothing was ersatz and now *everything* is ersatz, it seems to me.

To H.J.G., 7 March 1962   *Northwick Lodge*

Thank you tremendously for the photograph of the page from the log-book of the *Euryalus* [Captain Blackwood's frigate at Trafalgar]—which I found exceedingly moving. I've put it in a small frame I had, and it hangs next the fireplace. I wonder why it is that technical expressions, within certain contexts, are so *overwhelmingly* moving, in fact to tears. I've never quite been able to analyse why this should be.

'. . . thirty-three Sail of the Line, five Frigates and two Brigs—light winds and haze, with a great swell from the westward . . . took our station on the Victory's Larboard Quarter . . . the enemy wearing and coming to the wind on the Larboard Tack. . .' You almost feel you're there. It does more than whole reams of 'poetry' can do. And there's something profoundly touching about this very 'pre-Break' looking document with the pathetic and inexact ruled lines of the columns of the analysis of the signals given and received—I wonder whose job that was—some midshipman, do you suppose?—how totally other it all is in feeling from our streamlined, efficient, dehumanized set-up.

Anyway, I love looking at it, and thanks very much for sending it. It gives me great pleasure and much further occasion for my endless cogitation on this tricky business of—well, of our old friend 'The Break'—the endless ramifications of which seem *more and more* difficult to determine. As I am indeed finding at this very moment, for I'm engaged upon that bloody awful talk which I foolishly promised I'd do for [T. S.] Gregory on 'Poetry and Religion' [Third Programme, 26 April 1962][24]—'My colonial, wardha bagful!' It's hopeless, and, what's worse, I *can't any longer* seem to summon up enough interest (or whatever the word is) in the damned problem—or drag out that old laborious stuff about the 'utile' and all the rest of it. But that's all I can try to do. I ought not to have taken it on, because I've got so many things undone that I ought to have done—two or three 'commissions' (drawings), and I've made virtually *no* progress with the bits and pieces of 'poetry' that I'm supposed to be assembling for my next 'volume', for the prosecution of which I was granted that Bollingen thing.[25] I'm beginning to feel that I'm not fulfilling the contract, so to say, and like the bloke in the Gospel who failed to do business with his Lord's money and so did not enlarge it, and got a rocket in consequence. So, one way and another, I'm doing a good bit of mea culpa, mea culpa, mea maxima culpa, but to no effect. What a bugger it all is.

I listened to the radio all the afternoon when the American astronaut was circling the world—I found it terribly impressive —again because of this technological thing. I loved hearing his actual voice giving all kinds of unintelligible code numbers etc. to some other bloke down below. Jolly nice the way he kept on talking about the 'beauty' of what he saw. But what extraordinary limitations these American chaps have in expressing themselves—jolly nice in a way. I thought the exchange of words between Kennedy and Glenn at the end of the exploit were both moving and pathetic in the utter inadequacy of what they said. Talk about British understatement! It was just as though a mate of some bloke who'd just come off a rugby field had rung up to say 'Jolly good show—I'll be seeing you, what about a wet'. It's interesting how *all* Americans of whatever sort or condition use exactly the same language, no matter whether the occasion is trivial or profound. I've had opportunity to

[24] Published (as 'Use and Sign') in *The Dying Gaul*, pp. 77–85.
[25] In 1960 David received a grant from the Bollingen Foundation for work on the collection of writings which much later became *The Sleeping Lord* (1974).

notice that here in this house, where a year or so ago lots of U.S.A. personnel lodged—from G.I.s to chaps of some rank. It was always 'Gee, I guess that's fine', whether the cat had had kittens, or the electric light had been made, at last, to function, or they were discussing some momentous world event, or were looking at one of my pictures. They might have been business-men from Utah or corporals from Florida, but their speech-forms were *exactly* the same, no matter what the occasion. I should think it the most unified culture that has ever existed. Rather like that damned boring so-called 'Samian ware' that everywhere, from Mespot to the Clyde, was on the tables of the Romans.

To H.J.G., 22 May 1962   *Northwick Lodge*

Glad you liked that article about *In Parenthesis* by John H. Johnston.[26] All things considered, it's the only decent analysis of *I.P.* that's ever appeared. I agree that even he does not properly understand the altogether different point of departure of my stuff from the writing of 'poetry' or 'prose' as conceived by 'writers', whether good or bad, from blokes like Rupert Brooke right on through Sassoon and even Owen and Graves and *even* T.S.E[liot]. It is next to impossible for me to indicate what the difference is.

Certainly the impact on me of reading *The Waste Land* in *circa* 1926 or 1927 was considerable. And René read *Anna Livia* to me in about 1928, about the time I met you, when I had re-turned from Capel-y-ffin to live again in London.

Ezra Pound I had not read at all—except for some treatise on his sociological and economic theories and his book on Proven-çal poetry, and T. E. Hulme and bits of Aristotle and transla-tions of St. Thomas, and 'the pseudo-Denis', and Père Maurice de la Taille and von Hugel. These were the 'formative' works, as you know, which in those years much influenced me. It's all so totally different from the 'literary tradition' of the other

[26] 'David Jones: The Heroic Vision', in *The Review of Politics*, January 1962; an enlarged version is printed in Johnston's *English Poetry of the First World War* (Princeton, N.J., and London, 1964).

writers of the period, but it's damned hard to explain—in fact I think it's impossible at this date. I can *quite* see *why* chaps think *I.P.* and the *Anathemata* are based stylistically on Joyce or Pound, but it happens not to be historically true. As you know, and you are about the only person who does know, because you were the only person to whom I read the stuff and discussed it with you as it developed, all I tried to do was to see how the business of 'form' and 'content' worked in writing in relation to what I knew of how it worked in drawing. All of which is appallingly difficult to explain to chaps who, for one reason or another, think 'academically' or, on the other hand, 'imaginatively'—in the Yeats tradition. I feel that my stuff, such as it is, is much more 'prosaic' than they imagine. I really do try to 'proceed' (as old John-Baptist Reeves would say) 'from the known to the unknown'.

It's terribly difficult to find the words to convey this quite practical and un-highfalutin approach across to chaps. Indeed I despair of doing so. It's largely the same over my watercolours. Chaps refer to the 'mystery' or 'subtlety' or 'illusiveness' or 'fragility' or 'waywardness' or 'complexity' or 'fancifulness' etc. etc.—Well, Christ almighty! what else is there in a bunch of flowers or a tree or a landscape or a girl or a sky, but these qualities? By the severest logic one must somehow, if possible, capture *something* of these qualities if the thing is going to be any damn good. It isn't the artist's 'fancy' or 'imagination' that imposes these qualities on a work—the blasted stuff is there as plain as a pikestaff—the bugger of it is how to 'transubstantiate' these qualities into whatever medium one is using, whether paint or words or whatever. It's only about once in a hundred times that one can come near to doing this. Must go to bed, it's 2.25 a.m. Bloody tired.

Tuesday morn, about 11.30. Sequentia evangelii secundum Jones! ... sorry for the blasphemy. As I was saying, it's terribly hard to get the stuff we were talking of last night, yet in the interests of truth I suppose one must try.

In various letters I've written to Prof. John H. Johnston I've told him as best I could the circumstances of how *In Paren.* came to be written. It would be untruthful to say that Tom E[liot]'s

Waste Land and also René's reading to me *Anna Livia* did not influence the 'form' of *I.P.*, I think. But what I've tried to tell Johnston is that in my view the whole business of critics endlessly nosing around for 'influences' is a bore and virtually useless and deceptive, and gives quite a false impression of how an artist works. Trying to rack my brain for 'influences' makes me more and more convinced of this. It's more the whole conditioning civilizational situation into which one was born that determines the 'form'. Browning, for example, gave me a bit of a clue of how something *might* be managed, and then the sudden appearance of Hopkins and my reading of Skelton and one's interest at that time in 'negro spirituals' and God knows what all, seemed to 'click' in some way with all kinds of childhood things—nursery rhymes, early readings of Malory and, of all people, Macaulay, and fragmentary bits of Welsh stuff, and the Anglo-Saxon Chronicle and Norse sagas, and Caesar's Gallic Wars, and all kinds of popular cockney songs, and bits of the metaphysical poets, and Lewis Carroll and Lear and God! it's absurd to try to trace the differing and very disparate strands, and behind that being brought up on the Authorized Version of the Bible and the Book of Common Prayer. And then all this heterogeneous stuff given new point and cohesion by becoming a Catholic in 1921 and reading Maritain and meeting you and Tiger Dawson and Tom [Burns] and those various blokes we used to talk with in the late 1920s and early 1930s. But how the hell can one explain all this—you can't.

. . . I am at the moment in a very *great* muddle about 'religion', but I do still feel that the Church, in showing-forth the Passion under this art form, commits us irrevocably to this basic notion of 'art'—as a thing which 'shows forth' under another form existing realities. Even the old 'penny catechism' was nearer the mark as 'art criticism' when it says that the Mass is a showing again in an unbloody manner what was done once and for all in a bloody manner, or words to that effect. I am sure that some such concept is the inner secret and nodal point of *all* the arts.

The silly and misleading distinction between 'abstract art' and 'figurative art' seems to me now to be a more and more out-moded and 'period' distinction. Like all 'heresies', 'abstract painting' had the enormous strength of a single-mindedness, and re-asserted lost truths. But, unless I'm very mistaken (and I may well be), it can't in itself be sufficient. It's produced the most splendid and invigorating works of great sensitivity, and un-doubtedly had a kind of prophetic quality—that is to say our moving away from the animalic and the creaturely into the cosmic spaces—perhaps it'll work out all right—I just don't know. Perhaps one is too old to now grasp its development. That is a thing one must always bear in mind. It is *terribly* easy to fail in one's apperception of some newer thing. For example my own appreciation stops short at somewhere round about T.S.E.'s *Four Quartets*, and, in the visual arts, somewhere round about Harry Moore's work—especially his earlier work and especially his 'Shelter' drawings [1943]—so it looks to me as though one were getting pretty old and 'blimpish'. I just bloody well don't know.

I doubt, personally, whether I, myself, shall ever do any half as good as I used to do in the 1930s, as far as painting is con-cerned. I still believe in *The Anathemata*. I think that's O.K. and a lot better than *In Parenthesis*—but whether I've anything more to say seems to me to be bloody doubtful. The whole cultural situation has changed so *rapidly* and I work so *slowly* and with such misgivings—almost paralysing misgivings—that I just don't know.

Unless *certain* things are taken for granted it's well-nigh bloody impossible for my sort of stuff to mean anything. I don't resent this, and I see why it must be so, but it does account for my smallness of production. 'The Break', by Christ, what a break it is now! It is partly all this that makes me so worried about the new U.S.A. *putsch* on my behalf.[27] I feel bogus, and about as dated as *The Yellow Book*.

[27] In 1962 the Chilmark Press, New York, published an American edition of *In Parenthesis*, followed in 1963 by *The Anathemata*; paperback editions of both books appeared shortly thereafter in the U.S., *In Parenthesis* in 1963 and *The Anathemata* in 1965.

The term 'The Break', which plays so large a part in David's writing and thought, was first used, I suspect, by Hilaire Belloc, who applied it in a religious and political context to the move from the theocentric world of the Middle Ages to the man-centred world of 'modern history' and particularly to the breach with Rome and the snapping of continuity with Roman tradition at the Reformation. Eric Gill adopted the term, but took it further by extending it to what he regarded as an inevitable consequence of the humanism of the Renaissance, the rise of capitalism, industrial production, division of labour, and the 'reduction of the worker to a sub-human condition of intellectual irresponsibility'. David complicated the issue when he moved the term into the field of aesthetics and the fine arts.

To H.J.G., 28 May 1962   *Northwick Lodge*

... I'm trying to re-write that thing that you liked—the dinner party with the old Roman blimp and the girl and the subaltern in Jerusalem at the time of Our Lord's Passion.[28] I used to feel it was crude and impious, but on re-reading it, I think I can make something of it—at least I hope so. And I don't much care *any longer what chaps think*. I'm also trying to re-write a thing I did in 1940 (or thereabouts) about a conversation between Judas and Caiaphas. I think, perhaps, I may as well make public all the stuff *behind The Anathemata* that I had suppressed. They can be fragmentary only, but that's what I'm engaged upon. In a way they seem more 'contemporary' than when I wrote them. They are beastly in a way and brutal, but I suppose they had better come out—I don't know.

To H.S.E., 16 September 1963   *Northwick Lodge*

... I was greatly honoured and *extremely astonished* by a visit at Whitsuntide by Stravinsky and his wife. He was on a visit to London and apparently had read something or other of my work and wanted to come and see me. I said, when phoned up about it, that I would go to London to his hotel, as he is over eighty, but they said no, he wants to come and see some of your visual art. Well, they came, and were absolutely sweet, both of

[28] This is one of several unpublished sequences now being prepared for publication.

them, straightforward, direct, appreciative, amusing and re-laxed. They didn't stay for long because he had to be back in London, but it was a jolly nice visit. I was especially surprised because the world of music is largely outside my world—I mean I know so little about it—and don't get much beyond plainsong and early polyphony and folk- and primitive music all of which have for many years now meant a lot to me. (I seldom play the gramophone, but I have a record of Guillaume Dufay, lived about the time of Joan of Arc—an *astoundingly* beautiful can-zone, a setting to words by Petrarch, beginning *Vergine bella, che di sol vestita*, and a marvellous setting to the Antiphon *Alma Redemptoris Mater, quae pervia coeli* etc., and another in alternate verses of Dufay's polyphony and plainchant, of the *Vexilla Regis*, my favourite liturgical hymn.) I did not know at the time of his visit that he was a close friend of John XXIII, who, when he was Patriarch of Venice, had had all Stravinsky's sacral music played in the Cathedral at Venice. He also had lunch with him alone in Vatican after John had been made Pope. John had written a large work on St. Charles Borromeo, and Stravinsky is one of the world's greatest authorities, it appears, on some composer—forgotten his name [perhaps Gesualdo]—of that period, and they talked a lot about that, so that's a new light on John. I mean one had been told of his peasant virtues, his skill in diplomacy, his great and evident charity and holiness, his un-breakable determination, his humour and much besides, but not of his interest in, and real knowledge of, music. (It was Mrs. [Natasha] Spender who told me about this, Stephen Spender's wife, she's a musician and knew Stravinsky. Stephen came with Stravinsky when he came to see me.)

The 'Desmond correspondence' in the letter that follows is a series of letters written to Fr. Desmond Chute by David in the months follow-ing the publication of *The Anathemata*. They came into my hands after Desmond's death, and I returned them to David. What happened to Desmond's letters to David I do not know. Metrical or rhythmical analysis was tedious to David, so that the 'near-Alexandrine' of a line on the last page of the poem ('If not by this Viander's own death's monument') meant nothing to him.

To R.H., 27 September 1963   *Northwick Lodge*

I had written or half-written a long meandering letter to you but decided to start again, having just received your parcel with that Desmond correspondence in it. Thank you for sending it to me. No, I'm glad you had a look at it and found it of interest. I've just had a slight look at it but couldn't read it properly as it seemed a weary going over obvious points and the remembrance of the sweat of writing it all got me down. But it was jolly nice of him to want to know and take all the trouble he did and better still that he really did *like* it. I agree about the questions touching 'prosody' are a bore. It's a curious thing these chaps have. I remember having a *charming* letter from Laurie [Laurence] Binyon, in appreciation of *In Paren.* but which asked *all sorts* of questions as to why I changed from dactylic rhythm here to something or other else there and then to lines that could be—I don't know what, something else, well, I felt almost ashamed to say that I didn't know I had! It is, as you say, merely a question of making the bloody thing as you want it to be—so that the 'form' follows the 'content' and, as you say, you bloody well *know* if it's right or wrong, that is you know if it fits with what you intend. *Of course*, what you intend may be all balls, but that's another matter. But I find it incredibly hard to convince chaps of this. They somehow won't believe that that's how it works.

By a strange coincidence the same post that brought your packet from Munster, brought also a very large packet which I couldn't imagine the contents of. It turned out to be from Denis [Tegetmeier] with a complete MS of *In Paren.* And it appears to be the one from which the typescript was made which you used in setting up the thing in type. Damned odd looking at it now in that form. It tells me an interesting thing that I was very surprised about. At the conclusion of Part 7 it says 'finished at Pigotts Aug 18th 1932'. The notes and Preface were written mainly at Sidmouth in 1935—that I knew, but I *thought* I did bits of the *text* between 1932 and 1935. However, that's what it says. Do you remember us going in 1936 to old Dicky de la

Mare and wondering if they [Faber & Faber] could be persuaded to print the thing in long columns like a newspaper, in 'Joanna' type face—What a hope!—but actually it would have been jolly nice.[29]

To H.J.G., 1 January 1964   *Northwick Lodge*
... And I found a letter the other day among my indescribable muddle of fragments, from Lloyd George's Private Secretary to my father in Sept. 1914, which is damned funny to think of now. My father had evidently (unknown to me) written to Ll. G. personally asking him when the Government were going to make official the proposed formation of a London Welsh battalion, as his son was anxious to enlist in such a formation and would otherwise enlist in some English regiment, which was not what he would prefer. The Secretary's letter was just a brief note saying that the War Office would shortly be authorizing this battalion as part of the Royal Welsh Fusiliers. It strikes me as bloody amusing, for it sounds as if Mr. Jones's son was anxiously waiting to be given some post of High Command, instead of merely, along with everybody else, attempting to enlist in the ranks of some regiment or other.

Later in 1964 there was an upheaval in David's life: Northwick Lodge was closed, and later demolished; new quarters were ultimately found for him at the Monksdene Hotel, Northwick Park Road.

To R.H., 6 March 1964   *Northwick Lodge*
I'm terribly sorry for failing to answer at least two letters and now the *Cennin Pedr*, Peter's leeks (daffodils) came a day or so ago—it was kind of you to think of sending them. Yes, the news you heard from Tom [Burns] is true indeed, this house is being vacated and you can imagine the chaos of trying to sort out, pack up etc. the 14 years of accumulation in this room [17 years, in fact]. It all happened with some suddenness, but no one could help it—only it was an *awful* blow because I had dismissed from my mind the notion of having to move which had been so

[29] See above, p. 54.

worrying a year or so back as all seemed to be settling down nicely. Anyway, there it is. This can't be more than a note for I'm preoccupied with trying to cope and nothing is settled.

However, it is arranged that all the pictures go to a bank for safety and perhaps all my other stuff to store or maybe go to a sort of ' Residential Hotel' [Monksdene] (there is a room about as big as this there that a friend of mine found and the stuff was going to be moved and still may be, but there's some hitch in the arrangement—you know—there always is! We'll see) down the road for the time being—but it's too boring to go into all the details and this is only to thank you for your letters and the daffodils.

... I had hoped there might be somewhere on this hill, but there is nothing, all sorts of people have been terribly kind. One person in particular whom you don't know, a young man who used to live here during my first years here, now married and living in Chelsea [this is Stanley Honeyman], has taken crate-loads of unsorted papers etc. for the time being to a store-room in his house and has also arranged for the bank to take the pictures and all sorts of other things. ... I have bought a certain amount of furniture from the house, things I wanted, for not all the things in this room belonged to me and I shall need various things in my new room. But it's so appallingly difficult not to get the things one immediately needs packed up with things one does not immediately need. To add to the difficulties I've had an awful cold ... and the house outside this room like an ice-box. Well, it's useless cracking on, I'll write properly when I'm some-where and less distracted. I shall miss this room *terribly* for it absolutely suits me to perfection, but there it is. It's rather as when old Jerry suddenly broke through and the whole front system was *aufgerollt* and Corps H.Q. staff-wallahs were caught in their pyjamas and the Siege-Artillery impedimenta was hope-lessly mixed up with that of the Infantry.

To leave all that aside, I've had a quite surprising reception in the U.S.—or from certain Catholic quarters mainly—of *The Anathemata*: e.g. 'Candlemas Lecture' at Boston on *The Ana-themata* by Fr. William T. Noon of the Society of Jesus, Professor of Eng. Lit. at Loyola Seminary, Shrub Oak, N.Y.—that sort of thing. It would appear that there are among Americans chaps who are *far* more receptive, willing to worry-out the meaning of a thing, more generous, naive—yes, perhaps, but more open, yes, more perceptive, not so inhibited and unresponsive as the English—in spite of the American 'thing' being so awful, this does seem—at least that has been my experience over these few works of mine—to be true. . . .

P.S. Strange thing, I was tearing up masses of stuff and my eye caught a glimpse in a Feb. [1964] issue of the *Radio Times* (Welsh Home Service edition) of a girl's face and I thought Lord! that's quite like darling Valerie—suppose it's a South-Welsh type—and then I drew out the paper and it jolly well was Valerie in a Welsh-language television play, looking a bit different because of television make-up of course. Then I did my best to read what it said and after a bit about the play it said *Merch amryddawn yw Valerie Price sy'n chwarae rhan Tessa*—Girl versatile is V.P. who plays the part of Tessa. *Magwyd hi yng Nghwmllynfell ac ymhlith pethau eraill bu'n ffsiotherapydd, athrawes, model a phencampreg hyrdlo Cymru.* Nurtured (was) she in Cwmllynfell and among many things has been a physiotherapist, a (school) teacher, a model and champion hurdler of Wales. Well, it's the last bit that amuses me—I had never heard of her prowess as a 'hurdler'[30]—indeed I did not know chaps jumped hurdles—I mean as a specific sport—very puzzling. I knew about the other occupations—*ffsiotherapydd* is jolly nice isn't it for physiotherapist?

This same 'no more than a note' continues for some time to discuss the mutation of initial consonants, and ends with an almost conventional formula:

P.S. Have not read this through, so forgive any lacunae and scrawl and unintelligibilities—chap waiting to post it, as I'm not going out in this cold.   D.

---

[30] Valerie remembers David saying of their first meeting 'You leapt up the stairs like a gazelle'—'Shades of my hurdling days', she adds.

IV

ROLL ON DURATION
1964—1974

———————————*———————————

Harrow (Monksdene Hotel, Calvary
Nursing Home)

David moved in April 1964 to a large room—though not so large as the one he had occupied for so long at Northwick Lodge—at the Monksdene Hotel, in the flat suburban part of Harrow. There he remained until his slight stroke and fall in 1970, after which he spent his last four years in the Calvary Nursing Home of the Blue Sisters, on Sudbury Hill, Harrow. It was at this time that his need of money became pressing.

As we have seen, his friends had been generous to him: Prudence Buhler had left him a legacy, and another friend had made him a present of £1,000. He had had some income from his books, though the royalties were not in proportion to their reputation, and had been given various prizes and awards, including an Arts Council Bursary, which over the years added up to a fair sum of money. Of course he could have lived on the proceeds of pictures that he could easily have sold, but as I have said, he was unwilling to part with them. David was extremely obstinate. He might need the pictures—that is understandable, for to look at what one has done is important if one is moving on to other work. They were a reserve against a great emergency—but how grave would such an emergency have to be? Finally, and not very fairly, '. . . you know what *dealers* are . . .'.

David was not, as his friend Stanley Honeyman points out, either foolish or careless about money. He always knew exactly how much he had left, and he did not incur debts that he could not pay. Even in earlier years he had few extravagances: cigarettes, whisky, Bath Olivers, many wastefully squeezed lemons. Taxis rather than the Underground ('I can never understand', he said, 'why Tom Eliot uses the Underground—you know—Tom—he took me *on the Underground*: I said to him, "What's wrong with taxis?" '). In the days of his visits to Rock, Helen Sutherland would send him his fare for the long journey—his third-class fare, naturally enough. David confessed that he would travel first-class, one of his small luxuries, and move into a third-class carriage at the station before Alnmouth, where he would be met.

In 1964 Helen Sutherland died and left David £6,000. At this point Stanley Honeyman stepped in, arranging for the raising of more money and for the purchase of an annuity. It was only after this was bought that David was completely free from worry and embarrassment. He had known before that he could rely on his friends, but there was always the difficulty of letting them know how he was situated, and the consequent uncertainty. Moreover, he thought it quite just and reasonable that any friends who were able to help him should do so. He served society—indeed he gave his health and his whole working life to what he regarded as that service, and it was proper that society should recognize this through the medium of his friends. Finally, and most important of all, Stanley Honeyman emphasizes that David's friends regarded it as a privilege to help in any way the man whom they loved and respected above all others.

1964—1970

David wrote soon after the move to Monksdene:

To R.H., 27 April 1964   *Monksdene Hotel, 2–8 Northwick Park Road, Harrow, Middlesex*

It was with a genuine *Deo Gratias* that I read your letter, which has just arrived, for it so chanced that only yesterday, Sunday, Walter S[hewring] came to see me and alarmed me greatly by the news of your boat having run into trouble and though he assured me that you and Robin had been picked up by the Ballycotton life-boat, I feared that either yourself or Robin or both might have suffered some great harm by being in peril in the saltsea. . . . I am therefore thankful that, from your letter, you *sound* all right. Curiously enough, in the way one does, I thought, I wonder if he lost his glasses!! For I know how helpless I should be now if I lost my reading glasses. It does not matter however many spare pairs one has, one can never find the bloody things. But, more seriously, I *truly was very worried.* Some months back, when you first told me that you were getting a little boat, I thought, God, I *do* hope they can navigate it safely, for I seem to recall that those seas off the south-east coast of Iwerddon are a bit treacherous and difficult—but I may be wrong about that. Anyway, for heaven's sake don't take further risks before you know the conditions. It must have been a bloody nasty experience. Get some advice from dear Mick

R[ichey]. . . . It must have been appallingly cold in the water. How long did you have to wait before you were rescued—tell me more about it at some future time. I do hope neither of you got bloody awful chills, let alone anything else, from it all. Other people I know who've been in the water in some accidents always say the coldness is the worst part of it. How near in shore were you? At least you didn't have old Taplow's trouble 'been in the briny for one thing—which gorn in to save this full of a phemail as gorn over board god dam her etc.'.

Sorry about all this but I kept going through the bloody paper in trying to draw a map on other side. I find sketch maps awful things to make, one keeps on putting things in the wrong place. No wonder I was not much use at trying to make sketch-maps of Jerry trenches etc. when plumber's mate to the Battn. Intell. Officer in 1917 in the Bois Grenier sector.[1]

Well, I've managed, with the help of one or two good friends, to remove myself and junk (sixteen years of accumulated stuff) from my beloved high room on the Hill. It was *absolutely ghastly* trying to sort the stuff out and *very, very* difficult to find a place—much more difficult than I had anticipated, and I was never very sanguine as to the prospects. I mean of finding a room of reasonable size that I could afford at all. This place is not an 'hotel' in the ordinary sense—it's about six small suburban houses knocked into one. My doctor had suggested, some years back, that there *might* be a room here and, in the end, though various chaps tried to find various places, this turned out to be the only possible one. I feel very peculiar here, as yet, for although it's only about a half-mile as the bloody crow flies from Northwick Lodge it feels, and is, in a different universe—the whole milieu is quite other. It is situated in that flat part—fields a few decades back, below the Hill, behind the shops, perhaps a *fraction* nearer Northwick Park Station than Harrow-on-the-Hill Station—very roughly this is where it is [*see map on p. 204*].

'Tyburn Lane' is an interesting survival, isn't it. Just that seventy yards or so of road at the bottom of Peterborough Hill. I understand that once upon a time it was part of a path that led

[1] See below, p. 243.

south-east to near where Marble Arch now is, that is to Tyburn
Tree; or maybe the little stream, the Tyburn, rose from round
about here and meandered about to eventually become confluent with the Thames.

Forgive all the confusions of gender, number and case, word
order etc. of the dog Latin on foregoing sketch-map (but I enjoy
trying to remember what tiny amount of the words I know. I
shall never be able to manage the grammar. It's the same with
Welsh, I think there is something curiously wrong with my type
of mind).

You'll see I have descended from the heights down on to the
maze of suburbia—but there was no help for it. It's not so bad,
but it's strange in a way, for it's quite a step further from the
bloody shops and things than was high Northwick L[odge], and
unfortunately it's a devil of a way to church. . . .

I wanted it ['a Latin thing I wanted to know'] for an ordination card I'm going to try to do for a friend of mine. I've not done an inscription for ages because of my eyes, but they seem neither better nor worse, so I thought I'd have a crack at this inscription as the chap specially wants me to do it if I can and he's a bloody nice bloke and I would like to do it for him if I can.

Would you bloody believe it, some chap in Hampstead wants to produce *The Anathemata* in 'live theatre'. I can't begin to conceive what his idea is, but I suppose I shall have to answer his letter.

To H.J.G., 6 July 1964   *Monksdene*

... by some good fortune I got up in time and got to London for the Mass at the Convent of Augustinian Nuns at More House in Cromwell Road in ample time ['for the first Communion of my godchild Rebecca Rose Fraser'], and went to lunch at Hugh's and Antonia [Fraser]'s in Campden Hill Square afterwards, taking my inscription with me.

It was, I found, a moving experience. There were about half a dozen (or less) little girls making their first Communion, and they looked heavenly in their white tiffany of sorts and little wreaths of flowers twined round *lemnisci* of a kind about their little heads. This 'convent-school' thing is very remarkable, and a curious combination of something greatly to be valued and appealing with something one finds a bit much. But the *infinite* care they take, the obviously carefully thought out details both with regard to the little children and the guests coming to attend the ceremony—the soft drinks and cakes and biscuits and cigarettes offered to one in the parlour afterwards—just the care with which it was all done, makes criticism seem churlish and beastly, but what a hard-to-state something or other clings to it all. One can see how girls one has known regard that convent-school atmosphere and how priests one has known or still know speak of 'these good nuns' in a special sort of way, with a mixture of respect and a measure of exasperation. I really think the 'aesthetic' of the cards, little prayer-books etc. is getting worse and worse rather than better. For in place of the older tail-end of late sham-gothic intermeddled with baroque, there's a kind of Americanized colour-photography reproduction of appalling realism of a priest in *terribly* clean vestments (that somehow look as though they've just come back from the dry-cleaners) shown at different parts of the action of the Mass. Little glossy books that look like brochures for travel-agencies (Come to the Costa Brava for sun and relaxation, only when you look at the picture you find it's not a mahogany sun-tanned *puella* on a bloody yellow beach, but a *sacerdos* at some given moment of the Mass—interesting how there's no escape from artefacts of 'now'—at least not in anything supplied in bulk).

Was interrupted yesterday morning in writing to you and been doing things all today. My train of thought has now to be picked up. The nuns. Yes. Was annoyed with one of them—may have been the Superior, she had a marvellous face—elderly, serene, disciplined, wise she looked, but she said, 'Now, who are you?' (I had arrived a bit early and was waiting in a large room with a bust of St. Thomas More and a floor so bloody polished that I had to walk with care.) I told her what my name was and that I was Rebecca's godfather. She said, 'Ah, yes, Rebecca. Her sister Flora's the one—she's really a *marvellous* child.' I said that actually I had never met Flora. She said, 'Oh, but you must know Flora, she's the one.' Well, I thought that was a damned silly thing to say to me as Rebecca's godfather, and displayed a favouritism which should not have been shown, I felt.

Anyway, it was all jolly nice, and Rebecca looked heavenly. She's very pretty and affectionate.

. . . Incidentally, the plates for the *Ancient Mariner* have been printed just right. I'm very pleased with them. At least with the separate sets which are being enclosed in a sort of pocket at the back of each of the copies of this new [Clover Hill] edition.[2] The ones in the actual book I shan't like as much, because they did not use thick enough or white enough paper, but these extra

---

[2] David's plates for the original 1929 edition of Coleridge's poem, published from Bristol by Douglas Cleverdon, were used for the 1964 Clover Hill Edition issued by Douglas Cleverdon in London and by Louis Cowan in New York.

sets are fine. Better, I think, than the 1929 ones, about as perfect as could be. What a treat to approve wholly of something!

Hugh [Fraser] was very amusing about all this vernaculariza-tion of the Mass. We laughed a lot at a nice thing [Stanley] Morison and Tom B[urns] had sent me from the Garrick a few days ago. It was just a slip of paper in an envelope, signed S. Morison and Tom B., and read, simply, 'Theological reformers please note' (or words to that effect) followed by 'Lest auld aquinas be forgot'. I think it was a jest Morison (or Tom) had picked up in the U.S. recently. The assault on the medieval scholastics is very marked, to my great regret. No doubt it had all become mechanical and academic, and no doubt patristic and biblical studies had been neglected, but for some of us Aquinas and Scotus have, one way and other, been so life-giving that it is insufferable that they should be cast aside in any way. The human animal, whether a theologian, a politician, a painter or a mechanic, seems always to swing from one extreme to another, so that the baby is continually being emptied out with the bath-water. I detest these radical 'switches'—it becomes so like that business of 'double-think' overnight.

. . . In using the bits [for Rebecca's inscription] from the Mass of Corpus Christi, I wondered what on earth they'll do with that sublime composition when they sing it in the vernacular. How *can* you give the total oneness of the firm theological statement and the splendid poetry of *Dogma datur Christianis quod in carnem transit panis*, to mention but two lines. And the Christmas Preface (that the idiots eliminated from the Corpus Christi Mass some few years back)—it can't be done.

I feel bloody sorry for our hierarchy actually, for whatever they decide they will be blamed by both parties, by those who are all agog for thorough and complete vernacularization and by those (some almost equally tedious) who see no point in any change at all. I say 'equally tedious' because there are some who just want, out of mere custom, to have no change—rather like those cavalry officers of the 1st World War who were totally blind to the requirements of trench warfare and who, like Haig himself, as late as 1916 said that one machine-gun to a company

was ample. That sort of attitude is ludicrous, and *some* of the
stalwart resisters to liturgical change are a bit like that. So I felt
a sympathy with Archbishop Grimshaw's article in *Tablet* this
week on the difficulties the Hierarchy is facing. Where I felt out
of sympathy with him was where he says that here in England,
if it comes to the vernacular, we have to compete with a tradition of considerable greatness in liturgy and music (meaning the
C. of E.). This comparison seems to me *most unfortunate*. As for
the musical tradition of the Anglican Church—what does it
amount to? As for the 'beauty' of the Cranmer's liturgy—well,
yes of course it has all that 16th cent. English had—partly Cranmer's artistry, largely the particular excellence common to the
English language of that age. Eliz. I's English has the same kind
of perfection—and the beauty of Shakespeare himself owes a hell
of a lot to that accident of period. But do what you will with
Cranmer's English liturgy, it inevitably reeks of that age, and
that age chanced to be the age that broke with the Church. As
[Dom] Gregory Dix saw so clearly [in *The Shape of The Liturgy*,
1945], Cranmer intended a quite un-Catholic interpretation of
the Eucharistic Sacrifice. Later, Anglican churchmen tried to put
a Catholic interpretation on the carefully constructed artistry of
his liturgy, and the C. of E. ever since has had those who put one
interpretation on it and those who put quite another. Three
centuries later the 'Oxford Movement' tried to give the whole
thing a Catholic interpretation. When I was growing up in the
first decade of *this* century, the atmosphere, though less violent,
was much the same. 'That dreadful Revd. So and So, d'you
know he wears a chasuble at "Early Celebration"—and a coloured stole at other times—it's rumoured he even whispers the
words of consecration in Latin—he ought to be unfrocked.' It
all sounds incredible now, fifty years later.

Now of course the whole picture has changed. A generation,
two generations perhaps, of Anglicans have grown up accustomed to the use of Mass vestments, going to Confession,
with Sung Eucharist, not Matins, as the central morning service
and so on. Compline has been re-introduced, religious orders
flourish etc. But I noticed that when Convocation a little back

made the use of vestments 'legal' it added that no doctrinal significance was to be attached to the ruling, but that as so many clerics used them it seemed reasonable to remove any idea of illegality. What *masters* the English are at this game of super-pragmatism.

I think our boys are making the same mistake as those classical dons who used to say that the teaching of the Greek and Latin languages was maintained because it taught men to think clearly, to write clear English, to become competent civil servants or what not. Apart from being largely balls, the reasons are utile and so-called 'practical'. What the dons ought to have said was that the classics were an integral part of our Western heritage and should be fought for on that ground alone. Our Church leaders have even more reason to guard that heritage—for it is saturated with the sacral. It's not a matter of knowledge but of love. It's a terrible thought that the language of the West, of the Western liturgy, and inevitably the Roman chant, might become virtually extinct.

. . . At root, I don't believe it's a 'religious' matter at all. I believe it's only part of the Decline of the West. Perhaps I'm talking balls, I don't know. But the *kind* of arguments used I find highly unsatisfactory, and they have just that same tang that distresses me so over the language of my father's *patria*. They prove by statistics that the Welsh language is dying, and that it has no practical value anyhow. Damn such bloody arguments.

To H.J.G., 17 July 1964   *Monksdene*

Well, I've had a regular round of 'social engagements', for me. I went as arranged to luncheon at [the Rt. Hon. Sir] Alan Lascelles on Wed. with Barbara M[oray] and met and had a longish talk with Siegfried Sassoon. It was very pleasant, but a broiling hot day—it's a heavenly place, that 'Old Stables' of Kensington Palace. I did not previously know where it was situated in relation to Ken. Palace, but it's a little to the S.W. of it, at the end of an avenue parallel with 'Millionaires' Row' and just before one comes to it one passes the actual house, that looks now to our eyes, accustomed to vast and hideous buildings, a tiny cottage, where Wren lived and worked when building the palace and other places. I didn't know about that, but you probably did.

I found Siegfried S. extremely nice, gentle and pleasant, *much* older than I had supposed, and quite different in appearance from what I had imagined. We talked about dear Prudence, whom he knew pretty well through Miriam Rothschild & Co. and we talked about Blunden and Graves and the Welch Fusiliers— Mametz, Limerick etc. (he said that however much he tried he could never get that 1st War business out of his system, which is exactly the case with me. It's a curious thing—he said Alan L. was just the same, and Blunden also. And I recall Clarissa telling me that Anthony E[den], a very different kind of bloke, upon the slightest chance, would talk of and read books about 'the trenches') but I found I couldn't make much contact, if any, about *poiesis*. That was disappointing. We seem *all* to live in separated worlds, and as far as I could make out, his particular literary outlook offered few openings that I could infiltrate to discuss the things that most occupy my mind. It was *not* that we disagreed, but never seemed to get engaged on the central issues. He very much wants me to go down and stay where he lives in Wiltshire for a bit, and said he could take me over to Mells to Katharine Asquith—apparently they are great friends of Helen Asquith. I asked him if he was worried about the fate of the Latin rite, but he didn't seem to be much aware of what was involved—but a jolly nice chap and he *couldn't* have been more friendly and agreeable. I was glad he thought so highly of Blunden's *Undertones of War*, which I've felt to be one of the very best of those various accounts of that infantry war.

Sassoon told me an interesting thing. A Dr. Dun[ne], a medical officer in the Welch Fusiliers and out in France from the Battle of Loos to the end of the war, had written the most interesting and detailed account of trench warfare and the R.W.F.'s part in it.[3] But that no one seemed to know about the book and that it was very difficult to obtain now.

[3] *The War the Infantry Knew*, a compilation of officers' reports, published anonymously.

One rather difficult thing is that he is supposed to use false dentures which, very naturally, I think, he hates doing. But the consequence is that he speaks very softly without opening his mouth, and as I am decidedly deaf in one ear, the left ear, I could only make out about half of what he said—got the gist of the rest, but by some considerable concentration, couldn't keep on saying, Would you mind saying that again a bit louder. We were left alone in a jolly nice, quiet room, Alan L.'s study. Sir Alan L. was jolly decent about that, for after lunch he said, Let's now go and sit in the garden. But I said, Well, if you don't mind, I'd prefer to stay in this room as I loathe sitting in gardens. So he went and talked to Barbara and his wife in the garden and left me with Siegfried S. in the quiet and cool of his study.

Well, that was Wed. On Thursday, Louis Bonnerot (the Professor at the Sorbonne who is Catherine Rousseau's (*née* Ivainer) 'supervisor', the French girl who did that stuff [a thesis, 1960] about *The Anathemata*, came with Bobbie Speaight (can *never* get the vowels in the right order in Bobbie's name. They are nearly all there—it reminds me of that thing one used to be told as a child, 'A, E, I, O, U, and sometimes W and Y'). I had been looking forward to meeting Bonnerot for a long time, and was not disappointed, except that the visit was terribly brief, because they arrived some time before 12 noon but had to get back to the Garrick for lunch and Bobbie was doing some recording of T.S.E[liot] in the afternoon. ... Bonnerot said I must expect a number of letters from him asking various questions, which I said would be all right, as I never mind answering questions if I can about *The Anathemata*. It was awfully good of Bobbie to conduct him here, but it did mean that the conversation within the brief space was a bit diffused—very largely about Eric G[ill], for Bobbie is faced with some *extremely* delicate problems re E.G. in that biography he's engaged upon. He *is* an incredible chap, our Bobbie, there seems *no one* in the bloody world he does not know.

A new business has started up now, similar to my not being able to go to get my D.Litt. from the Univ. of Wales.[4] I told

[4] See above, p. 183.

you I'd had an awful sweat writing letters and getting things framed, photographed etc. etc. for the Visual Arts section of the National Eisteddfod at Swansea. Well, I thought I'd heard the last of that, but no, they've awarded me the Eisteddfod Gold Medal for the bloody things and my general supposed services to the Welsh nation in the arts, and are beseeching me to go and get the thing at *9.30 Ac Emma*, on *August Bank Holiday* in a blasted park in or outside Swansea—I ask you. I can't describe the touching telephone conversation with a chap who said, I do implore you, Mr. David Jones, to come. I understand that you have a phobia which prevents you from going to places, especially to functions, but I do ask you to understand that this is not in any way difficult but homely and more than friendly—and is there not Scriptural authority for believing that love casteth out fear?—and the love that we bear towards you here in Abertawe and in all Cymru will surely overcome your phobia, and so on and so on. Oh dear! it *is* difficult. If one has a broken leg or even a cold in the head chaps understand, but, even now, these things to do with psychoneurosis only few understand.

My blasted back is troubling me a bit, after a long period of freedom from that fibrositis. It was partly my own fault, for on Friday I ordered a taxi somewhat late in the afternoon to go to the shops to get things for the week-end, and the taxi-man, having been kept waiting for some while at one of the shops, said, 'Can't you do your shopping earlier. I'm supposed to be off duty at five o'clock', which made me so angry that I said, 'Well, you can stop this taxi—what is the fare?' and had of course to carry the large parcels home. There's simply no bloody end to the impudence one can expect nowadays—how the devil was I to know when he was off duty, nor did it in the least concern me. But I only, by paying him off in impatience, had to carry those damned packages, which I knew might hurt my back. . . . So tired, must go to bed. Wish I did not feel so *terribly* tired all the time.

Saturday July 18th. A rather nice thing happened on July 10th (Mametz Day!). I had to go to lunch here in Harrow with the Malans (he's a master who used to live next door to Northwick

Lodge but now, no longer being a housemaster, has moved over the Hill). Anyway I was asked there to meet an archaeologist, a friend of Audrey Malan's sister. Her name was given as Nancy Sandars, and they said she wanted to meet me as she wished to quote certain passages from something I had written. She's writing a book on pre-history for Penguin. They said you *must* have heard of her, she's a very eminent Oxford archaeologist. I said I was sorry but had never heard of her, but that the name *Sandars* rang a decided bell as the author of some book I'd read. Anyway, after lunch, Miss Sandars came here and we talked for an hour or so about all sorts of things of mutual interest—the Celts, Celtic art—painting etc., and then just as she was about to go I happened to say what an exciting translation that was (which you, incidentally, had sent me), *The Epic of Gilgamesh*, and she said, 'I'm so glad you like it—I don't really know the Sumerian language of the original texts, you know.' And then I suddenly realized that 'N. [K.] Sandars' was the translator. I had taken it to be a man's work. You may recall how impressed I was with that Epic.

Previously I had known only of bits of it years back when chaps talked much of the Flood motif in that epic, and how it long antedated the Biblical account of Noah's Flood. But actually the Flood part is but a small part of it. It's a marvellous epic —a *proto-epic* containing ideas that filter through into Greek and Celtic mythology. But it was nice that I had not connected 'Nancy Sandars' with the 'Sandars' of the translation. Rather like that occasion in about 1942 or so when I first met old Jackson Knight and said a friend (yourself in fact) had given me a *marvellous* book called *Cumaean Gates* that had had a profound influence on me. At which Jackson got up, bowed, gave me his hand and said, 'But I *am* Jackson Knight—this is the first time I've been complimented without suspecting a desire to please.'. . .

12 August. Since I've been here, it's odd, but I've not had my little wireless installed nor have I read the newspaper, because I used to have the *Times* from a shop on the Hill, but this is too far away for the boy to deliver it and I've never bothered about getting a newsagent nearer to do so. I can't say I've missed either! However I did get the wireless fixed to hear how *I.P.* sounded [rebroadcast on the Third Programme] after an interval of some nine years (I think 1955 was its last previous performance) but more because Douglas [Cleverdon] had managed to find a 'hard' recording of the 'Boast of Dai' read by Dylan Thomas in the 1949 [1948] production. This production could not be used in 1955 because it was a 'soft' recording and they deteriorate quickly. So D. had to make a fresh recording in 1955 but Dylan was then dead. However somebody or other had made a hard recording of Dylan's reading of 'Dai's Boast' so that was inserted into this 1964 production, and Dylan was *perfect* for that bit—and I wanted to hear it again and did. Otherwise it was as in 1955 and my reactions were about the same. It's awfully rum this transference from one art form to another.

In the case of *I.P.* the 'poetry' suffers very gravely, the 'narrative' becomes more predominant. Some things *put in* enrage me—far more than anything that is left out. However I try to think of it as a separate thing altogether from the book, as one might think of an opera based on well, anything you like, *Pilgrim's Progress* let's say. It's very ingeniously done in many places. It must be a bugger of a job to reduce a written work of that sort and length to two hours of radio-production.

Of course, some chaps, who find the book very hard going indeed, are *enthralled* by the radio version and say 'Well, now I understand, it all comes alive'. . . .

Louis Bonnerot was very amused when he discovered that I'd never read a poem by Yeats about Leda and the swan—I'd never even heard of the bloody thing. He said, Ah, that's so happy for you artists, you need read only what you wish or require, whereas we unfortunate tutors or professors of this or that have to read *everything* pertaining to our particular subject, whether we want to or not.

To H.J.G., 2 October 1964 *Monksdene*

. . . Wish I could report better of my settling in here. I seem in as great a muddle as I was three months back and more. Can't find any of the books I want when I want them. The extra two feet of width in my high room on the high Hill—that is to say two feet along a wall of twenty-three feet—just made all the difference in the world. I feel permanently cluttered-up and constricted, and still greatly regret that high open view and the casement windows. Otherwise not so bad. Quite comfortable, but this bit of Harrow is suburbia per se, whereas somehow the Hill isn't.

... So you saw the television thing about the battle of Passchendaele (what an awful word to spell, as difficult as the vowel sequence in Bobbie S[peaight]'s surname). Am naturally gratified they used bits from *I.P.*—from Part 7 (final Part) I suppose. ... Please, some time, if you would when we next meet, tell me about it. I mean what was the *terminus a quo*—the opening attack on Pilckem Ridge in July, which my battalion were in? or much later? because that was only the opening phase of what turned out to be the Battle of Passchendaele, which lasted until November all told. We were involved only in the first bit and in late September or October moved into another sector. But we had been in that Boesinghe sector for a full year previous to the battle and were involved in all the preparations. There was hardly a moment's let up, and during the last part of the time the artillery on both sides were continuously active. Guns of every imaginable calibre were simply everywhere, and munition dumps rose like slag heaps on every available bit of ground—*more or less* camouflaged with bits of foliage.

I remember our digging a new 'Assembly Trench'—it had to be dug in one night, seven feet deep about (and we were ordered to wear our gas masks because there was a heavy bombardment with gas-shells mixed with H.E. and shrapnel) and then covered over with branches of trees etc. before it got light. The leafy branches we cut from a hedge just behind the new trench, and I remember thinking of 'The wood of Birnam/ Let every soldier hew him down a bough'. I also recall how the C.O. walked up and down *in the open wearing no gas mask* but threatening blue murder on any man taking off *his* mask—the temptation was great for the masks at that date were ghastly to wear for very long, especially if one was exerting oneself—they became a filthy mess of condensation inside and you couldn't see out of the misted-over talc of the eye-vents. There evidently were very few gas-shells 'intermeddled' as Malory would say, with the H.E. and shrapnel, otherwise the C.O. could not have strolled about above us without his mask. But his doing so in that rather heavy shell-fire which was falling uncomfortably close was very typical of him. They were a remarkable breed of men, those Regular officers. I've forgotten his name, but he succeeded Col. Bell (the 'Well Dell!/and into it they slide' etc. of p. 154 *I.P.*) and though totally different in all other respects had that same outward calmness and immaculate attire as though he were paying an afternoon call in Belgravia, in which *I*, at all events, found a mixture of exhilarating morale-making and extreme amusement—also there was something *aesthetically* right about it. I suppose it may have still a continuity in some other form—don't know. I know only that I found it both consoling and, which is perhaps much the same thing, amusing, pleasing —*Id quod visum placet*! But it was very much a *non placet* to some.

To R.H., 5 November 1964 (Poor Guy   *Monksdene*
Fawkes. He was a brave man.)

Thank you so much for your letter or letters rather, it was awfully kind of you to write—I know how *awful* this writing letters is—I seem to do nothing else—and as you say the time goes by like lightning—it seems only about a month since I came here from Northwick Lodge and now it's winter and bloody cold. So glad you got over to Barbara M[oray]'s house and liked her pictures. She came to visit me on my birthday on Sunday afternoon and spoke with affection of Joan and yourself and said the house (your house) was lovely. I never knew, curiously enough, where her house was in Ireland—she's never talked much of it—but I understand that it's not a great distance off as things go nowadays. She's a wonderful person and has been very kind to me. I especially love her straightforwardness and total lack of affectation about anything. Dear Mick R[ichey] rang me up from Brighton the other day—I'd not heard from him for a while, but he'd been away. He said that Robin had done especially well at that training place he's in [H.M.S. *Ganges*]—I'm so glad. Yes, I liked your description of Rosalind and her friend on the horses in the red light. Must have been very beautiful. . . .

They held the 50th anniversary dinner of the 15th (London Welsh) Batt. R.W.F. on Oct 29th and had asked me to it as a guest, because of being in the 15th and because of writing *I.P.*, but I didn't feel well enough to manage that—apart from the usual stuff I've been suffering from some damned boil or irruption of some sort on my backside or very nearly—bloody painful and depressing. Anyway, had a nice letter from a chap who used to be adjutant of the battalion in the latter part of the war—he's been secretary to the Association for years and years. He sent me the souvenir of the dinner celebration—it was odd to see photographs of faces so familiar fifty years ago, such as Major-Gen. Price-Davies, V.C., C.B., C.M.G., D.S.O., the Brigadier, photographed here in full-dress uniform with a white-plumed hat—I recall him only in khaki—he used to wear a specially designed (and extremely sensible) waterproof attire difficult to describe, but a sort of tunic with pull-ons over his legs, so that he was *entirely covered* in lightish khaki rain-proof. And he used to carry a very long stave rather like a surveyor's measuring rod and marked in feet and inches, and he used to put this against the trench-wall and if it was an inch or so less or more than the regulation height, he made one get it the *exact* height by taking out headers and stretchers of sandbags and empty a little earth out of them, or add more to them, as the case might be—*very popular* on a pitch-dark night in forward trench, as you can imagine. Also a photograph of Col. R. C. Bell, D.S.O., of the Central Indian Horse, who commanded us over the whole period covered by *I.P.*—he was a jolly nice bloke—he is the 'Colonel Dell presumed to welcome' of p. 154 of *I.P.* I felt rather awful about not going to the dinner as the souvenir includes a whole page about *I.P.* and Douglas C[lever-don]'s radio adaptation of it.

I had asked Capt. Fitzsimons (the adjutant mentioned above) if Fr. Daniel Hughes, S.J., M.C., was still alive—he was our

Catholic chaplain [the Fr. Martin Larkin of *I.P.*] and I used to talk with him when we were in the Ypres sector and he lent me a book of Francis de Sales . . . and it was really from then that I began to think of the Catholic Church. Well, alas, it's too late to write to him now, because he died, Fitzsimons told me, in 1960, and moreover Fitzsimons told me that he was sad about this because he was a mate of his and they had both received part of their education at St. Francis Xavier's College, Liverpool —so I suppose, from that, that Capt. Fitzsimons is a Catholic too, which I did not, of course, know. As you can imagine nearly all the officers in the battalion were Nonconformists, at least the Welsh ones. Well, God bless you.

Talking of Fusiliers, I was astonished and pleased to find in Dr. Smith's Eng.-Lat. Dict. hand-grenade, *malleolus bombardicus* (with a mark of interrogation between 'grenade' and *malleolus*).

Not read this newspaper [much abbreviated above] through so heaven knows what rubbish it contains.   D.

The next letter, begun on Epiphany 1965, was broken off and continued a week later:

To R.H., [January] *1965*   *Monksdene*
. . . I'm so glad you've seen Mick R[ichey]. And awfully glad that Rosalind has been integrated into the life of Eire. Yes, I'll give Barbara M[oray] your message when I next see her or speak to her on the phone.

Yes, I expect in spite of your loving being in Ireland and that lovely place you do feel a bit in exile at times. But as a matter of fact *I* feel *utterly* in exile of late, more and more. Everybody one *really* knows is separated and inside me for all this 'interest' (in e.g. U.S.A.) about my work etc. I feel completely isolated in some curious kind of way.

It was an awful blow to me to hear of the death of Tom Eliot [on 4 January 1965]. They had kept the fact of his illness very dark. At Xtmas time I had a card from him and his wife Valerie. Since I've moved from Northwick Lodge I've not been taking in any newspaper. Never got round to getting a nearer newsagent to send me the *Times*. So if there was any indication in the *Times* of his illness I should not have seen it. But though I hardly ever use the radio now, I switched on by chance the evening that he died, for the late news bulletin, but missed it except for the last few words and heard the voice of old Auden talking about someone but did not know who until the announcer said 'That was Mr. Auden paying tribute to Mr. T. S. Eliot who died this evening'. Next day I spent most of the time trying to write a letter to his widow, which I managed somehow, but Lord! how difficult such letters are to write and how damned stupid all the words sound.

I see from the *Tablet* that he is buried in East Coker from where his ancestors went to America in the seventeenth century.

I reproduce the whole of the Belloc sonnet which David copied at the head of the next letter for a special reason.

To H.J.G., 4th Sunday after Easter 1966   *Monksdene*
Dearest Harman, merely a tribute to your [Third Programme] reading of the selection of old Hilary's (as Fr. John O'Connor used always to call him) verse . . . God! he could manage the special sort of biting wit with undertones of deeps possible only to a man who was part of the untranslatable . . . *omnibus orthodoxis, atque catholicae et apostolicae fidei cultoribus*, and at the same time was part and parcel of that particular politico-social milieu of the first couple of decades of this century. I think the 'comic' ones are *much* better than the others, judged purely as made works. The 'form' and the 'content' is achieved in them far more than in the 'non-comic' ones (badly put—it's more complex than that—for the more 'comic' they are the more 'profound' they are. The 'uncomic' ones *tend* to be a bit lightweight or even slightly embarrassing—don't know). I *adore* one called 'The Ballade of the Unanswered Question' that begins, 'What dwelling hath Sir Harland Pott/That died of drinking in Bungay', and as for the *whole* of the Newdigate Poem, I tend to read that (when I can *find* the bloody book) whenever I'm particularly depressed. The only one that, strange to say, I know by heart, is the 'non-comic' sonnet written overleaf, René used often to recite that one

from memory, and I expect that's how I came to remember it.[5]

VENIT·SVMMA·LIES·ET·INELVCTABILE·TEMPVS
DARDANTÆ·: FVIMVS·TROES·FVIT·ILIVM * * * ‹

Sonnet XXViii

But O, not Lovely Helen nor the pride
of that most ancient Ilium matched with doom.
Men murdered Priam in his royal room
and Troy was burned with fire and Hector died.
For even Hector's dreadful day was more
than all his breathing courage dared defend,
the armoured light & bulwark of the war
trailed his great story to the accustomed end.

He was the city's fortress, Priam's Son,
the Soldier born in bivouac praises great
and horns in double front of battle won.
Yet down he went: when unremembering date
felled him at last with all his armour on.
EKTΩP: the horseman: in the Scæan Gate.

... I don't suppose my liking for that sonnet is based on un-
biased aesthetic judgement—not for a moment—it's for the same
reason that made me write a few of my favourite lines in *The
Anathemata*, pages 56, 57:

> Little Hissarlik
>
>> least of acclivities
>
> yet
>
>> high as Hector the Wall
>> high as Helen the Moon
> who, being lifted up
>> draw the West to them.

[5] Many years ago, in London, David used often to pick me up at my place of
work, and after we had had a couple of drinks he might say, 'Well, I'm going
up to Hampstead now to see Jim and Helen'; and in tribute to Helen Ede I
would start 'But oh! not Lovely Helen. . .'.

Hissarlik, traversed Hissarlik
> mother of forts
> hill of cries

small walled-height
> that but 750 marching paces would circuit

first revetted of anguish-heights
> matrix for West-*oppida*
> > for West-technic
> > for West-saga

down

Hilary B. would have thought all that pretty deplorable rubbish, wouldn't he?

It's all a very rum business, this tangle of comprehensions and incomprehensions of overlapping generations—well, and overlappings of all sorts. I'm coming to think that almost *everybody* is much more *separate* from *anybody* else in a way, than I used to think.

To R.H., 8–16 June 1966   *Monksdene*

... You see, knowledge of theology, great and deep understanding of the Xtian tradition in *any* of its aspects, or other religious beliefs and cults as well, not spirituality, nor a profound understanding of psychology or of phenomena of all sorts, seems to be of much help in making chaps see the particular dilemma touching this business of effectual *signa*. For the question is anterior to *all* the varied beliefs and practices and behaviour of human beings and (maybe) of some other 'animals' also if we knew enough about them, but for the time being anyhow, we'd best confine the question to human beings; for one thing the evidence of 'ritual', i.e. non-utile practices among certain creatures is a study of various specialists in non-human animal behaviour and is in its infancy and few conclusions can yet be drawn. But with regard to *homo sapiens*, well, not only do we know about him because we are him but we have at least 60,000 years and *maybe* a *hell of a lot* longer, of evidence of this 'ere *signa*-making in man.

None the less it is extraordinarily difficult to get chaps to see what one is *really* talking about when one says that, e.g. the Sacraments of the Church are a total impossibility, wholly unacceptable unless man is *essentially* a creature of sign and *signa*-making, a 'sacramentalist' to the core. It is so hard to make it clear that one is *not* talking about 'ritual' in the sense of degrees of ritual. Here Catholic 'apologists', especially now, confuse the issue just as much as other chaps, in that they *tend*, in various ways, or give the impression that—I don't know how to put this—that the sacraments are in some way helps to our 'infirm' condition rather than absolutely central and inevitable and inescapable to us as creatures with bodies, whose nature it is to *do this*, or that, rather than *think* it.

. . . I believe the *essence* of Protestantism is that the Xtian religion is a matter of inclination of the heart and soul, an interior disposition, resulting in virtuous works of all sorts—all most admirable and unquestionably that's all contained in the Catholic tradition also, but with the crucial difference that certain manual cult actions and verbal formulae are of the *essence* of the Xtian religion, not, *primarily*, because such actions are 'commanded' or appear to be commanded in the Gospels and were the practice of the 'early Church', but because such is the nature of man.

But if this diagnosis is anywhere near true it is pretty easy to see that kinds of Protestantism are more acceptable to the main trend of our phase of civilization than is the Catholic insistence on the crucial position of Sacrament, of *signa*. It is perfectly true that all kinds of non-Catholic Xtian bodies (the Methodists I think for one example among many) are tending to return to a 'liturgy' and the Eucharist is taking a much more prominent position among them than it did only a few decades back, and again in the C. of E. the change in, I suppose, the majority of churches is so great that my parents, let alone my grandparents, would not have conceived it possible. But I don't think any of this, at bottom, affects the situation, any more than I think the enormous 'interest' in the visual arts, the radio discussions and talks on the Great Masters, whether it be Giotto or Tintoretto or Goya or Turner, alters the situation—which doesn't mean that I'm not pleased that such interests are shown.

Damnation, more meandering.

What I am really trying to say is that the turn that our civilization has taken, the 'positivist' Hegelian turn, affects the Catholic thing in a special way. I suppose one can trace it, in embryonic form, to late Nominalism—something I read from Meister Eckhart the other day made me think. It was about Our Lady, about that text where the woman in the crowd says 'Blessed is the womb that bore thee etc.' and Our Lord said, 'Nay rather, blessed are they that hear the Word of God and keep it.' It's used as the Gospel in the Common of Our Lady. Aelred of Rievaulx in the 12th century I remember said in a sermon that the *Fiat* of Mary was primary to her physically bearing the Incarnate Word and that everything depended upon her *Fiat mihi*. Now, that is perfect. But when we come to Eckhart, the difference is subtle, but jolly important, he says:

Thursday 16th: 'It is more worthy of God that he should be born spiritually in every virgin or good soul than that he was born physically of Mary'. Sounds all right, but the next step is to 'demythologize' the story of the physical Incarnation and say that what matters is that all chaps should be awfully good, which is, roughly speaking, more or less what the present notion of Xtianity boils down to. And that is not the difficulty in our civilizational phase in at all the same way as a religion of Sacrament.

Older Protestants from the Reformers of the sixteenth century to the last century did, generally speaking, take over a great deal of the Church's structure, observances etc. intact—the Canon of Scripture taken very literally, hence the Incarnation was of as much importance to them as it was to the Catholic religion. They rejected the Mass on various grounds, but retained the Commemorative rite of Holy Communion. Without questioning the sincerity—and just considering the matter in itself—the penetration of the timeless into time at some long past historic date is more easy than accepting an analogous event in the historic present—I mean in the words of the 14th-century carol—

> The flour sprong in heye Bedlem
> That is bothe bryht and schen

is 'more easy' of acceptance, because more remote in time apart from being in the written Scriptures, than is a later verse in that carol or poem

> The thredde braunche is good and swote
> It sprang in hevene crop and rote
> Therein to dwyllun and ben our bote
> *Every day it schewit in prystes hond.*

Yet the 'difficulties' of giving credence to the birth in the reign of Caesar Augustus (itself no less a *signum* and what is signified) [are no less] than the 'difficulties' of giving credence to that sign which is also what is signified shown 'every day' in 'priest's hand'.

But leaving aside the truth or otherwise of the Catholic belief in this matter, it is clearly at odds with the thought process which conditions all men of our essentially positivist, de-sacramentalized civilization, whereas a religion of the mind, of aspirations of interior 'faith' issuing in 'good works', is not, fundamentally, at odds with 'modern man'. It is for this reason that I think it useless for those who hold the Catholic belief to— I don't know—gloss over or something, this business. (It's difficult to put into words and I'm getting *less and less able* to put *anything* into words—but even apart from this business of valid *signa*, there is a pervasive feeling, at parish level, of something like 'It's all perfectly straightforward and understandable etc.'. A priest at a church that a friend of mine goes to said, for example, only last Sunday, 'We must get rid of all this accumulated stuff—Latin and all that obscures.') . . . These blasted liturgists have a positive genius for knocking out *poiesis*.

Must stop, dearest René, forgive this appallingly long and entirely useless letter. I've not read it through, so God knows what rubbish it contains.

What is printed above is hardly half of this characteristic and illuminating letter.

'Did I tell you (I think I did),' David writes in June 1970, 'of the young man who wrote to me last November who'd chanced to hear Douglas C[leverdon]'s radio version of *I.P.*, then bought the paperback and then decided to take a holiday of four days from his job and visit

Mametz Wood and district.' This was Colin Hughes, whose in-valuable work on the Welsh Division, the 15th Battalion in France, and the attack on Mametz Wood in July 1916 has already been mentioned (see above, p. 25). David writes at considerable length of his great pleasure and interest in meeting Hughes, but the subject that most concerned him—the close connection between *In Parenthesis* and the historical facts—is best studied in Hughes's own work. The new friendship led David to commit to paper a great deal that came back to his mind, as will be seen in the extracts that follow from letters to Hughes (A.C.H.):

To A.C.H., 18 November 1969   *Monksdene*

... Zero hour was 4.15 a.m. [i.e. of 10 July] for the infantry to go forward. A heavy artillery fire began at 3.30 a.m., concentrating on the south-west corner of the wood, and the 16th Batt. R.W.F. were the first wave and suffered *very* heavy casualties, including their C.O., and were, I understand, twice repulsed by machine-gun and other German fire. It was then our turn, and together with the depleted ranks of the 16th we advanced to the edge of the wood and then into it. We, or anyway I, as far as I can remember, had little or no information of the previous assault, but in retrospect it was because of that assault that we found in the first German trench at the edge of the wood (pages 166-8 of *In Paren.*) little but dead or dying Germans (at least in the few traverses I saw)—we had expected otherwise. So it may be that in spite of the great losses of the first wave, the Germans had more or less retired from that front trench—but this is largely surmise. ... Even at the time one had only the vaguest notion of what was happening—but later one vividly recalled this detail or that, and a rough idea of the sequence of events.

Here, before we move to the last stage of David's life, is a mere fragment—that word which serves David as maid-of-all-work—from a draft or copy:

household enamel baths are incredible and again full of 'poetry' —I think old Bonnard makes Degas (by comparison and in general terms) much less great—enormously skilful and a superb draughtsman and painter—but somehow 'worldly' and lacking in the quiet, indefinable poetry of Bonnard.[6]

1970—1974

After the slight stroke and later fall, in March 1970, referred to in the following letters, David was taken to a private ward in Harrow Hospital, Roxeth Hill, where he spent a month or more, then to the Bethanie Convent, Hornsey Lane, Highgate, and finally to the Calvary Nursing Home, Sudbury Hill, Harrow.

To R. and J.H., 16 April 1970   *Harrow Hospital*

This can't be a letter, as I'm too weary, dull-witted and half-asleep to think—and filled with various forms of drugs they dole out—but, damn and blast it awakes like anything during the night, mostly but I feel I *must* write this note to my old pall for both letters—one a bit back and the other yesterday. Thank you and Joan for all you say and much love.

Yes, Mametz again, as you say, but a bloody sight worse. They reckon technologically speaking it's been perfect. You know how the femur bones turn in at the top called the 'head' and are joined to the pelvis by a large round bone—forgotten its name—anyway in falling I smashed the bone on the left side—I think they've put in a steel one instead—in negative it looks like a pure white circular ball—of steel—well, *right* leg is O.K.—I now have to practise trying to walk with a steel frame, hands pressed on a bar of steel contraption—down the corridors—it's not so easy as it sounds and damned exhausting . . . thinking for hours on end of all the trials, pains, miseries, of the human race, I'm beginning to think that these 'ordinary' accustomed things are more demanding of 'bravery' or whatever the word is—I suppose that's why one has always thought of women as more 'brave' than men, because they take for granted these things of

[6] Cf. his earlier (1963) comment in a letter to Jim Ede: 'So good old Braque has died. I reckon he was the best of those chaps, and before him Bonnard. I'm glad I met him at your house in Elm Row once.'

[226]

the body (as childbirth and all that) whereas we think and can more easily endure active pains, as in war etc.—I suppose all my stuff has on the whole been central round the Queen of Heaven and cult hero—son and spouse. Anyway you know what I mean. Seen a number of Irishmen of late. And, incidentally, before my accident, I have been re-reading a lot from your Chanson de Rolant . . . I do wish it could be reprinted with French opposite English. Can't manage more now. Much love to Joan and yourself.   DAVID

Valerie [Wynne-Williams] has been here during the last week and sends you her love.

Later (from Highgate):

Yes, this and the Harrow Hospital would make *perfect* material for a Taplow acconnt—but I can't rise to it as yet, anyway.

To H.J.G., 15 November 1970   *Calvary Nursing Home*
I'll tell you about Laurie Cribb next time the Powers give us a chance to talk. He was[7] one of those Londoners of the sort I so often met in the army. Always working, willing and, once given comprehensible orders, carried them out competently and well, and with a kind of resignation, which did not prevent them 'grousing' almost continually. E.g. 'Would you believe it —no bloody oil now—with rifle inspection in half an hour's time—wire-cutting fatigue tonight, and feel the edge of them wire-cutters—wouldn't cut wool' and so on and so on. One would go into Laurie's workshop at, say, Pigotts. 'Hello, Laurie—that's a bloody beautiful inscription.' 'Do you think so —very glad you like it, but have you ever seen a stone like this— impossible—bits of flint all over—and this chisel's like shaving with a blunt razor—and see that water dripping from the roof. Shift the bench? No good, light wrong there—I've had enough for one morning.' . . . He was one of E[ric] G[ill]'s apprentices for years and *by far* the best cutter of inscriptions known to me. I have not seen any of his work since the 1940s, but at that time anyway he was better than Eric—as Eric was the first to admit.

[7] Laurie Cribb died in the summer of 1978, at the age of eighty.

Laurie was *wholly* free of art-school aesthetics *and* from any awareness except that he was simply doing a job—the result was as though he were a stonecutter within a tradition, without knowing it. Of course he learned the craft solely from E.G.

... Tomorrow I am hoping to see Nancy Sandars—she's coming in the afternoon. She much hoped that I would be well enough to go to the marvellous exhibition of Celtic artworks at the Hayward Gallery on the South Bank. It was organized by Stuart Piggott ... God! he managed to get together some marvellous stuff—both from the Hallstatt beginnings and then La Tène—the latter from Gaul as well as Britain. The gold work torques etc. is *incredible*. This delicacy and refinement and aesthetic ingenuity is an astonishing phenomenon when one remembers that their makers were true 'barbarians'—savages, very savage savages, without any 'civic' life at all, but none the less, even just 'technically', *extremely* able—not only in weapons of great beauty but wheeled vehicles—waggons with most skilled and differing arrangements of hubs and spokes of wheels. .... It is the natural genius for the 'abstract' that is the dominating feature. They borrowed motifs from the Mediterranean world or from anywhere and immediately made it 'abstract'—and usually *asymmetric*—even when it looks symmetrical you find it's most subtly asymmetric in all its details.

18 November. .... I find in various matters akin to those you discuss in *The Painted Kipper*[: *A Study of the Spurious in the Contemporary Scene* (1970)] that not only one's terminology but the whole of one's ideas behind that terminology have less and less meaning—and this has happened with alarming speed. One can't be sweeping, because sometimes quite unexpectedly some very young persons clearly feel what their immediate seniors fail to see at all. They may 'know' no history for example, but they very often have a sense of loss—it may be that the revolution (for it amounts to something like that) in the 'finds' of archaeology, at least in some fields, made possible by scientific methods of all sorts, will be on the side of the angels in at least bringing to light the splendours that Man can and did achieve even while he was a 'savage' but a cult-man—at least for some it may 'ask the question' and destroy (for some) the inevitable progress of the whole man that evolution etc.—that was the fond but sustaining belief of most men, popularly voiced by Wells, Shaw—the list would be interminable—not forgetting such brilliant minds and nobility of blood as the recently deceased [2 February 1970], perfectly mannered, kind, aged gentleman referred to in, I think, Part 6 of *In Paren.* on a sunny chalk down where I lay with three of my closest friends[8] on the eve of our assault on the Bois de Mametz as 'Mr. Bertrand-bloody-Russell'.

That was straight reportage—and though, no doubt, merely a shorthand expression for all 'conchies' and without any knowledge of the man's remarkable character, did express what a middle-class Lewis-gunner from Monmouth (I think it was he) along with most of us on that July afternoon awaiting (already in a state of all but total exhaustion) the final orders to take up our battle positions from which the enemy was to be wholly dislodged from the wood left of the central ride. The other half of the Division being allotted the clearance of the wood right of the central ride. Having reached the first cross-ride the two halves of the Division will move forward in close co-operation and clear the remaining area and dig-in at the far edge of the wood in the direction of the two Bazentins, or words to that effect.

Perhaps Reg Allen may be excused his 'Mr Bertrand-bloody-Russell'. Leslie Poulter merely muttered something which meant 'Those who are appointed to die salute Caesar'.

I don't think I said anything as far as I can remember, but I had a rather empty feeling in my stomach when I thought of the long frontage of that wood and guessed it to be pretty deep and certainly a tangle of perfect defences. But Leslie's poker face (if

[8] As the text (*In Parenthesis*, pp. 139, 143) says, and as his conversations confirmed, David was one of three, not four, his companions being Leslie Poulter, of the Signals, and Reggie Allen, Lewis-gunner. The former is mentioned fairly often in letters, but David seldom spoke—hardly at all until the later years—of the latter. Reggie is the only individual mentioned in the Dedication to *In Parenthesis*, and the friendship was, I believe, so valued that David suffered more from Reggie's death in the winter of 1916–17 than from anything else during the war.

that's the right word), anyway his appearance of complete un-
concern when he made these perfectly chosen remarks—that for
some reason were always extremely amusing—could not fail to
make one grin.

Damn, meandering again, but it was that notion of things
'getting better' in every way borrowed from the evolutionary
theory that led on to minds of people able as Russell and sus-
tained the hopes of ordinary blokes. . . .

To A.C.H., 5 December and later, 1970   Calvary Nursing Home
How did you come to learn of this confounded accident of mine
that actually occurred just before Whitsun about March 19th I
think? Apparently I had had a stroke of some sort, very mild, I
did not even know of it, but I had been feeling pretty off-colour
for some time previously. But someone was coming to see me
and came and insisted that she called the doctor, who immediately asked if I ever looked in the mirror, because my
mouth was a bit out of the straight. Anyway, next day I felt
decidedly better, and better I think the day after, then I had
breakfast as usual and made my bed and piled it with its usual
conglomeration of books and papers, as you've seen it. But I
was just carrying the remaining papers and books—the last load
as it were—when I came down with a crash to the floor. To cut
a boring story short, I was taken to the casualty ward at Harrow
Hospital and the X-ray showed that I had smashed the round
bone at the head of the femur which fits a cavity in the pelvis—
so that had to be operated on. I understand they replace the
smashed bone with a steel circle. Anyway the operation went
well and after some time at Harrow Hospital I was removed to
a nursing home in Highgate and was there for about six weeks
and then came to where I am now.

In the same letter David continues his memories of Mametz:

. . . The shortage or absence of water—that interested me very
much, for I had, during the action in the wood felt the great
desire for a mouthful of water, and noticed that those about me
evidently had the same desire—as that of the hart in the psalm

quemadmodum desiderat cervus ad fontes aquarum, 'like as the stag desireth the water-brooks' in one English version, but the Welsh *Fel y brefa hydd am afonydd dyfroedd*, 'As the bleat of the stag towards the rivers of waters' I think I like best, for it physically evokes the hard-breathed quarry, the bleat-cry of a hunted creature on its last lap to gain a river-course—sorry for all this interpolation—but it's a verse which I've felt to be not only extremely beautiful, but especially relevant to us all in all sorts of differing situations—and it certainly seemed relevant to me parched-tongued in the waterless wood and the dry chalk approaches. But when some usually uncomplaining cockney came up and said in a parch-throated whisper, 'Blimey, chum, gotta drink o' water in y'r bottle?—just a drop, mate. I'm not a bleedin' scrounger, but I give me last drain to that sod Major Lillywhite, just after they got him so it were sheer waste, for he snuffed it almost immediate—but what could I do?'

To H.J.G., 4 September 1971   *Calvary Nursing Home*

... dearest Harman, *why* oh why, in all the varied stuff from 'fans' and admirers or from those hostile or most critical, is this pivot round which all one has ever stated depends, this utterly crucial matter, the distinction between the utile and the extra-utile, between, at its highest conceivable level (for Catholics, anyway), the *Oblatio* at the Supper, a ritual act and words wholly extra-utile, and the entirely utile acts whereby he who was already self-oblated was made fast by iron hooks to the wood of the *stauros*. We speak of the 'Altar of the Cross' only on the *presupposition* that the extra-utile ritual oblation at the Supper had already placed Our Lord in the state of a victim awaiting immolation. I am not here concerned with the profound theological terms involved or even how best to state the vast mysterium of the Passion, but it is clear that the *inutile and* the *utile* are both involved—otherwise the rite at the supper and the execution on the Tree have no substantial connection nor, necessarily, the Sacrifice of the Mass with both. Whereas we are committed to something more than a connection of some sort, but rather to an actual real (substantive) identity under differing forms.

[231]

This was a matter I used to discuss in 1919 at Westminster art school in what may seem a curious context: that of the post-Impressionist *theory*. I said, Well, the insistence that a painting must be a *thing* and not the impression of something has an affinity with what the Church said of the Mass, that what was oblated under the species of Bread and Wine at the Supper was the same *thing* as what was bloodily immolated on Calvary. Post-Impressionist theorists, however bad their paintings, were always loudly asserting that their aim was to make a 'thing'— let's say a mountain or a table or a girl that was one of these objects *under the form of paint*, and not an impression of 'mountain', 'table', or 'girl'. And that this idea was, *mutatis mutandis*, similar or analogous to what, I understood, the Church held with regard to the Mass. I said I had no idea of the theology of this mystery, for I was not yet formally a Catholic, but I wanted to know from my Catholic friends at Westminster if they had any idea on this matter. Needless to say they had not, and moreover could not see at all what I was driving at! This was, of course, some years before I had met with John O'Connor or Eric or heard of Maritain or de la Taille's *Oblatio victimae immolandae* (of the Supper) and *Immolatio victimae oblatae* (of the Tree).

... But my next point in all this meandering is that *now* among our mates and contemporaries, this business of utile and inutile is virtually impossible to get across.

All the bloody sweat of half of *Epoch and Artist* simply evidently had no meaning. You will remember how we were a little surprised at the time that no one took up the questions raised. They are or are not real questions. As you say in your letter, it's not much good saying that it must be remembered David Jones is not a philosopher—of course not—but that implies that 'a philosopher' would find the answer to this extremely difficult question concerning man's innate and million-years' habit of making inutile acts—in fact his greatest achievements up to the other day have been at least largely of an extra-utile nature. Rembrandt was wasting the party funds no less than Mary Maudlin if the extra-utile is not a necessity to man.

As for the Lascaux caves—well, there (if the specialists are right), the superb forms of great horned creatures with a dart or two depicted in flank or neck, is about the nearest thing to the acts and words of the inutile Oblation of the Coena Domini, while outside on the bitter tundra the great beasts fall before the highly utile spears of the tribe.

I know what the psychologists say—that the animal, man, has this 'wish-fulfilment' thing and the inutile is part of that. Well, that does not get one far.

Do you think, the main reason for lack of any comprehension of our question is that it is so taken for granted that men make *signa* that it's futile to say, for instance, that the Church can't have seven Sacraments with a cap 'S' unless man is a user of sign and sacrament with a small 's'—they say, Well, of course man is a maker and a user of *signa* with a small 's'—but they *don't seem to have grasped the actual situational fact* that technological man is fast losing that habit of thought, or at *every* level the capacity to understand what one is talking about.[9]

To H.J.G., 9 October 1971   *Calvary Nursing Home*

. . . As you know, I've an innate, inordinate, loathing of 'changes' of these sorts, anyway. I think I told you of how it chanced on one occasion that I was due for leave during the precise week when my parents had just moved from one house to another, and I knew exactly what that would mean, but could not see how to avoid being present. So I went to the adjutant and asked him if I could postpone my leave till some later date. He looked up in some astonishment and said, 'Well, we get plenty of requests for leave before it's due, pleading "some trouble at home", but never in my experience a request for postponement—you realize it may mean cancellation or anyway considerable delay? Anyway, what's your reason?' This was a

---

[9] The analogy between the artificer and the High Priest of the Cenacle is at times taken to further extremes. Thus David speaks of his friend Desmond Chute as an *artifex*, in virtue not of his engraving or lettering but of the exercise of his priestly function. So, too, in a MS draft, it is said of the priest as he pronounces the words of consecration, 'Here a maker turns a hard corner'— the very phrase David uses to indicate that critical point at which the picture may be enlivened by form—the sign will be effective.

bit difficult. But he was a bloody nice chap and possessed of a sense of humour, a Welshman. I can't recall what I said except that it would be very inconvenient at home. He laughed loud at this and said, 'Same old game, but in reverse!' He consulted the Orderly Room sergeant and asked if there were a vacancy on the leave list for a few weeks' time, and he said well he could swop with Pte. Griffith, who'll no doubt be delighted. 'What about—ah, yes, the 14th—that's ten days ahead, would that be all right "at home"?' 'Yes, sir, perfectly. Thank you very much, sir.' 'Well, change those dates, sergeant.' 'Yes, sir.' 'By the way, what's she look like?' and a further amused grin. 'You realize this is a chancy as well as a most unusual request? Remember, *anything* might happen between now and the 14th. There's always the Boche—he's quiet at the moment but . . . anyway, you've asked for the postponement, so don't blame me.'

. . . A vague and no doubt very inaccurate account, but I saw no other way to avoid spending ten days leave assisting at where this sideboard should go or hanging pictures or unpacking half-packed packing-cases.

. . . O dear, the point I was coming to in all this meander about the Mass is virtually lost owing to my inability not to stray off the point. But while the sacrifice of the Altar 'made sense' in the way I've tried to express—within our tradition and in all sorts of contexts—the 'God offered to God' did not for all its total mysterium, did not worry one. I have wondered about 'the Fall' that necessitated this stupendous act—it's plain enough in our dogma, I know, but I'm hazy about what outside—Xtendom mankind makes of 'original sin' as we put it, what precisely was the *felix culpa* that merited so great a Redemption. We answer that first the revolt of the angels, followed by a corruption in human creatures, was the cause—and that too 'makes sense' within a certain framework. But *humanum genus* as such is (I take it) aware that something pretty fundamental has gone awry, and certainly that great misery and appalling wrongness abounds and that the lachrymose valley is the habitat of most (if not all) of them—this is not the same thing as 'sin' as postulated by the Church—on the contrary I imagine they feel that the gods have placed them in this predicament. The Schoolmen called the Fall the 'deprivation of original justice'—but that does not greatly help.

As for that blasted Milton's *Paradise Lost*, his passage of how the pair in the Garden, when realizing their criminal state, immediately sought consolation in sexual embraces, well that's the bloody limit and a most outrageous perversion of Xtian doctrine and of the conjugal condition as well. But we need not take heed of him, for his theology was not Xtian at all, but unfortunately not a few of those *orthodoxis atque catholicae et apostolicae fidei cultoribus* from the 'early Church' onwards have been and are infected with this Miltonic stuff.

No good, shall have to try in some later letter to say what I mean. Must stop now. . . .

P.S. Re the Ulster etc. situation he hinted at the sort of attitude of some in his last letter to me. It must be particularly embarrassing for his clear and supremely intelligent mind.

My eyes have been playing me up a lot lately.

In 'my' war we used to sing a cockney rhyme that went *something like this:* 'I've lost m' rifle an' baynit, I've lost m' four-betwo, I've lost m' hold-all m' oil-bottle an' pull-through, and now I've got f. . . all, and I've lost you.' That about reflects what I feel like at the present time.

> David was at any rate slightly cheered to be reminded of Kipling's
> . . . And I've lost Britain and I've lost Gaul,
> And I've lost Rome, and worst of all,
> I've lost Lalage.

A letter to Harman Grisewood of 22 March 1972, writing of a chance acquaintance:

. . . his cut of suit rather suggested the turf—but then so did that of Sickert, which did not prevent him from being the best English painter since Turner (in my view).

And to the same, 15 April 1972, when discussing the disuse of the maniple:

. . . actually my thoughts went straight back some forty years and more when serving Mass for John O'C[onnor] and vesting him in, I think, Pigotts sacristy—I was exceedingly nervous and he in an early morning temper and high blood-pressure. 'Now, David, I don't want those bloody maniple-tapes tied above my elbow, but at the wrist. That's better. But you want to concentrate on the job. That *is* prayer in serving at Mass—doing what is required properly, exactly and carefully, and not too long about it, either.' But it was an alarming experience.

To H.J.G., 17 May 1972   *Calvary Nursing Home*

. . . I virtually *never* listen to the radio now, but occasionally for the news summary, and it so happened that I turned on the blasted machine, very soft, late one night, and the first words that came across announced the death of Edward, and the memory path led straight back to what we felt in that wretched December of 1936. It is impossible to convey to people now *what* we felt, but in your book (I think it's in the autobiographical one) you *express it to perfection*, deeper than our suspicions, anger, fury and what not, we knew that, irrespective of the tangled situation, something had happened that was *terminal*.[10]

To H.J.G., 6 October 1972   *Calvary Nursing Home*

. . . I've also wanted to write to tell you of the result of the changed pills etc., but wanted to leave it for a reasonable while. The fluid about my ankles was got rid of with remarkable speed, my physiotherapist is very pleased and also I feel more alert—I think more able to work without going to sleep—but it's impossible to explain in a brief note—these blasted balances are of the subtlest nature, and considering my history of breakdowns and recoveries over the years, followed by this damnable fall, and preceded by a stroke of some sort, it's all a pretty complex mess and has so many aspects it is virtually impossible for me to speak of it except at unconscionable length, and even not really then, for one knows only what one experienced, and that is as impatient of exposition as, say, why I consider this watercolour

[10] See Harman Grisewood, *One Thing at a Time*, pp. 101-5.

got more or less what I wanted, while this other watercolour of a very similar sort is no bloody good.

One matter in my talk with MacLellan [the doctor] interested me in that I'd wondered about it myself: i.e. the precise relationship of 'the stroke' (and there is no question but that I had a stroke, however slight) with the fall two days later that smashed the head of the femur, or rather the round bone that connects the head of the femur with the cavity in the pelvis. It is not a hundred per cent certain to what degree the stroke and the bone-crashing fall were connected. There was a huge rent in the carpet, over which I tripped, carrying an armful of books, papers etc. to the bed, but I had already carried three or four such bundles without feeling any weakness in the arm, and had had breakfast and made my bed as usual and did not feel unwell —so it may be that Humpty Dumpty had a great fall by tripping over the carpet, and that accident was independent of the stroke of two days previous . . . but in either case as MacLellan agreed the breaking of the hip bone, operation etc. would have no good effect on the nervous system, especially in the case of a bloke such as myself who had a fair bout of prolonged neurotic troubles. You see, Dr. Stevenson in the summer and autumn of 1947 really did by his great skill as a psychiatrist work marvels in my case. He made it possible for me to make the major part of *The Anathemata* and most of the stuff in *Epoch and Artist*[11] and the large inscriptions and the watercolours I did at Northwick Lodge, but there was one thing he could not manage me to conquer—the fear of going to places. I always had a return of feeling ill when ever I went away—for example to South Wales in 1954. Otherwise I was perfectly well, as you know, from 1947–8 until this blasted thing in 1970.

In the next letter David is writing of the *Word and Image* exhibition of his work, seen at the National Book League in London in 1972, which I saw later in Cardiff:

---

[11] The mention of *Epoch and Artist* is a confirmation, incidentally, of the view that David's essays are more artefact than argument.

To R.H., 1 January 1973   *Calvary Nursing Home*

... Naturally I am exceedingly delighted that you found the stuff looked all right and not a disappointment after the lapse of years—for so often things that one may have liked, perhaps quite a bit, disappoint on seeing some time later. Like Taplow of certain humans 'their girlhoods had worn off'. Glad you chanced to notice that portrait of yourself made in the billet—for I'm pretty sure it is the best 'portrait' *qua* portrait—'likeness'—of any I've attempted. For portraiture in that sense has never been a thing I could manage very well. I remember it has through the window in the distance a couple of hayricks towards that path that led to Little Pigotts, if my memory is right, and your forearms look very powerful from pulling that hand-press. A chap called [Ellis] Cemlyn Jones owns it and says that he owns the largest drawing made by D.J.—I forget who told me that.

Talking of 'largeness', it's very gratifying that you felt things like *Aphrodite in Aulis* seemed larger than you had thought. That was very consoling for so often things disappoint a bit by seeming of less 'mass' than one had thought.

Talking of 'mass' and what the scientists tell us of velocity causing weight—I suppose that's why when a machine-gun or maybe rifle bullet passed clean through my left leg without touching the fibula or tibia—but merely through the calf, it felt as if a great baulk of timber or a heavy bar of some sort had struck me sideways, in fact I thought a ponderous branch of one of the trees of the wood had been severed by shrapnel and had fallen across my leg but couldn't account for the *extreme violence and weight*. I did not realize it was S.A.A. until I tried to stand up and felt the wetness seeping from the wound, then I realized I'd been hit by a mere little bullet—but the disproportion of the smallness of the nickel projectile and the great bludgeoning weight of the impact astonished me even at the time. Of course I have little or no idea of the distance that separated me from the rifle, or maybe machine-gun, that loosed off the shot. Might have been a few yards or a hundred yards or more and it was extremely dark and a general confusion—I mean firing coming from various directions and suppose the 'mass' created by the velocity stands in some exact relationship to length of the trajectory line. Anyway it remains odd that being hit clear through the leg by a round of S.A.A. should give me the impression of being swiped by a bloody great baulk of timber such as a ship's boom suddenly by some accident slewed round. I've never, curiously enough, asked of anyone who'd chanced to be hit in the same way by a rifle bullet if they had this same impression, of not being pierced by a bit of metal but of being subjected to some great weight. I expect it depends on a number of different factors.

I was hit in the chest by a bit of a bullet that went through a whole wodge of stuff in my tunic left pocket and just reached and grazed the skin, but that I didn't even feel, it must have been practically spent before it came to me, and was, anyway, a ricochet of some sort, none the less rather surprisingly had still sufficient impetus to go through the wodge of stuff, letters mainly, in my tunic pocket and 'cardigan', waistcoat, shirt and vest—so I can't account for not feeling its impact. On another occasion some very heavy bit of stuff with evidently a sharp edge came down on my shrapnel helmet and just failed to penetrate it but left a kind of herringbone pattern on the *inside* from side to side, that did knock me out for a little while, a few moments I suppose, and pressed the tin hat down over my ears and eyes, but the only effect of that was a *very* stiff neck and painful that lasted for a week and more. But I haven't the least idea what that was—might have been any old bit of iron—it was thrown up by a mine explosion just outside the trench, so was merely a bit of falling debris—not a discharge from a gun, I mean, and dropt, so to say, out of the sky.

To H.J.G., 5 April 1973   *Calvary Nursing Home*
... Oh! how much I agree with what you say touching the *Divina Commedia*. For among the people I have known and respect you are the only one who feels it to be 'conceptual' and not 'of this flesh'. I of course having no Italian have read only in Laurence Binyon's English translation with Italian text opposite

page by page, and have put down the failure on my part—to find it cold and unmoving except in a few places. Beatrix, as you say, is not a compelling girl of total pulchritude in all her members, impossible to resist because of the radiance in flesh and blood, not a 'smasher' as the pre-Raphaelites would say ['stunner', surely?]. Not in any sense a Helen of Troy—but a disembodied creature of some sort. Dante appears to have forgotten (in spite of his work being so based on the Schoolmen) that Aquinas says that though we are, *in order of 'Being'* a little lower than the pure Intelligence of the angelic creatures, yet we have this advantage of having bodies and so senses that are necessarily denied the incorporeal hosts. This, from the 'Angelic Doctor', is very much to be remembered. But I had supposed that failure to feel the greatness of Dante was due to my inability to read him except in English translation because it has been my experience to find that among people of extremely differing temperaments and professions, once they read Dante (in Italian, of course) they either openly or otherwise place him as by far the poet they most love, and regard him as by a very long way the greatest poetry Christendom has produced. To name a few such, Tom Eliot, as far as I could tell from conversation with him, appeared to be in no doubts as to that. Then I discovered that Mr. Plumtre, the Classics master at Harrow School until his retirement a few years back—a marvellous man who I imagined was wholly and most deeply concerned with the Greek and Latin authors, was in fact even more devoted to Dante. And dear Bernard W[all]—a very different bloke in his wide appreciations, I think, puts Dante at the top of the list, and various friends, once they got on to Dante, virtually dismissed or anyway considered other poets as far below Dante. Laurence Binyon himself, I know, was of this opinion. So I couldn't but feel that my lack of appreciation must indicate something wrong in myself, even apart from my reading him in English translation only.

However that may be, I was greatly consoled to hear that you find Dante fails to convey 'this flesh' or the whole desire for feminine thing embodied in this flesh. His Beatrix seems to me a 'have on'. A kind of convenient 'figure' necessary to his worked-out scheme, and his scheme itself borrowed from the Scholastics —and he appears to be very much a Nominalist, not a Scotist kind of Nominalist but more like William of Ockham. I mean he was pretty anxious about the rights of King and Emperor not being impinged upon by the Holy See. Well, I can see the case for that, but I do think that Nominalism led to the break-up of Europe—or, as the Tiger used to say, the growth of nationalistic states of later times. I have a feeling that Dante was more interested in power politics than he was in Beatrix—forgive this useless meander. But I want you to know how consoled I was by what you say of Beatrix.

In the following letter the secrecy about David's unit is most puzzling. I had long known—as did all his friends—that he belonged to the London Welsh battalion of the R.W.F., but did not know the company or platoon. He gave others exactly the information he gives here to me. They, too. may well have been told that it was most confidential, for such is often the habit of hoarders.

To R.H., 15 April 1973   *Calvary Nursing Home*

Well, and this is for your personal information since you ask it. (I mean this for I've always deliberately made it vague in my writings, so this information is confidential to you.) My Division was the 38th (Welsh) Division and I was in the 113th Infantry Brigade of the Div. and the 15th Batt. R.W.F. I was in 'B' Coy of that Batt. in Number 6 Platoon. At least for practically all the time—for a while I was in the Field Survey Company.[12] But only for a few months. Got the sack from that job because of my inefficiency in getting the right degrees of enemy gun-flashes—as I've told you long ago—I remember how amused you were about how we were not allowed to mention on the field telephone the probable calibre of weapon, e.g. 4.2 Howitzer firing

[12] A copy survives of David's New Year card for 1917. It was printed at his father's office, with a reproduction of a drawing by David and a greeting from

> Private W. David Jones
> No. 22579 B Group
> 2nd Field Survey Company
> 2nd Army Headquarters
> BEF France

at so many degrees and seconds, but had to follow a list of dogs' names from terrier up to Great Dane according to the size of gun we took it to be by nature of flash, hence 'Foxhound barking' (or I believe 'baying' was the correct term for foxhound) at such and such degrees and seconds. But my trouble was that in the process of getting hold of the field telephone I usually managed to jolt the dial of the theodolite and so gave an inexact bearing. It was in a pitch-dark half-smashed windmill that was swaying in the wind and one was allowed only a *very small* electric torch to be on to get the bearing and of course it was all too bloody easy to jolt the blasted contraption just a tiny bit in finding the speaking-end of the field telephone—anyway it was no job for me. And on St. David's Day 1917 I found myself in full pack making some good few miles to the railhead to get back to where my battalion were then stationed, north of Ypres. But in spite of all protests a railway transport officer insisted on my getting into a train that instead of taking me north took me south-west and I found myself in Rouen or rather in a large camp on a hill above Rouen. Naturally when I reported to the authorities there, they said in effect, 'But we have no information about you. Your unit is in the Line in the Boesinghe sector, north of the Ypres Salient'. I explained how the Railway Transport Officer at X had insisted on my taking this train. They said, 'Sounds pretty fishy, but we'll have to wait till we get confirmation from y'r battalion—in the meantime you'll have to stay in camp here'. It took them about three weeks or four, to get the required information. Eventually I was returned to my battalion. . . .

When he returned to France, after recovering from his wound, in October 1916, David had for a time been posted to 'D' company. Cf. the following, from an undated draft or copy:

When I returned to my unit I was greeted by my friend Leslie Poulter who was a corporal in Signals and on good terms with the Reg'mental Sergeant-major, who said there was no need to proceed to my company, and as it was very near to my twenty-first birthday we had better celebrate with some rum and some bottled cherries Leslie produced from somewhere. Which we did. I can't remember any further immediate details about my return. I did a short period with my company, now 'D' Coy, whereas up to the Somme I had been in 'B' and still don't know why I was transferred, and men hate being transferred from one company to another. For a certain domesticity is very strong and changes of any sort are resented. Soon after Nov. 1st I was transferred to Battalion H.Q. for certain duties. The Intelligence Officer, hearing that I had been an artist, thought I might be useful in making some maps and perhaps going on patrol with them and making sketch drawings of the place where Jerry had put up some new wire or other defences.

The letter of 15 April 1973 continues:

One advantage of my short stay with the Field Survey Company was that I saw bits of our front line that otherwise I would have missed, for the Observation Post in the rickety mill was one of three posts we used in that sector, one being in or just in front of 'Plugstreet' wood which was an amazing place with a complex meander of entrenchments, a bit more like a German 'defence in depth' than our usually flimsy trench lines. That very great distinction, both at the time and ever since, was most marked. We developed something a *bit* more like the German, but not to any extent. Kipling's 'thin red line' seemed to be innate in our tradition. I always remember Tiger Dawson again and again in conversation referring to the cardinal difference of the German or French etc. being in column, while we marched in column only to deploy in line.

I remember once in particular being in a working party (in the Bois Grenier sector) sometime in late 1917, one lieutenant, a sergeant and about half a dozen or less privates, with about thirty Portuguese to wire a support or reserve line. When we arrived there was nothing but a slight indentation in the soil with some white tapes placed in position by the R.E.'s. It was a very quiet bit of frontage, but a few Jerry shells were falling a bit further back—the Portuguese simply got down into a ditch by the road-side and nothing would move them. I'm not implying that the Portuguese were cowards, but they were peasants suddenly finding themselves in an essentially industrial type of war and shell-fire they would not put up with—man for man any of them would have taken on any of us with ease, and in fact there were all sorts of stories of them knifing and fighting chaps over girls—but however that may be I do know that shell-fire they could not abide. Sorry for that digression on the Portuguese, for the point was that there *was* no support (or 'reserve' would be more accurate) trench—and we didn't know quite what to do. The lieutenant and the sergeant and the few privates tried to put up what wire we could and made some attempt at deepening the shallow indentation left by the R.E.'s. But it would soon be the beginnings of dawn and the young officer in charge of the party was almost in tears for he had to report back before it was light that the job had been accomplished. . . . The Welsh sergeant was almost beside himself with rage but as there was no common language, his threats to 'shoot the bastards' not only fell on deaf ears but also received a most alarmed reprimand from the unfortunate lieutenant. It was a most unhappy affair.

There was another point you mentioned but can't remember what it was—ah yes! It chances that *Tales of Army Life* is the only book of Tolstoy I read properly and I remember being amused about how 'He' is for soldiers those opposed to them. It was certainly universal with us. I don't think Robt Graves is right in saying [in *Goodbye to All That*] that officers used—now I've lost your letter—but was it 'Fritz'? whereas the ranks used 'him'—I can't recollect any difference—in the ranks certainly 'Fritz' was very commonly used, I think the term 'Boche' was more used by commissioned ranks—but more, maybe, among the higher commissioned ranks—on the other hand my friend Leslie Poulter very frequently spoke of 'Bosches' (can't spell it) but Leslie was partly Swiss I think or anyway, though tremendously 'English' in the sense that Harman is 'English', had many continental affinities. In the ranks we often used 'Squarehead' of old Jerry—'That poor old "squarehead" they brought in from last night's raid looked pretty far gone to me'. 'How many of our mob caught a nasty one?'—'Yes, and that's not counting the covering-party.' 'Maybe, but Sergeant Hughes and Mr. Talbot looked to me in a very bad way and are probably dead by now.'

Forgive this wholly boring stuff, René, but yr questions recalled in me incidents of the post-*I.P.* period.

The paragraphs that follow are extracted from one of the longest, but by no means the very longest, of David's letters; in some 9,000 words, with the usual digressions—'meanderings'—of which this is one, it deals with the relation between *In Parenthesis* and his own real experience. The date made it an anniversary letter.

To R.H., 9–15 July 1973   *Calvary Nursing Home*

. . . What astonishes me about Owen whose poems I have been familiar with only in recent years is how on earth he was able to write them while actually in the trenches, it was an astonishing achievement—I can't imagine how it was done—a unique and marvellous detachment—but I don't like his identification of the grimly circumstances and maims and 'dole and tray and tene' with the Passion of the Incarnate Logos—yes the bit you quote from the letter is an astonishing *tour de force* and, as you say, 'terrific'. But, none the less, I don't like the analogy— the very consciously stated analogy. Its brilliant artistry and skill and plain stated factualness, down to the right way to tie the leather thong of Field Service boots[13]—do not, for me, at all events, justify what I think is the unfortunate theology implied, well, more than implied, but quite explicit.

It may be, indeed it may well be, that Owen (*lux perpetua luceat ei*) was so sincerely a believer in that particular tradition of 'Christ crucified' that has been from the beginnings as far as Wales is concerned in the first quarter of the eighteenth century, its height in the middle or latter part of the nineteenth century, *the* religion of Protestant Wales, for though Owen was born and nourished in the English Low Church tradition of the English shires bordering the Welsh lands and I don't think he ever

[13] Cf. *Wilfred Owen: Collected Letters*, ed. Harold Owen and John Bell (1967), pp. 457–60.

spoke of his Welsh ancestry in his poetry, but he may well have inherited much of the same religion of Bryn Calfaria, whereby, if he did, he might well however unconsciously, quite naturally as an infantry officer see in all the mutilation and death an image of the immolated *geong haeled thaet waes God Almihtig* of the A[nglo]-S[axon] *Dream of the Rood*. Perhaps it may even have made it possible for him to write these poems when actually in action. And it may very well have caused him to write, under such immediate pressure, of that 'old lie' to rhyme with *pro patria mori*. Whereas had he not himself become one with those fallen, but had survived to consider 'in tranquillity' he *might* have hesitated and seen that there was no 'old lie', but something more akin to Isaias' *non est species ei neque decor, et vidimus eum et non erat aspectus*. However that may be, I again have meandered, for I merely wished to indicate that in writing *In Paren.* I had no intention whatever in presuming to compare the varied maims, death-strokes, miseries, acts of courage etc. of the two contending forces, ours or those 'against whom we found ourselves by misadventure', with the Passion, self-Oblation and subsequent Immolation and death of the Cult-hero of our Xtian tradition. For that is a unique and profound Mystery of Faith.

... To return to this matter of my Catholic thing that some critics have said that I've introduced into *I.P.* notions imbibed in subsequent years. This is a misunderstanding but which I can't inform them of, but which I can speak of to you, even if it's a bit embarrassing. Long before 1914, when I was at Camberwell art school—old Solly ['born to failure' Reginald Savage, of Canon John Gray], my attempts at 'figure composition' nearly always of some medieval subject introducing a vested priest, and my interest in Morris's poetry and Rossetti & Co. And dear old Hartrick in quite a different way was a kind of oblique Catholic influence or at least, if 'influence' is too strong a word, opened my mind to the European tradition, this would be 1910–14.

Much earlier still, when I was a child of I suppose about seven, I recall that one Good Friday my father had gone to what, in the Anglican Church, is called the Ante-Communion service.... I can't recall where my mother was on that particular

Good Friday morning or my brother and sister—and I wouldn't have been left alone in the house but all I can recall is that I was in the garden and the flower beds had along their outward edges longish slats of light wood to keep the earth from spreading over the path or grass lawn or what not. I decided that it would be a 'good thing' to make a recalling of Feria VI in Passione et Morte Domini by taking up a length of this light wooden bordering and then finding a shorter piece and nailing on or in some way fixing the two together to make a cross-form, and carry it round the limited space of the garden. In the middle of this child-ritual my father returned from his Ante-Communion Service—as I cannot recall with any precision what he said and do not want to invent words that were never said, I can do no more than say that he was much distressed that I should have disordered the flower beds and broken one piece of wooden slatting in making the cross-bar and of getting into the greenhouse to find a nail and in doing so had smashed two or three red earthenware flower pots and all this on this most solemn day of the Christian year. I can recall no more except the whiteness of his face which always was a sign of repressed anger or sorrow in him. I have a vague idea that I tried, through my tears, to say that it was because of it being Good Friday that I had done this thing. But I fancy that had I attempted this, the true cause of my actions, I should remember his answer, which I do not, so I had best leave it at his not unnatural displeasure and regret with my behaviour.

Some years later, and here again I am vague as to the details, or perhaps it would be more true to say that I am reasonably clear as to the details, but altogether vague as to time and circumstances. In the church we attended it was considered papistical to kneel at the words in the Creed 'and was made man'. I found that something almost in the nature of a compulsion at some time in my teens—made me kneel if only on one knee, at these words, but as no one else in the congregation made any such gesture and boys at all events greatly fear being thought odd, it was a battle between what I considered was in harmony with the herdsmen from the fields of Ephrata when they in obedience to the wonder-tale of the angel came into the caved stable and saw between the patient animals the Babe and She whose womb-burden that Babe had been, and my teen-age fear of acting other than was customary in that congregation. Sometimes the fear of oddity would win, sometimes the sense of bodily latria would prevail. A relative, most likely my mother, would say, 'Why will you make yourself conspicuous, you know perfectly well that it is not customary in this church' and my answer was that I didn't think anyone would notice, but if you like I'll drop my handkerchief or something, and kneel, *apparently* to pick it up, but actually because I think it right that the words demanded this bodily action.

. . . I don't know whether I ever told you of my first sight of a Mass.

It was after the Somme, I think, so when I had returned to France from being wounded. Anyway when or where it was I can't exactly place. But as I was always cold, one of my main occupations was to hunt for any wood that was dry and could be used to make a decent fire. We were in some support trenches and I said to the people I was with, 'I'm going off to find some decent firewood'. Just a little way back that is between our support trench and the reserve line I noticed what had been a farm building now a wreckage in the main, owing to shell fire. No individual of any sort was about and I noticed that one bit of this wreckage a byre or outhouse of some sort still stood and its roofing appeared to be intact and its walling undamaged at least from a little distance.

I thought now that looks to be most likely the very place where there might be not only wooden objects of one sort or another, broken cart-wheels, or other discarded bits of timber but, with a bit of luck, a wood-store perfectly dry and cut ready for use. So I went to investigate and when I came close to the wall I found there were signs of its having been more knocked about than appeared from a few hundred yards away, but there was no door or opening of any sort on that side, but I found a crack against which I put my eye expecting to see either empty darkness and that I should have to go round to the other side of the little building to find an entrance. But what I saw through the small gap in the wall was not the dim emptiness I had expected but the back of a sacerdos in a gilt-hued *planeta*, two points of flickering candlelight no doubt lent an extra sense of goldness to the vestment and a golden warmth seemed, by the same agency, to lend the white altar cloths and the white linen of the celebrant's alb and amice and maniple (the latter, I notice, has been abandoned, without a word of explanation, by these blasted reformers). You can imagine what a great marvel it was for me to see through that chink in the wall, and kneeling in the hay beneath the improvised *mensa* were a few huddled figures in khaki.

Only a very few, for of course most of the R.W.F. were of some Nonconformist sect and the Londoners mostly C. of E. But there was a big-bodied Irishman and an Italian naturalized Englishman, represented under the forms of Bomber Mulligan and Runner Meotti in *In Paren.* on page 121 and Mulligan as 'old Sweat Mulligan' on page 117 and one or two others. I can't recall at what part of the Mass it was as I looked through that squint-hole and I didn't think I ought to stay long as it seemed rather like an uninitiated bloke prying on the Mysteries of a Cult. But it made a big impression on me. For one thing I was astonished how close to the Front Line the priest had decided to make the Oblation and I was also impressed to see Old Sweat Mulligan, a somewhat fearsome figure, a real pugilistic, hard-drinking Goidelic Celt, kneeling there in the smoky candlelight. And one strong impression I had (and this I have often thought about over this last ten years of change when clerics of all sorts declare that the turning-round of the *mensa* and the use of the vernacular and much besides made the faithful more at one with the sacred minister and so get back nearer to the Coena Domini) for at that spying unintentionally on the Mass in Flanders in the Forward Zone I felt immediately that oneness between the Offerant and those toughs that clustered round him in the dim-lit byre—a thing I had never felt remotely as a Protestant at the Office of Holy Communion in spite of the insistence of Protestant theology on the 'priesthood of the laity'.

I then had to seek elsewhere for my fire-wood—I can't remember what I managed to gather.

And another thing that puzzles me a bit is that I can't fit in this incident with any place we were in *after* the Somme in July 1916, for when I returned to France in Oct. 1916 we were in the sector north of Ypres and remained there until Sept. 1917 when we moved south to the Bois Grenier sector—that place of incredible quiet where convolvuli grew over the revetment frames of the communication trenches and where a little French boy used to come up and blow a little horn of some sort to let us know he had issues of *Le Matin*.

To R.H., [? 11 December] 1973   *Calvary Nursing Home*

... It [his new book] will contain all those various bits and pieces of mine that were in *Agenda* and is called *The Sleeping Lord and other fragments* and also I've included some stuff that I made immediately after *In Parenthesis* was more or less finished, made partly at Sidmouth and Hartland Point and in that 'cottage' on the Stanmer estate [The Mill House, Falmer] where Prudenceand Lady Chichester lived—I was going to call it *The Book of Balaam's Ass* but I abandoned the project as it would not come together. *Sat. Dec. 15, morning.* To continue, I found one section that I thought might do. It's 'about' a later phase of the war and a remembered conversation of the immediately post-war years, 1919–20 or so. Anyway with a bit of work it would serve. It's about that 1917 trench war north of the Ypres Salient, for after my getting wounded in Mametz Wood on the 10th of July or more accurately the small hours of July 11th, I was evacuated across the Narrows[14] and after nearly four months returned to the West Front—and found my battalion indeed the whole 38th Division was occupying the most northerly bit of the British

---

[14] 'By a curious chance,' David writes in an undated draft or copy, 'the little steamer that I embarked on was called the *St. David*. I also recall that while waiting transit a jolly nice fair-haired nurse with a strong Canadian accent kissed me on the face and said, "You ought to be in a kindergarten, how did you manage to get attested?"—"Twenty last fall! You can't kid me!"'

Front north-west of Ypres—having no map with me here I can't explain exactly the position we held, but it was mainly along the Yser canal with dugouts using the south bank of the canal and they opened on to a road with trees on either side in the usual French manner, but between the road and the dug-out entrances, there ran a little stream that we called the Yser Lea across which were planks of wood with 'rustic' hand-rails here and there, I suppose I remember them because they were so humane when contrasted to their setting, in that most uninviting of areas. There is a passage in Chaucer about the Palace of Mars that I felt and feel, has words best descriptive of it.

The Division occupied this bit of front for the exceptionally long period of virtually a year, that is from some time in Oct. 1916 to Sept. 1917. I arrived back from England a little before my twenty-first birthday on Nov. 1st and during my period we spent virtually all the months consolidating or repairing and extending the trenches or rather the trench system. New communication-trenches—one I can recall was a very solid affair of carpentered revetting frames and in general making the place a formidable *defensive* position—I recall seeing dumps of artillery ammunition that ordinarily would be more out of sight of enemy observation—but of course all this continued labour was in preparation for the British Offensive that was launched at the end of July, or August 1st 1917, and which was destined to continue until sometime in November 1917 under indescribable conditions and enormous casualties.

The 38th (Welsh) Division with its numbers of labour companies of Welsh miners from the mining villages of south-east Wales were obviously of great use in all this building-up period and it has been suggested by some that the reason or part reason for the Division's prolonged stay in that one sector—but for various reasons I should doubt if that decided G.H.Q. in this matter. However that may be, after we had been engaged for nearly a year in this building up of the line in this sector we were withdrawn to another sector away to the south of Armentières in September 1917. But the Division was involved in the first phase of the offensive, its objective being Pilckem Ridge in

the first days of August. From what little I saw of that advance,
I can't speak of the incredible nature of the warfare in the months
to come, but I saw enough to guess something of the assaults
over a terrain of churned-up mud, water-brimming shell-
craters, not a yard of 'dead ground' not a fold of earth the length
of y'r body and sighted with his usual accuracy his sweep of
fire from narrow slits of concrete pill-boxes covering all the
approaches, heavy mortars operating from behind each stark
ridge.

As I say above I can speak contactually only of the first day or
two, in late July or early August and even then hardly in the
thick of it, for I was posted to a reserve group. (I think it was
called 'Battalion nucleus'.[15] As casualties mounted and mounted
G.H.Q. formed groups of Battalion nuclei round which new
men could be formed so that the life of the battalion or unit
would retain its identity, and its life would not be wholly
extinguished.) But no one present at all in the terrain of battle
could fail to feel the land bereft of its natural foliage and given
over wholly to the desert of war—could altogether forget its
feeling—the rain also made matters worse and by October one
can well believe (what I was told later) that men were literally
drowned in liquid mud.

Those of us of my unit who had been in the contest in the
woods of the Somme in July 1916 felt the great change that
'mechanization' in one form or another had unconsciously
changed things quite a bit. Some, by a chance give-away word

[15] The account continues in another draft: 'I was detailed among this Batt.
nucleus. I went to the Adjutant to ask him if I could be removed from this list.
I thought the best line of argument would be that I was unmarried and that
would it not be more appropriate for some married man to be on this list. This
was a mistaken move on my part for all I got was a rating for pretending to
wish to be a bloody hero, knowing full well that men detailed for or not for
this or that duty would not have any option in the matter. Further that I should
consider myself remarkably fortunate on this occasion and that the war was not
likely to be over for a long time so there were plenty of other opportunities,
and that anyway, the nucleus was likely to be called upon on this occasion, and
that he, the Adjutant, only wished he had been detailed to remain with this
nucleus—no such luck however. I felt extremely foolish and tried to explain
that I didn't mean it in that way at all.'

betrayed their feelings, their 'instress' that they would, if they could, bring back that sylvan terrain where so many Agamemnons had cried aloud.

To R.H., 9–11 June 1974   *Calvary Nursing Home*

It is a great goodness, a very great goodness and kindness in you to send the letter re the de la Taille thing—I very nearly tore my half-illegible meandering messed-up scrawl for I felt it unfair to bother you with the matter, so I feel particularly grateful to you for this clear and detailed answer, giving also the authorities. . . . And I've still to thank you *very very greatly* for the most careful explanatory, word by word of my beloved 'Six Dukes'.[16] The odd thing was that I had in the back of my mind about the dukes standing before him and the twelve that raz'd him from the grōn, but I can't imagine where I got that from, but I didn't like it very much the switch to 'Lords' and felt that twelve dukes were too many for the job whereas six would be more likely. The nine lords that followed after him in the black mournin gōn. Black was the mournin and white was ther wand and see (that rang a bell, heaven knows where from, for I recall hearing the 'Six Dukes' only from Fr. John O'Connor and, later, from Eric)—for so—yaller was the flamboys what they carried in ther and. (Tremendous the dialectal locality changes intermeddled with 'standard' English.) I know that 'they go like that—like bleedin' lead' (somewhere in *I.P.* [p. 46]) but somehow I prefer the six dukes to go before him, the six dukes to raise him from the ground and six dukes to follow after him. Anyway again I thank you dearest René for checking up on the whole matter and the pronunciation so subtly differing in the vowel sounds throughout—and very remarkably—I was sorry to see that 'what they carried in their *hond*' goes by the board—

Now about the de la T[aille] thing. I'm glad the Greek letters were in Latin for I have so very 'little Latin and *no* Greek' or

[16] This had simply to be copied from Percy Grainger's *British Folk-Music Settings*, no. 11. It was the only song that David himself sang, in a true, reasonably strong, tenor voice—apart, of course, from some most indelicate soldiers' songs.

rather I never can recall more than a few 'lower-case' Greek letters. Greek caps I can more often follow. I have in this room Liddell & Scott but owing to this block-headed inability to remember the lower-case letters, I sometimes spend hours trying to find the spelling of some word I want. I remember how delighted I was when I was writing 'The Wall' I wanted to use the word 'bucinators' and for some reason I wished to know the Greek word for trumpeters—maybe because Lewis & Short give *bucina* as derived from the Greek and I wondered if there was some way of suggesting that waxed-moustache feeling that, apart from sergeant-majors and some other N.C.O.s who have served in the Boer War and were now along [with] us in the 1914–18 affair, there were bandsmen in my mob who retained the Regular Army fashion. (There was, for example, the bandsman who played the large drum, Marx by name, middle-aged, with whom I shared a room in a billet in Llandudno early in 1915. He was an inveterate drinker and I had to keep awake till he came in very late always smoking a cigar which he refused to put out before he was in bed and I feared that the ash from his cigar would get the bed on fire, but it was no use. When I thought he really was asleep I would walk across the room to where his corner was, but he always heard me and *would not* allow me to remove the cigar. He used nearly always when he came into the room, to say, 'Gounod, Gounod—*what* a musician!—and always drunk, thank God!')

Anyway, in Liddell & Scott, I chanced upon 'lancer-whiskered bucinators'. It seemed to be too good to be true for it had the exact feeling I wanted—merely had to slip in 'bloody' and the bottom lines of page 22 of Fabers' *The Sleeping Lord* were given to me on a plate.

. . . God! I was distressed when Bernardine Wall phoned one evening to tell me her father had died the previous day (a Thursday) [2 May 1974] and that they felt, knowing my close friendship with dear Bernard that I ought to be told, lest I should hear from some obituary. I can't take it in yet—in fact it's terribly difficult to 'believe' that death has removed a person so close to one in feeling.

[254]

By chance I had not seen him for some while because he was unwell, but twice very shortly before his death he had come over here, once with Kathleen Raine and then on the after[noon] when you were here, he was a very remarkable bloke, much more learned and perceptive, too, than was generally understood.

... So glad that dearest Joan's sprained ankle is much better, but she should take care for a bit. Anyway, no R.S.M. to bawl out 'Put that stick down'. Glad Joan liked 'Put that stick down'— I *marvel now* how I was so stupid after 3 years in the army to say to a R.S.M. quite flatly, 'No sir', but I think I was so angry with the set-up of what is now called 'bull' and all the rest of it. God! they did pile it on at Limerick, because it was thought that those who had been in the actual fighting in France or elsewhere required some smartening up. But I'm glad I spent those couple of months in that place, otherwise I should never have seen the astonishing girl in red skirt driving a red cow in a red sunset—it was an absolutely pre-historic Celtic sight.[17]

At least you won't have to hear our R.S.M. Jones, being a man subject to authority and saying three times, 'Put that stick down'. 'No, sir: the M.O. gave it to me.' 'Put that bloody stick down.' 'No, sir.' 'Put that stick down.' 'No, sir.' 'Very well: fall out yous two men' (I've never discovered why, but so often 'yous two' in place of 'you two' was employed—especially by Scots

---

[17] David had mentioned these two, the R.S.M. and the red girl, in earlier letters. He was carrying the stick because he had twisted his ankle when climbing over an obstacle in an 'assault course'.

Here is the 'red girl' passage, from a letter of 11 January 1956: 'It was a red sundown and I was coming with some other fusiliers along a wet hill-road by a white-washed cabin and we met a girl with a torn white shift of sorts with a red skirt with a plum-coloured hem to the skirt which reached a bit below the knee; and she had auburn hair floating free over her shoulders and in the wind, and her feet and arms were bare and she had a long stick; she was driving a red-coloured cow before her and the evening sun bathed all these differing reds and bronzes. . . . For some reason that's another image I associate with Troy—the red sunset on the red cattle-girl in Munster . . . cattle-raiders, horse-raiders, soldiers, queens, queans, and the red as of flame—and the great dignity —well, *fuit Ilium.*'

Cf. *The Dying Gaul*, pp. 78–9.

N.C.O.s, but this beauty was a Londoner, not a Scot) 'fix bay'nets—*At the slope if you don't mind*, and escort this man to the guard room. Tell the sergeant of the guard to place this man under close arrest.'[18]

From another, undated letter of this time:

... Your mention of the Ulster men celebrating the Somme battle and that of Boyne Water on the same day made me recall that in some early draft of *I.P.* it ended with the words 'to Hébuterne' (can't spell it) and have no map of France so can't even guess where the place was, 'to bury the Irish dead'. [Hébuterne is some 10 miles north-west of Mametz Wood.] I can't recall how I came to write those words, but I suppose for some reason I wanted to make a recalling of events subsequent to the Division or Bde or what not being relieved after the capture of the wood, by some other troops on I think the night of July 12th.

... I'm glad that you make the contrast by reference to there being no 'Queen of the Woods' in that later place—for bare earth and mud, rusted barbed-wire hedges, concrete pill-boxes—you would be put to it to find the material required for the sacramental signa of daisy chains and floral crowns of any sort and the Queen of the Groves, no less than any other sacral award-giver, cannot function without what the earth yields—such offerants can do no more than make petition 'spiritually' 'mentally' with words maybe, as *essential* protestant belief maintains—in direct contradiction to what is crucial and central to the Catholic faith and which does but ratify and set the seal to what 'man' *qua* man consciously or unconsciously holds.

I hadn't looked at *I.P.* for some long time so was surprised that Major Lillywhite was decidedly unpopular with us from our first billets in the soggy fields somewhere in the neighbourhood of St. Omer (the H.Q. of British Forces in France).

I.P. page 15—poor Lillywhite is already 'that shit Major Lillywhite' and remained so until he had the death stroke in Mametz

[18] So far as I know, this was the only time David was 'crimed', and he was lucky in that the charge was reduced from 'refusing to obey an order' to 'hesitating to obey an order'.

Wood, but whom the 'Queen of the Woods' found worthy of a daisy chain—and Her awarding is not to be questioned.

The odd thing is that I cannot recall who it was that the name Lillywhite disguises—but usually in *I.P.* apart from change of name, I have in mind two, or sometimes three, persons, mixing some of the characteristics of one with something typical of the other. But in the case of Lillywhite I can't recall a Major of whom we had so persistent a dislike. I think I must have accidentally heard some men of another unit mention a Major Lillywhite and then recalled the qualities of certain officers of my own unit and fused these dislikeable qualities—anyway I can't sort it out now.

In another letter David, after turning his mind back to the Twenties and speaking of *The Beggar's Opera*, continues:

To R.H., 27 September 1974   *Calvary Nursing Home*
Another 'stage play' Frank Medworth and I went to whenever it was possible was because of the line 'Gascon cannon never recoil', I don't know how it sounds in Frog but we used to drag it into any conversation when possible and laugh like anything.[19]

... by a curious chance Colin H[ughes] ... came to see me on Sunday afternoon and brought with him part of the typescript of a thing he's working on about the 38th Welsh Division and much besides. He's an incredible bloke for accuracy and has spent oceans of time reading all the official matter available both English and German (the latter in translation) and for me, at all events, it was a great treat and also revealed to me things that I knew nothing of before. Among other matters that long march from the La Bassée area down south to the chalk lands of the Somme, aspects of which Part 5 of *I.P.* is concerned with, was a

[19] The phrase, and the period, suggested Edmond Rostand's *Cyrano de Bergerac* to me: and so it is, Act IV, Scene vii: 'Le canon des Gascons ne recule jamais'. Cyrano was being played in London in 1927: Charles Hawtrey? Hawtrey certainly appeared in another play of about that time, which amused David enormously, called *Ambrose Applejohn's Adventure*. This was the source of 'the man from Amsterdam' who is introduced into the beginning of *Balaam's Ass*: a very good and buoyant period for David.

much wider curve than I had thought. I do on page 119, middle of page, speak of the south road gleam scorching white with its wide-plotted curve, you couldn't see the turned tail of the column, for the hot dust, by ten o'clock. But that might apply to almost any movement in column of route. . . . And before moving south we stayed in the vicinity of St. Pol and for awhile the 15th battalion H.Q. was at Bailleul-aux-Cornailles and the whole Division made a so-to-say 'dress rehearsal' of the place it was supposed we would attack in actuality. Now I cannot recall at all any of this Divisional practice-ground in full scale. Not a single bloody thing remained in my mind when I was writing *I.P.* nor can I now recall *anything at all* of this extensive rehearsal. Strange, isn't it?

I took the opportunity of asking Colin H. about the matter of Hébuterne and the Irish dead . . . it appears from the diary of the 15th R.W.F. that on July 17th they moved into let's call it 'Z' Corps and from July 18 to 24 'supplied working-parties' in the Hébuterne trench sector. . . . (I, of course, was cosy in hospital in Birmingham, for it was some time after that that I was sent to the Nursing Home between Stratford on Avon and Banbury Cross, where I got into trouble for being seen having tea with one of the nurses and her mother on the lawn, trying to eat strawberries and cream *which I loathe*. But was far from loathing the heavenly nurse. But it was a strict rule of the place that on no account could one visit the homes of the Staff. But as the house and garden was near by we thought we'd chance it—but the daughter of the Scots doctor (who ran the place) and was a nice enough chap but had the maddening habit of a certain sort of Scot of great solemnity and moralizing—'Almighty God made the universe subject to certain rules—all human institutions, even this nursing home, similarly have rules etc'.—but his red-haired daughter was matron and somewhat of a R.S.M. type, must have spied on us from a top window and evidently reported having seen the little tea-party, maybe out of *invidia* of some sort (I don't mean out of envy on my account but just a general female spite)—don't know, but even now nearly 60 years after, I harbour an unforgiving feeling towards her. But to go further into that episode would require a song of deeds of some length.)

October 6th. . . . 'Damn in the classroom, Blast on the rugger field, but bloody hell I will not have.'[20] I so often think of your story of your schooldays, and also how the Abbot could not read certain passages in the *Iliad*, I think you said, without shedding tears. What was his name? Was it 'Met' [headmaster of Ampleforth, later Abbot Matthews] that you called him—so did Harman. That breed of men are not to be found now, from what I gather.

. . . But this can be added [to the account of his being wounded at Mametz]. . . . I record it here for you as it is amusing and indicative of the general muddle as related on page 183. Finding that I could not stand up or walk I crawled away in the opposite direction—that is in the direction of our own lines thinking that that there might come some chance R.A.M.C. man. I don't know how far I crawled and my rifle with bayonet fixed I had somehow managed to sling over my shoulder and it hung a dead weight and somehow 'fouled', as sailors say, with my tin hat, but I did not want to be without my rifle, partly for the obvious reason that I had no other weapon, and after all for all I knew, there might well be groups of Germans about, though what I imagined I could do with my rifle under the circumstances I can't imagine—after a bit more crawling I found I should have to abandon it, which I did, still with a sense of shame and a feeling that can only be described as real affection (akin to the feeling of leaving a mate or something—or as when a child has to leave a toy it has had an affection for. 'The fair flaw in the grain, above the lower sling-swivel' on p. 184 corresponded to an actual streak in the wood) for what I was leaving. My gas mask I kept on grounds of sheer ungraced, pure utility. At some point I found myself looking at a corporal whom I recognized as of my own battalion—I did not know [him] at all well but I can see his kindly Welsh face—a countryman's face, even now. I can't remember what he said but recall

[20] To be correct: 'Blast in the passage I can tolerate, and Damn on the football field, but Bloody Hell in the classroom *I will not have.*'

only his lifting me up and carrying me on his back. We had not got far when in the darkness or half-darkness a tall figure emerged who happened to be a Major and 2nd in command of our battalion, a Major and a Welshman, much liked, and very able, good-looking, and I *think* in civilian life in the legal profession. He said, 'Is that you, Corporal X?' 'Yes, sir. I was trying to carry Pte. Jones a bit nearer the advanced dressing station or find some stretcher-bearers, sir.' 'Corporal X, you will no matter *who* he is, drop the bugger *here*. If every wounded man is to be carried from where he has chanced to fall, by a corporal or any other of the rank and file, we would double our loss of fire strength and that's not overmuch as it is. Put Pte. Jones (of 'B', I think?) down immediately. Stretcher-bearers will find him within a short time. Don't you know there's a sod of a war on.' (That last bit amused me, even at the time, for it was pretty obvious that a war was indeed on.)

I had written to David for Trafalgar Day, 21 October. He started the following, his last letter to us, on the 22nd, continued it on the 25th, and it was postmarked the 28th.

To R.H., 22 (?) Oct 1974. Now Oct 25th   Calvary Nursing Home
Many thanks for your letter that did reach me yesterday afternoon so it did come on the day intended, the hundred and sixty-ninth October since . . . they closed like a forest . . . in thirteen fathom water . . . in the worsening weather . . . the shoals of Trafalgar on the lee quarter or however it goes in the account—I know I've quoted the passage somewhere [*The Anathemata*, p. 114] but can't find where. It's quite awful how one's memory lets one down. I did not know that y'r Robin's birthday was on Trafalgar Day. I send him birthday greetings. I write this brief note only to thank you for letter—it crossed a long meander of mine to you enclosing a printed extract written by dear Louis Bonnerot that his widow Luce gave me when she came to visit me last week, but it evidently had not reached you when you wrote, but I expect it will have arrived at Shanagarry by now.

Seeing we are on the subject of Trafalgar I can't resist a

matter (Mick Richey would laugh at this because from time to time I've mentioned it). You know the account says that when Nelson was hit by a musket-shot fired from the maintop 'platform' or anyway from the lower masthead where cross-timbers formed a 'fire-bay' for marksmen to pick off their targets from their high perches but at mortally close range, for, unless I've got that wrong too, there was between the *Victory* and the French ship little leeway. But that's not what puzzles me. Nelson was pacing the quarter-deck when he fell, but a few moments before one of his officers had fallen and the account says that the actual spot was scattered with fragments of timber from the *'fore-brace bitts'*, i.e. the heavy baulks of timber to which were belayed the braces (of cordage) of the fore-mast to which the fore-mast sails were bent.

(I understand that quarter-deck derives from a time when a 'half-deck' extending over half the length of the vessel had above it a much smaller deck right in the stern roughly covering almost a quarter of the ship's length. That makes sense of the words 'quarter-deck'.)

Bitt or bitts could be used nautically of other contrivances, but it is obvious in this context . . . that what had been hit was one or both of the heavy uprights that supported and were part of a heavy cross timber to which was belayed the cordage of the fore-mast yards and so determined the manipulation of the sails of that fore-mast. Generally speaking, rightly or wrongly I say sometimes to myself, Remember 'braces' go aft, 'stays' go forward and *shrouds* go from beam to beam or rather from mast to outboard beyond top-strake and made fast by heavy-sheaved blocks and dead eyes to wale above where her bulwarks 'tumble home'. (What a *perfect* term to express the inward inclination of a ship's bulwarks.)—I fancy her shrouds are set *very slightly* to aft of the mast they supported but this is purely from memory and may well be wrong. I've still not come to the question that no doubt has a perfectly simple answer. If the timber called the 'fore-brace bitts' was on the quarter-deck, that is far to the stern of the great vessel, from all time the place of command and helm and admiralty—part in medieval vessels, of the After

[261]

Castle, are we to suppose that the cordage of the fore-mast yards run the whole, or a large part of the whole length of the *Victory*, that her hemp or sheets had their belaying bitts that far aft?

If so, where were the braces of the mainmast yards belayed— or more difficult still, where were the sheets of the mizzen-mast yards, for if braces being part of the 'running rigging', run aft, to what brace bitts were they belayed? Ludicrous question of course and foolish for the answer is, without any doubt, quite simple. But those bloody 'fore-brace bitts' that got a nasty one (presumably from a cannon shot) shortly before the discharge of a mere musket laid 'that great Ammiral' low on the quarter-deck of the 'leading vessel of the weather column' still seems odd.[21]

I'll thank you Captain Harvey to keep y'r place in line. Do you remember how we enjoyed that.

A bit back quite by chance (I *think* in *The Mariner's Mirror* that I take in) that an analysis of the ship's company in the *Victory* showed that of nearly a thousand men the vast majority were English, a number of Scots, about 30 or 40 Irish and but some 18 Welsh men, so far as I can recall.

Yes, *Agenda* did advertise the *Ken[sington]* *Mass*, in that same issue [Autumn–Winter, 1973–4] that has in it a fragment of a draft of it—The issue with the *Drystan ac Esyllt* watercolour reproduced on the cover in colour. But it just announces that they hope to print the whole 'poem' if it is finished, in 'later this year'. You'll find the editor's note on page 11 of that issue. But I have told William C[ookson] that it can't possibly be finished within the year. He quite understands that. He has already received some orders for it, but says that's O.K. and the delay is perfectly understood. My trouble is that it, the *Ken. Mass*, is very differently *gesceapenne* from the thing I made in the '40s and indeed from what I thought it would be in this '74 attempt—

---

[21] Did David misunderstand, or deliberately pervert, the meaning of Milton's 'great Ammiral'? The latter, I think, taking this passage in conjunction with two references in his 'Introduction to *The Rime of the Ancient Mariner*', *The Dying Gaul*, pp. 220, 223.

indeed I'm beginning to wonder if I can manage what I wanted but I must make the attempt somehow.

I agree wholly with a little Moses in the wattle *basawd* in the form 'ship shape' it lifts up a bodily image strange how one finds delight in some few simple words that define and hold up a visible and evocative thing.

In the Welsh Lucan narrative of the Birth where the Gospel says et pannis eum involvit *et reclinavit* eum *in praesepio*, the last few words are translated *y dyn bach yn y preseb*—the *little man* in the crib—I have not here a Welsh version and can remember only the *dyn bach yn y preseb* which is comic and very unusual for you'ld have thought *baban* would have been used.

Oh Lord I had more to say but the kind person who takes my letters to the post is literally waiting for me to put this in an envelope ready.

Much love dear René.   DAI

(Not read through. Do hope my other letter with Bonnerot thing in it reached you. Love to Joan of course and Ros. DAI)

The David of those last years, and then those last months, in the Monksdene Hotel and the Nursing Home of the Blue Sisters, is recorded with great tenderness and affection in a memoir by Peter Orr (*Agenda*, Summer–Autumn 1977). 'That weekend', he writes, 'David was told that he was to be moved to a room upstairs, a fate he had dreaded for some time, since he so hated change. In the early morning of Monday, 28 October, David was ready to receive his breakfast. Sister Joseph, of the Little Company of Mary, had just gone upstairs, when a call came through for her on the internal telephone: "Mr. Jones has gone", was the bleak message.'

Nest Cleverdon telephoned to us in Ireland on that Monday evening. From no better, kinder or gentler person could one receive such news. As I put the telephone down, I could only say, quoting my friend, 'Bugger, bugger, bugger'—and then I remembered, no saint though I am, what he had also said, 'the Bugger! Bugger! of a man detailed'—to go or to stay—'has often about it the Fiat! Fiat! of the Saints'.

Index